running

the

spiritual path

The Seattle School
2510 Elliott Ave.
Seattle, WA 98121
theseattleschool.edu

www.stmartins.com

The Essential Rumi translated by Coleman Barks with John Moyne, A.A.Arberry, and Reynold Nicholson, San Francisco: Harper, 1995, excerpted here by permission of Coleman Barks.

Library of Congress Cataloging-in-Publication Data

Joslin, Roger D.
    Running the spiritual path : a runner's guide to breathing, meditating, and exploring the prayerful dimension of the sport / Roger D. Joslin.—1st ed.
        p. cm.
    Includes bibliographical references (p. 245).
    ISBN 0-312-30885-X (hc)
    ISBN 0-312-30886-8 (pbk)
    EAN 978-0312-30886-5
    1. Running—Religious aspects. 2. Runners (Sports)—Religious life.
3. Spiritual life. I. Title.

BL629.5.R85J67 2003
248.8'8—dc21   2003043114

10 9 8 7

running

the

spiritual path

A Runner's Guide to Breathing, Meditating,
and Exploring the Prayerful Dimension of the Sport

Roger D. Joslin

St. Martin's Griffin ⚞ New York

In the spirit of gratefulness, I dedicate this book to my beloved parents, Hollis and Lillian Joslin.

contents

acknowledgments

Above all, I would like to acknowledge my debt to Donna Egen Mata Joslin, whose labor of love was to read and edit this manuscript through its, and our, innumerable phases. I wish to especially thank two of my friends, Cass Ray and Dr. Terry Muck, whose willingness to read and comment on the book is greatly appreciated. I am thankful for the love of my children, Nate and Lillian, who continue to patiently endure their father's eccentricities. I am indebted to my agent, Natasha Kern, who found the right home for my "baby." Thanks very much to my editors at St. Martin's, Diane Higgins and Nichole Argyres. Their belief in the project, along with their fine editing skills, brought the book to life. Thanks to the faculty and my fellow students at the Episcopal Theological Seminary of the Southwest for their encouragement and their kindness in allowing me to talk incessantly about "the book."

Stillness is what creates love. Movement is what creates life. To be still and still moving—this is everything.

—DO HYUN CHOE

In reading this book you are being asked to go with me on a spiritual journey taken on foot. The book started as a journal, a chronicle of my experience of seeking God while running. Please view what you read as a work in progress. Many of the ideas that I explored and found useful in the early stages of the development of the practice of running meditation are no longer part of my personal routine. I have included them because some of you, at different stages in your quest to know God, might also find them useful. The practice continues to evolve. I have stopped here only to put it into print because bookbinding is a static process and requires that the writer stop writing somewhere. My fervent prayer is that my words may assist you in the development of new ways in which you may learn to love God.

It would be extraordinarily pretentious of me to suggest to you that I have found an exclusive path to the Divine, or that the path that I will describe to you is the path that you should take. The truth that I have stumbled upon, as countless others have discovered before me, is that God's presence can be made manifest in an infinite variety of ways. We each have a unique spiritual character, a propensity to find God readily accessible to us in widely differing circumstances. God calls to some people most directly through the expression of ancient liturgy, practiced in majestic high-church settings. I have a dear friend to whom God speaks most clearly when he is fishing for striped bass. Some know God through silence. Others experience the Transcendent most completely while working for the betterment of those most in need of God's love. The world's great religions provide well-trodden avenues for those seeking God within the established traditions.

My comments are aimed primarily at the runner—at those who choose to run down the spiritual path. Running the spiritual path doesn't mean that you are going to attain enlightenment in a hurry. Running is simply another means of traveling the path. The path is both circular and spiraling. There is no hurry and goals are meaningless. God exists all along the path and at all levels. Our task is to be aware of that Presence as we move along it. The true runner can see God more clearly while running. We will explore ways that enable the runner to open his eyes to the presence of the Divine while running. Those on a spiritual quest seek God among those things that we know and do not know. This is an exploration of the unknown within the familiar. You may have been running for decades and received only brief glimpses of a spiritual world that is present with every breath you breathe and every step you take. Attentive running can take you into that world.

The book is less a how-to manual than a description of a singular experience with running. I am certain that my personal experience with running is not universal. Glean from it what you may and discard the rest. Much of what I have learned may be applicable to a variety of activities in which the physical and spiritual can be linked—in walking, swimming, rowing, and cycling. The foundation for the book is a running journal I kept from 1993 until 2001. Occasionally I have retained in the book certain passages from the journal that have seemingly little or nothing to do with running. I will admit that the connection may sometimes be stretched, but it is there. My own spiritual formation was informed by my involvement with running prayer. Experiences that took place outside of my running life were processed while running. Conversely, my running experiences greatly influenced the events of my larger life. I think it may be easier for the reader to relate to my running life if some aspects of my life apart from running are understood. I have therefore left some journal entries intact, and hopefully, they will aid you in integrating your own running life into the larger context of living and being.

Most of the journal entries chosen for inclusion in the book describe peak running experiences. This may be misleading for the beginning runner. Know that for every run in which I describe a transcendent experience there were many more that were either ordinary or, from an athlete's perspective, utter failures. Both spiritual and physical conditioning can be difficult processes. Accept each run for what it is, remembering that this is a spiritual practice that, like any discipline, requires persistence through episodes of success and seeming failure.

Why run? To the casual observer the reasons might seem obvious—an increase in cardiovascular conditioning, a chance to be out in the fresh air and sunshine, improved concentration, a positive effect on physical appearance, or stress release. I was always aware of the benefits of running, but, in truth, for many years I ran simply because it felt good. Running offered an effective physical release from the day's mental activity. When I ran I felt liberated, free from the burden of obligations, expectations, and ambitions.

This might seem reason enough. The apparent benefits of running provided sufficient reason to keep on going, and those reasons would probably still be enough to keep me running even if I hadn't realized that running had become much more than putting one foot in front of the other. To state it simply: Running became prayer. I don't mean, merely, that I began to run in a prayerful fashion. It is not that I engage in verbal prayer while I run. (Although, on occasion, I might.) It is not enough to say that I pray while I run. It is, quite literally, that running has become prayer.

I am speaking of prayer as communion with God, as an awareness of His presence, as a conscious recognition of the divine spirit that dwells in each of us. Definitions of prayer are as numerous as the paths to God. My favorite was penned by the most secular of Trappist monks, Thomas Merton, who offered the encouraging and sustaining words: "Prayer is the desire to pray." It is this dynamic of intention that most clearly separates the runner who merely runs from the runner who prays. Running, at its core, is a joyful, invigorating, playful experience. Expansion beyond that, to a spiritual realm, is based on a foundation of intention. Running has become, for me, a way to communicate with God. The act of lacing up my running shoes is the beginning of a prayerful exercise aimed at divine union. A visitor once said of Dov Baer of Mezritch, a Ukranian rabbi known as the "Great Preacher," "I didn't travel to Mezritch to hear him teach, but to see how he tied his shoelaces."

Why running? Why choose this particular avenue to prayerful meditation? Aren't there more traditional and perhaps less strenuous paths? This has been my choice primarily because it works. For many years I have practiced a sitting meditation. This continues to be the way I start each day, and the practice has changed my life. Yet the practice of sitting meditation has been one that I have had to cultivate. I have always been physically active. The notion of sitting still and waiting for God was not an idea that I accepted readily—at least in my early attempts. I understand this practice better now and, especially as I have grown older, find a silent, sitting meditation to be essential to my sense of well-being. The practice of running meditation, on the other hand, has been completely natural. When I know that I am going to spend an hour of a beautiful afternoon on the running trail, I can hardly wait to get out the door.

Running and prayer may seem an unlikely combination when first considered. Yet for those who are familiar with the practice of meditation, it is not such a foreign concept. The focus on breathing, the attention to rhythm and cadence, and the heightened sense of awareness are among the many common features of both a sitting and a running meditation. To a large degree, learning the art of prayerful running is a matter of applying many of the principles of a sitting meditation. The application is relatively straightforward, with only a few twists and nuances that make the adaptation of the practice an interesting challenge to the already committed runner. Prayerful running is an attainable goal. If you already meditate and run, you are almost there.

I pose the question again, "Why?" Why combine two perfectly

useful practices? The activities of running and prayer (or meditation—I use the terms interchangeably) are complete, in and of themselves. Why try to merge them? Wouldn't the ancient Buddhist advice "When you cook, cook!" suggest that one's attention should be focused on a single activity? There is truth in that elemental wisdom and I grappled with that apparent inconsistency for some time. The resolution of the conflict came about during one of those rather frequent revelations that drop into my head while running. It is not simply that I desire to pray while sitting quietly in a lotus position, or while reciting the liturgy in church, or while focused on the syncopation existing between the sounds of my breath and the crunch of the gravel beneath my running feet. My desire is to pray always—to follow St. Paul's admonition to "Pray without ceasing." It is all practice. Sitting meditation, formal church-bound worship, yoga, walking labyrinths, and prayerful running are all structured, carefully designed ways of practicing what I aim to do at all times. So, why running? Why not a business-lunch meditation, a final-exam cramming meditation, a commodities-trading meditation, or a shopping-spree meditation? Why not, indeed? The answer for me is that I'm not there yet. Maintaining a heightened level of consciousness comes easier in a setting conducive to prayer. The time-honored methods of a traditional meditation practice are, for most people, the appropriate place to start, but if one's prayer life never moves beyond the meditation pillow or the hallowed sanctuary of a church, the depths of prayer have not been explored. Sensing the presence of God while walking through the woods, sweeping the floor, planting a garden, gazing at the stars—these are obtainable goals. The question is how do you remain conscious of God's presence when you argue with your mate, discipline your children, or receive criticism from your boss? Running meditation is a small step forward in that direction. It is probably more of a challenge to remain in the presence of God while running than it is while sitting alone on a mountaintop gazing at the sunset. Unfortunately, most of us spend little time on mountain peaks overwhelmed with God's splendor. We are usually engaged in more mundane activities. Finding God in the mundane, in the place where we are now, this is the challenge. We live in an action-oriented culture. Opportunities for inner reflection are few. Contemporary culture seems to be fashioned in a way that prevents us from exploring our inner reality. Society's emphasis on doing, rather than being, keeps us distracted from the business of knowing ourselves.

Running meditation is one way of venturing forth from a comfortable conception of prayer and to begin testing the boundaries of what it is possible to know about the nature of God. It is a small step, similar in many respects to traditional meditation, but operating on ground dissimilar enough to encourage the seeker in the hope that if God can be found on the running trail, he can be found elsewhere. What can we do about this? Our culture has this orientation toward action and we are not likely to be successful in combatting it head on. Rather than try to campaign against the innate resistance to sit and meditate, it may be more fruitful to simply take an orientation toward action and channel those energies in a meditative direction. Clearly there is the need for spending time exploring the inner self, for exploring the empty chambers of the heart-mind. Using running meditation as a tool, the action-oriented individual can accomplish many of the same goals implicit in sitting meditation, and still follow the ingrained drive to keep moving. I am advocating taking our culture as it is and finding ways to connect with the Divine within it. In the agrarian societies in which sitting meditation developed, *zazen,* or sitting meditation, served the dual purpose of allowing the practitioner to both rest from his labor and seek enlightenment. Running meditation, at the end of the day, allows the student of this practice to explore the spiritual realm while getting the physical exercise he didn't receive while working behind a desk. In this way a more healthful balance in the day's activities can be achieved. If your work is largely physical, if your day is spent walking and standing and lifting, then it is unlikely that you have the physical energy to run at the end of the day. A sitting meditation is probably more appropriate for you. If your work is not physically demanding, then there is a good chance that the release of pent-up physical energy at the end of the workday can be accompanied by an opening into the sacred realm, if only one's intentions are properly focused.

It is also possible, whether or not the society in which you live is oriented toward action, that you simply have trouble sitting still. Here is a way for those not naturally blessed with the contemplative spirit to engage in contemplation.

> *All the runners at the stadium are trying to win, but only one of them gets the prize. You must run in the same way, meaning to win. All the fighters at the games go into strict training; they do this just to win a wreath that will wither away, but we do it for a wreath that will never wither. That is how I run, intent on winning; that is how I fight, not beating the air. I treat my body hard and make it obey me, for, having been an announcer myself, I should not want to be disqualified.*
>
> 1 Cor. 9:24–27

In this letter to the church at Corinth, St. Paul compares the rigors of the Christian life with athletic competition. He speaks of training hard and running with an intention to win. Paul was primarily using running as an example illustrating the rigors of spiritual discipline. It is, however, an illustration of how running, itself, can also be a spiritual discipline. The focus, the concentration, the willingness to submit to hardship play a role in the spiritually disciplined life, whether that discipline involves more traditional forms of sacrifice (fasting, simplicity, study, submission, etc.) or the sacrifice required when seeking God through the practice of running meditation.

Paul's reference to the wreath that will never wither is significant. When you run, you may or not be intent on beating the competition. It matters little whether or not you receive an award for first place. We run to achieve a victory of awareness. Each run becomes a race that can be won.

running

the

spiritual path

intentions and preparations

Therefore I do not run like a man running aimlessly; I do not fight like a man beating the air.

1 COR. 9:26

If you walk toward Him, He comes to you running.

MAHAMMAD

It is possible to begin a meditation run simply by stepping onto the pavement and putting one foot in front of the other. In fact, the simplicity of this is one of the great joys of running. No elaborate gear, accessories, or training are required. One can simply step into the run and see what unfolds.

However, a clear declaration of the intention can give the runner a sense of purpose that increases the possibility of fulfilling the objective of sensing the sacred. There are many good reasons for running. Hopes of achieving physical fitness, releasing stress, or enhancing one's appearance motivate most of the runners you see on a city's tracks and trails. These goals, as well as the thrill of competition or just a simple appreciation of the joy of movement, are all worthy. However, running meditation is a practice with a singular purpose and many side benefits.

It is very likely, since you have undertaken the task of reading this book, that you have felt some sense of the sacred when running. The connection may have appeared to happen accidentally, without any desire or action on your part. This kind of experience often emerges at a time of need, whether or not we are aware of the need. We find ourselves reaching out for help in all directions. Our call for assistance, perhaps in the form of a prayer, but perhaps not, is answered as we find within ourselves the presence of the Divine. This realization of God's closeness is always a matter of grace. However, we have to be ready to receive that grace. We can take steps to prepare ourselves to recognize that grace awaits us. In preparing for a run, we can ready our mind and body to be receptive to a power that is always present.

Preparation for a Run

For many people, it may be useful to sit quietly in meditation before beginning a run. Personally, when I am eager to begin running, I find it difficult to sit still. At the end of a workday, having spent many hours behind a desk, I crave movement. I have realized that I can find God in that movement as easily as I can find him in stillness. However, if your schedule and temperament allow it, you might try to first solidify a connection with the Divine through silence and stillness before beginning the run. Generally, when engaged in sitting meditation, I will sit for a minimum of twenty minutes. That length of time is not necessary here. A shorter period, about five to ten minutes of silence, should allow you to move into the run fully prepared.

If you do not choose to sit in silence before a run, do allow a few moments for recollection. Focus your attention on your breathing for a minute or two. You might ask God to make his presence known to you on the run. In some way, make the purpose of the run known to both your mind and body. Simply stating to yourself that the run is intended to bring you in touch with the Transcendent can be helpful. Along the way you will undoubtedly lose touch with your goal, but a firm declaration of your intention before beginning the run will make it easier to find your way back to your objective.

The Sufi al-Sarraj speaks of the preparation and attitude that are essential before entering a state of prayer. When elevating running to a form of prayer, the same kind of preparation should take place. Al-Sarraj advises us to enter into a state of meditation and recollection, free from thoughts of anything but God alone. He advises that those who enter into prayer with this kind of recollection will find that the state remains even after they have ceased to pray and lasts from prayer time to prayer time. This is what the meditative runner strives to achieve as well, a continuation of the state of recollection from one run to the next. The frame of mind stretches from before and after each run, each an intentional conversation with God, until the peace is continuous.

If you stretch before a run, treat each stretching position as a prayer posture. The Islamic practice of prayerful kneeling and bowing toward Mecca is similar to a runner's stretch. Christians often kneel in prayer. In both the Hindu and Buddhist traditions, mudras, or elaborate hand and arm positions, play an important role in bringing the body into alliance with the mind and spirit while meditating. Central to the many disciplines of yoga is the harmony and health of the whole person. Within the yoga of postures, or *asanas*, the focus given during each movement and holding of a pose can almost be described as sacramental. This intent not only allows for the fullest physiological benefits from the *asanas*, but also makes the practice one of mindfulness. Imagine that, in addition to stretching your muscles, you are stretching your spirit and giving it the flexibility it needs to engage the Transcendent. Each stretching exercise is transformed into a pose of prayer.

A Beginning Exercise

Prepare mindfully for the run. Dress slowly, methodically, as if you were a devout priest and your running clothes were sacred vestments. Pay special attention as you put on your socks and shoes, lacing your shoes carefully. Just as a priest uses his hands to prepare the sacrament, your feet will be the contact point between your body and the sacred earth. Hold on to an awareness of that fact.

If you begin by stretching, focus all your attention on each muscle being stretched. Just before you begin to run, say a silent prayer, asking for God to be present on your run and to aid you in your effort to be present to the Divine.

The first quarter of the run: Start out running slowly, focusing on breathing. When extraneous thoughts arise, acknowledge them, and then simply return to the breath.

The second quarter of the run: Shift your attention to your feet. Be aware of the contact between the soles of your feet and the earth. Listen to the sound of your foot striking the various surfaces you encounter. Hear the differences in the sounds that gravel, sand, concrete, and asphalt make beneath your feet. Step lightly on the earth. Be aware that you are running along the surface of a spherical planet. When thoughts arise, let them go and return to an awareness of the interaction between your feet and the ground.

The third quarter of the run: Practice the Mother Teresa Run. Look kindly in the eyes of every person you meet. Whether or not your gaze is returned, offer them a slight smile and a silent blessing.

The final quarter of the run: Come home to your breath. Let go of thoughts that arise and return your attention to your breathing. If it is helpful, count each breath up to ten and then start over.

Finish the run by stretching mindfully. Zen-walk to your door or your car. When you undress, disrobe as a priest removes his sacred garments. Shower as if you are being baptized. Extend the heightened awareness of God's presence into as much of the day as is possible.

Intentionality

As was noted earlier, the Trappist monk Thomas Merton once defined prayer as "the desire to pray." During the period in my life in which I first read these words, I felt an overwhelming desire to pray, but I was not sure how to go about praying in the way I thought I needed to. The prayers I had learned as a child no longer seemed adequate to express the depth of longing that consumed me. I found great comfort in Merton's words—learning that out of those depths of desire to connect with the Divine came the realization of the desire. I understood that I was already praying. From that point I began to study and practice many different forms of prayer and meditation. Undoubtedly, my understanding of the myriad ways to connect to the Transcendent has been enhanced by this study. However, always at prayer's core is the simple desire to pray and it is that desire that transforms the most elaborate ritual or the purest moment of silence into a divine encounter.

The same is true with running meditation. Without the desire to join with the Transcendent, even with the most studied preparation, a run will be no more than a jaunt in the park. With the intention of establishing a connection with God, even a run that is full of outside noise and mental distractions can become a sacred act. If, in running, the desire is to connect with God, to pray, it is already happening. Keeping that desire at the forefront of your thoughts, remaining conscious of the intent, is critical. Merton's description of prayer can also be used to encourage the meditating runner who is concerned that his efforts are not bearing fruit or who asks, "Am I doing it right?" If the desire is to run with God, then the specifics of the techniques used don't matter very much. Hopefully, an exploration of the practice of running meditation will provide new avenues to the Transcendent. However, it is grace alone that has provided us with the desire to run along those holy avenues.

One Saturday morning, as is my custom, I went for a run in the hills. I ran for more than three-quarters of the run before I began praying. Eventually I settled into the Jesus Prayer, a prayer used in Eastern Orthodox churches since the sixth century. I often allow my thoughts to drift aimlessly for a brief period of time before moving into prayer. At times I question the wisdom of allowing my thoughts to wander, even on the first part of the run. It may be that reserving running time, or at least specific runs, for meditation only would be better. The phenomenon may be similar to having particular places for working or studying. When you settle into the place to study, then studying is more likely to occur. If your mind identifies running as the place of communion with God, then there may be less of a tendency to use the run for other mental activities. On the other hand, your mind needs some time to process the events and thoughts that have transpired during the day. But if you can, use other, more idle time to process thoughts. Utilizing this less valuable time (such as when you're commuting, or driving to the running track) may allow you to save your running time for prayer.

Know that from the beginning, this is to be a run dedicated solely to communication with the Divine. When the random thoughts arise, acknowledge them and gently move back into the present.

The various forms of asceticism, such as fasting, abstentions, and self-restraint, can train us for the actual event of prayer. Running can be viewed as a seeking of simplicity, requiring a turning away from comfort and pleasure and moving toward discipline and self-denial. Its importance as an act of asceticism is dependent on the intention behind the self-restraint. Physical fitness alone may be a goal sufficient to justify the self-imposed hardship the runner endures. For the runner who is seeking communion with God, the self-denial involved in maintaining a challenging running routine is more than an aspect of fitness training. The act of self-denial prepares the runner, readies him to receive the Divine Spirit. A degree of asceticism is a necessary preparation for running in the presence of God.

Why is this so? I believe it's because the needs of the body and the spirit are so closely intertwined. If the motives behind fasting are correct, the physical hunger can lead to a spiritual hunger. The self-denial of earthly appetites for comfort, wealth, or control can lead us to an understanding of our need for more sustaining spiritual sustenance, for which the more superficial desires are only substitutes. When we run, we tire, we thirst, we ache, and we seek relief from the immediate physical demands of our bodies. However, when our running is done to intentionally establish a God connection, each self-imposed hardship is inextricably linked with our overarching desire to rest in God's arms, to drink of God's love, and be soothed by the Divine Healer.

Seek God, and you will find God and every good thing as well. Yes, truly, with such an attitude you could tread upon a stone, and that would be a more godly thing for you to do than for you to receive the Body of our Lord.

MEISTER ECKHART

Christ asked that the sacrament of Communion be performed, "in remembrance of me." It is the act of remembrance, not the tasting of the "Body and Blood," that is of paramount importance. It is a matter of seeking God in all things, including "treading on stones." While it may be true that the road to hell is paved with good intentions, it is also true that the path to God can be more direct if the proper intentions are declared before embarking on the path. If our intention is to find God, then we will—in every head wind, in every rocky trail, in the blazing sun, but also in the smile of a stranger and the relief of shade and a cool breeze.

Acting as if You Have Already Received

Of course, it would be foolish to expect to experience a state of Divine Union on the first attempt at the practice of running meditation. In fact, you might even feel like an imposter—like someone who is only pretending to pray. You can expect for some time to feel as if you are only acting like you are engaged in the practice. You may be attempting to focus on your breath—perhaps on your heart beating—but you find you are so distracted that your intentions to pray are lost in a muddle of random thoughts. Remember that it is the intention that sets you apart from every other runner you meet on the trail. It is your intention and your willingness to persist in the practice that will eventually move you beyond simply acting as if you are praying. It is much like the Islamic practice of *zhikr*, or repetition of Divine Names. What begins as simple recitation of words for God gently eases the practitioner into an awareness of the Divine Presence. The prayerful runner is quite literally "going through the motions." Yet it is this process of simply going through the motions of running prayer that leads you to the point where you are doing the prayer, and ultimately to the time when you are receiving prayer. This is the stage in the process where control over the exchange has been handed over. You are not acting, not doing, but instead are the recipient of grace.

Imagine that you are running toward God and know that far in the distance God is running toward you. Hold this image in your heart, pick up your pace, and move with the expectation that you will encounter a God that is racing to meet you. As Bayazid al Bistami said, "For thirty years I sought God. But when I looked carefully I found that in reality God was the seeker and I the sought."

November 7, 1998—Intentions and Choice of Chant
Cool weather has arrived. I was able to run a fast hill run—fast

enough that I'm contemplating adding another run up Mountain
Climb to the routine. Donna asked me about the question of inten-
tions before my run this morning. She wanted to know if I planned
the run beforehand—if I knew what kind of run I was going to do.
Sometimes I do and sometimes I don't. This morning I began the
run chanting, "Holy God," and later in the run, as my pace and
breathing accelerated, I chanted, "Onward, to the One." I think
that it is not so important to have a specific plan as it is to have a
declared intention to connect with God. I might intend to look into
the faces of all I meet and offer them God's blessing and find myself
drawn more inward to a prayer of the heart. The critical matter is to
be resolute in my intention to seek God through the run, not to al-
low myself to be overwhelmed by wandering thoughts, nor to give up
on my intention to focus on God's breath moving through me.

Before beginning a morning run I sometimes read the headlines
or a lead story from the day's newspaper. I remember in 1998, the
President of the United States was embroiled in controversy over
the Monica Lewinsky affair. Special Prosecutor Kenneth Starr had
just issued his report and most of the newspapers had published ex-
tensive accounts of the investigation. Probably like most readers, my
eye was first drawn to the sections of the report titled "Sexual Encounters." I felt that it was none of my business, but still I was
attracted to the sordid details of the President's sexual relations with
a White House intern. I read the article, laced up my running shoes,
and headed out the door. I realized ten minutes later what poor
preparation for running reading about this tawdry affair could be.
My mind was engaged in ruminations about the presidency, politics,
illicit sex, the press, special prosecutors, hypocrisy . . . all topics that
disconnected me from the place I wished to be while running. It took
some time, and a lot of breathing, to reorient myself to my surroundings and to regain my proper sense of self. Once again the importance
of appropriate preparation for running meditation was clear to me. If

I am going to read, then it is better to read Rumi, the Psalms, or Thoreau, not explicit accounts of a troubled President's sexual adventures.

Is God There if We Are Not?

A Polish rabbi depicted in E. L. Doctorow's novel *City of God* was faced with the methodical and complete decimation of his village by the Nazis. Asked why he continued to pray when God appeared deaf to the tortured cries of his people, the rabbi replied, "I pray to bring Him into being."

Can running be a spiritual practice whether or not the runner regards it as one? Perhaps. Attending religious services or reading scripture can be spiritual practices even if done in a mindless way. It is clear that people often go through the motions of religious practices for a variety of secular reasons, and God touches them anyway. People attend church for social or business concerns, or for their children's well-being. It often happens that they find themselves fed spiritually even when their objectives were more mundane. The same can be said for running. A conscious intention to allow the running experience to become an opportunity for intimacy with God makes it much more likely that an intimate encounter will occur. However, even if your intentions are only the usual desires for exercise, tension release, or fresh air, the opportunity for communion with the spirit still exists. You have placed yourself in a situation where you are open to the Divine and the Divine can speak.

Some people take active steps to prevent the likelihood of feeling God's presence. Running with the radio blaring through headphones will likely keep one's brain occupied enough to prevent an opening for spirit. Purposely working on mental tasks while running also makes one less open to divine intervention. Not making any effort to still the incessant chatter of mental activity means that the stillness of mind that is fertile ground for God's intervention does not exist.

Much can be done to encourage or discourage the transformation of running from a secular to a sacred experience.

Winding Down the Run

For most of us, the number of hours spent running can be only a small fraction of the number of hours in the week. Even if running time becomes a richly rewarding time of communion with the Divine, it remains only a tiny portion of the time we have available to be in relationship with God. I urge you to extend the running meditation time beyond the run itself. End the run by stretching slowly, methodically, and with the same level of awareness that you achieved during the run itself. When stretching is complete, walk mindfully back to your car or your home. Be aware of each step; notice the sense of well-being remaining from the run. Take the time to savor the heightened sense of God's presence that has been experienced while running. Consciously extend the feeling as long as you can. Don't be too quick to plunge into the events of the day. Resist the temptation to turn on the radio for the drive home. When thoughts of the day begin to intrude, you might acknowledge them, and then let them go and practice returning to an awareness of God breathing through you. Eventually, the demands of the day will win over your thoughts. However, if at the end of every run you attempt to remain fully conscious for as long as possible, an awareness of the Divine spark within you will be retained for longer and longer periods. You will be sustained and strengthened by the remembrance of the time spent in God's presence.

You may find that the time immediately after concluding a run, and after stretching properly, is an excellent period in which to engage in sitting meditation. Your mind is uncluttered, you are probably tired and willing to sit quietly, and you are likely still enjoying the sense of well-being that lingers after a satisfying run. Take advantage of this state of mind to move into an even higher state of consciousness. The run has already elevated your level of awareness and it remains for you to allow a quiet focus on your breath to transport you to new realms. You will find that you are unusually receptive to stillness and quiet. This experience has been especially rich for me during the times in which I have completed a run by a body of water. After a brief plunge in cool water, I emerge refreshed. Sitting quietly, I am aware of all the sounds and sensations around me, but so much more aware of my presence in a larger universe.

Do I Need This?

The preparation for the individual run is also a preparation for the inevitable crises, disappointments, and losses that accompany life. I began to run seriously in the midst of crisis. Running, simply for the escape it provided from the pain I felt, was valuable as a harmless anesthetic. However, if my practice of running meditation had been more highly developed at the time, it would have been much more useful. If you have an already developed meditative practice, you already have a place to turn when you need it. Starting from scratch, in the midst of crisis, it is sometimes too difficult to even put one foot in front of the other. Preparing for these difficult times, developing a running meditation practice—becoming familiar with a well-trodden path to the Divine—can give you the assurance that even your most feeble steps toward God will be answered by God's running toward you.

If you are new to running, be assured that speed and distance covered are of little consequence. Start running slowly. If you find that you are tired after running only a short distance, stop and walk until your breathing is less labored. Then pick up the pace and run until you feel the need to walk again. Over time, as you begin to get into shape, you will find that you are able to walk less and run more. I often walk in the midst of a run—either to catch my breath or simply to savor the experience of being where I am.

Despite the fact that I love to run, there are also days when I simply do not feel like running. Many times I have dressed and headed out the door, only to return after running a half of a block down the street. On those days, I might take the dog for a walk, practice yoga, do a few push-ups, or maybe do nothing. Running requires some measure of discipline, but a rigid adherence to the practice can take the joy from the experience. Run in a way that allows you to find pleasure in the experience.

emptying the mind

The only real test comes
when you are alone with God.
Live in the nowhere that you came from,
even though you have an address here.
RUMI

The emptier the spirit, the more is the prayer and the work mighty,
worthy, profitable, praiseworthy and perfect. The empty spirit
can do everything.
MEISTER ECKHART

Only a few months after I began to practice contemplative prayer
with some degree of consistency and devotion, I became aware of
an intense bluish aura that would sometimes appear as I moved
deeper into a meditative state. Usually, as I sat silently focusing on
my breathing, I would see only the darkness of closed eyelids. Occasionally, however, this sense of lustrous, light-filled blue would
move across my field of vision. The blue would occupy all that I
could perceive with any of my senses, enveloping my being. If I
focused too much on this "blueness," it would dissipate. However,
if I was able to follow the practice of letting go of any vision of
this kind and focusing on breathing, I could sometimes rest in the

peace of this blueness for several minutes. I consider this experience to be one of what Teresa of Avila called God's small favors. St. Teresa cautions against seeking after or relying on these experiences; however, she acknowledges the pleasure and encouragement that these gifts from God offer the seeker of communion with the Spirit. Her counsel is not to be attached to these favors, but to acknowledge them and let them go.

I interpreted the experience of the blue light as a sign that I was on the right path. The blueness offered to this easily discouraged seeker an indication that the path I had chosen offered some recompense along the way. I recognized that if I didn't chase after the incentives, and stayed with the path, the ultimate reward would be far greater.

As I began to incorporate the practice of contemplative prayer into my running, I found myself wondering if and when I would receive one of St. Teresa's "small favors." In particular, I began to look for the presence of something akin to the "blue light" as a readily recognizable sign that I was on the correct path. This thought often accompanied me as I ran through the heavily wooded neighborhood where I lived. Obviously, it would not be practical for me to run with my eyes closed, searching for a vision from God. Still, in the newness of this quest for God on the running trail, I sought affirmation that this practice could be as rewarding as sitting meditation had become for me. In retrospect, my desire for a sign seems foolish and naive, but in the way that God looks after small children and fools, I was granted a simple insight.

As I ran, with my eyes focused on the portion of the distant sky I could see framed by the early autumn's still-green leaves, the clouds parted and all I saw was blue. To my amazement, the color of the sky was exactly the same color as the blue I had often seen in my deepest meditations. It had never occurred to me before that the blue I had been seeing in sitting meditations, and seeking while I ran, was a brilliant sky blue. The revelation was that all I had really needed to do was open my senses to the sights and sounds and smells that already surrounded me. My "small favor" that day was an awareness that God's small favors were available to me all along, if I only accepted them. Perceiving the blue aura was not a matter of experiencing a mystical vision; it was simply a matter of receiving God's grace.

I learned a critical lesson from this incident about the difference that exists between sitting and running meditations. In sitting meditation, it is advisable to minimize the sights, sounds, and sensations of the external world that tend to disrupt a silent meditation. In running meditation, it is impossible to avoid the influence of external stimuli. As you run, you encounter an endless stream of sensory impressions. It is impossible to shut them out. The lesson I learned from the realization that I could see the blue aura simply by opening my eyes to the sky in front of me was that I should fully engage the senses while running, not ignore them.

On the other hand, it is essential not to be a slave to the endless barrage of sensations encountered on the trail. The goal of creating an empty space in which the Divine can dwell remains the same. In order to accomplish this goal while running, it is necessary to direct your focus of attention on specific sensory impressions. For example, attention is concentrated on the feel of your lungs as they fill with air, the sound of your feet as they touch the ground, or perhaps the view of the hill in the distance. It requires some discipline and practice not to allow your mind to follow the wanderings of your eyes and ears, but it can be done. The reward is a movement toward the Transcendent.

The Need to Quiet Your Mind

The practice of sitting meditation was developed in a time when most of one's day was spent engaged in physical labor. Meditation provided a respite from those labors, a change of activity as well as a change of pace. However, in contemporary Western society most people's workdays are spent in more sedentary tasks. They work in offices, at computers, on the phone, or sitting at a desk most of the day. Their bodies cry out to be used, to be active, to be physically challenged. The idea of being still to meditate, when they have already been sitting most of the day, may not be an appealing notion. The need to quiet one's mind is more pronounced than the need to quiet one's body. We may return home from work exhausted, but we misinterpret the nature of the exhaustion as physical rather than mental. We may be compelled to collapse on the sofa and doze through the evening news, when our bodies and minds would be better served by a stillness-creating physical activity.

At the end of the workday, I am ready to run out the door. Part of this is my recognized need for physical exertion. In addition to that, I feel the desire to empty my head of the day's activities. People accomplish this in a variety of ways: stopping for a drink on the way home, spending a half hour unloading the burdens of the day on a spouse with her own concerns, or burying themselves in the mindlessness of television. Another way to accomplish this, and perhaps one that more directly addresses the source of our mental overload and fatigue, is to go for a run—a run with the clear intent of creating a place for prayerful meditation.

The Rev. Lauren Artress, in speaking of the calming effects of walking a labyrinth, has written, "The labyrinth can be a tremendous help in quieting the mind, because the body is moving. Movement takes away the excess charge of psychic energy that disturbs our efforts to quiet our thought processes." The same can be said for running, and perhaps even more so if the proper intentions behind the run are present. If the movement of walking discharges psychic energy, the more vigorous exertion of running is likely to be even more charged.

Which Is the Successful Run?

On some days running is effortless. My legs are light, the air is crisp, and I am fully conscious. I can run for miles, absorbed in the present, savoring each moment, and moving easily to the next. Through my own breath I sense the God-instilled life that surrounds me.

Other days are hot and muggy. My legs feel as if they are made of iron and my mind lacks focus. My thoughts jump from one topic to another. It is a struggle to bring focus back to my breathing. Over and over again I must retrieve my thoughts, recognize them, and let them go. It feels as if attention to my breathing, to my footsteps, to my immediate surroundings lasts only a few seconds before that attention is again displaced by seemingly random and distracting ideas. The entire run is a battle, an effort to stay aware of the presence of God amid a constant barrage of interference.

Which of the runs is the most fruitful? The first run is clearly the most enjoyable. On such a run a smile rests easily on my face. I feel a connection to the earth, to God's spirit, a sense of unity that is the reward for being open to God's presence. The whole experience is a delight. It is, however, the second kind of run, the run that is a struggle, which is most beneficial on the spiritual journey.

On such a run, I must constantly practice returning to God's presence. I am distracted, become aware of the distracted state, and return to my breath. I rest in God's presence for a few moments and before I know it, I am overwhelmed with thoughts large and small. Then something snaps and I am often able to return to an awareness of my place in the universe and I breathe the breath of God again. It is this constantly repeating return to the breath that is so useful for those seeking an awareness of God's presence that extends beyond the focused meditation session. Living a God-centered life requires constant practice returning to that center. The repeated shifting back and forth between random thoughts and a focus on breath serves to illuminate the path that leads back to God. The more practice you have returning to God, the clearer the way becomes.

The times when it is easy to remain in God's presence are gifts. Enjoy those small rewards along the way, but know that the most productive work will likely come on those days when God's presence seems most elusive.

Percolation of Thoughts

Sometimes, during the first few minutes of a run, I allow my mind to drift aimlessly. This wandering happens naturally, but it can also be quite intentional. Before moving into a rhythmic state of consciousness, one conducive to prayer, it is necessary to allow time for that rhythm, or pace, to develop. As I run, I slowly move into a place where my mind and my body are in synchronization. Until I feel this happening, I may allow my thoughts to roam. This also has the effect of cleansing my mind. Some thoughts cry out to be heard. Some events of the day demand that they be mulled over. I seldom make any effort to try to stop this from happening. I'm not sure that I could. However, slowly and gently, as I feel my mind being touched by the rhythm of the run, I nudge my thoughts away from the concerns and happenings of the previous hours and toward the present.

On occasion a thought is too overwhelming to be dismissed. I sometimes feel that I need to dwell on a thought for a short while, or perhaps even an extended time. I can remember my first realization of the strong connection between meditation and strenuous, repetitive physical exertion. (Here I am referring to meditation in the Western sense, focusing on a particular idea, theme, or passage of scripture—dwelling on it, looking at it from various angles, seeking its inner meaning.)

I was twenty-three years old and just less than a week into my first of two cycling trips across the United States. I was to spend many weeks pedaling through the solitude of the plains and mountains that stretch from Canada to Texas. The scenery was spectacular and the ride, at times, thrilling. I will never forget crossing the Continental Divide—pedaling up and up and up, in my lowest gear, all morning long and then having one exhilarating, tear-filled, and terrifying thirty-minute ride down the east side of the Divide. Yet the trip was mostly filled with the monotony of the plains, routine and constancy. I occupied my mind with meditation, as I knew it then.

I would decide what topic I would dwell on that morning. I remember clearly saying to myself (as a solitary traveler, I often talked quite openly to myself, a habit I haven't completely broken), "I think I will consider the question of the existence of God," or "What kind of a career path should I seek when I return from this trip?" or "Do I really love this woman who may or may not be waiting for me back in Texas?" It wasn't really the profundity of the topics that strikes me as interesting now, but the degree of concentration I was able to maintain on a particular theme. With very little interruption, I could hold an idea in my head and explore it as if it were a tangible object held in my hand.

As I look back on this experience, I attribute the singularity of focus I was able to maintain partially to the repetitive nature of the physical experience. The steady cadence of each downstroke, the pistonlike movement of my legs, the constant breathing, the sound of my heart beating—all contributed to clarity of thought. Even today, it is those thoughts and the unique thought process that make up my clearest memories of that trip. Although I experienced exhaustion, exposure to severe weather conditions, life-threatening danger, and glorious encounters with man and nature, my encounter with meditation was what I retained.

Exhaling Extraneous Thoughts

When running, think of the breathing process inhaling God and exhaling extraneous thoughts. You are allowing the thoughts arising from your head to move through your body and be expelled through your breath.

February 25, 1999—Sacrificing of Thoughts
I have begun to think of this letting go of thoughts as a sacrifice—an offering up to God of all the thoughts, hopes, dreams, concerns, fears, and ambitions that drive, perplex, trouble, and please us.
"Offered to God" sounds too much like hollow God talk, but each

of these invading ideas need to be blessed, enveloped, and enfolded in God's love. I have an opportunity while running to present the issues of my life to God. A tremendous unburdening can occur, or it can be a very reluctant letting go of thoughts to which I am firmly attached. As I settle into the practice, the letting go becomes more natural.

As with sitting meditation, thoughts continually arise; grow neither distracted nor frustrated by their arrival. As Father Thomas Keating says, "Adopt a friendly attitude to the thoughts that arise." Don't try to force them away; acknowledge their presence and let them pass through you. There is a need to process these passing thoughts, but no need to dwell on them. Rigorous physical activity can stimulate these kinds of insights. I view them as gifts to be considered with a wary eye. During one particular run, I received a new way to view and understand the Trinity—an idea that was undeveloped but might significantly contribute to my appreciation of a concept central to Christianity that has often eluded me. But my intent of this run was to rest in God's presence, to listen to the Silence. At the same time, I did not wish to discard the gifts of insight that seemingly fall from the sky when I have cleared my mind of the rubble of life's temporal concerns. So my method of dealing with these kinds of thoughts is to pause for a moment and catalog the idea. Taking no more than a minute, I visualized the equation linking the Father, the Son, and the Holy Spirit with the mind, the body, and the spirit. I could then record the idea in my brain until it could be considered at a time when it did not interfere with the running meditation. Not wishing to feel ungrateful, I thanked God for the insight and then resumed my focus on the breath.

Burnt offerings are no longer a common component of contemporary religion, but the opportunity to offer a meaningful sacrifice of the mundane in exchange for the sacred can be found in every quiet moment. It takes genuine effort to give up our appealing and interesting thoughts. After the run, the truly important thoughts resurface, but most are usually far less enticing than earlier perceived. It is amazing that they can seem so important when competing with God's presence for space in your head.

January 3, 1999—The Percolation of Thoughts, Ideas, and Concerns

On Saturday morning, the second day of the new year, I went for a run in the hills. My intention, as usual, was to focus on the breath. I did so, but found that my attention stayed on breathing only a short time before an extraneous thought would pop into my head. I had been to a New Year's Eve gathering, had a very bad fight with Donna, and had been ill on New Year's Day. I had not meditated, sitting or running, for several days. Under such conditions, there is always the need to process the events that have transpired since the last run. The thoughts surrounding my experiences rise to the surface of my consciousness. It is as if the act of conscious breathing compels these thoughts to percolate through both body and mind. During the run, I do not deliberately choose thoughts that need processing. In fact, the thoughts that appear at the surface are often not the ones that I would have predicted would appear. For example, I had to re-experience and let go of the embarrassment I had felt New Year's Eve when I gave an over-the-limit credit card to the waiter. However, the very intense argument I had with Donna did not emerge. I have no way of knowing what thoughts will appear, though I am certain that they are the thoughts that need the cleansing attention of the prayer run.

Again, whatever thoughts materialize, I must treat them the same. Acknowledge them, recognize that, for whatever reason, they are significant—and let them go. Return to the breath. It may be that, like on this Saturday morning, the time spent focusing solely on the breath will be brief and a whole series of thoughts will line up in the queue, waiting for attention (while some thoughts sneak back into the queue, needing an additional treatment), waiting for the creation of the void that breathing creates.

When I return from a run like this, I usually feel better—as if a burden has been lifted from me. I no longer feel that the concerns that had been waiting below the surface are directing my thoughts. It is much easier to remain in the present when, in the run, I have allowed the concerns of the past and the future to dissipate. However, after a run like this I do feel the need for another run. The run in which thoughts and concerns continually arise is healing. The run in which you have moved beyond the petty concerns of life, and focused completely on the breath of the moment, is uplifting. Although it is the uplifted state of mind I seek, the healing must take place first, then I can move on.

Similarity Between Therapeutic Effects of Centering Prayer and Running

There is, however, a step beyond this level, where running becomes therapeutic. My thoughts on this topic stem primarily from the work of Father Thomas Keating and his teachings on centering prayer. For Father Keating, centering prayer is a form of meditation that involves the recitation, over and over, of a "holy word." This is done as a way of focusing the attention on the breath and minimizing the distractions that arise by repeating the self-chosen holy word throughout the entire twenty- to thirty-minute sitting.

A major insight of Father Keating's involves what happens to the thoughts that inevitably arise during the prayer or meditation session. Keating recognizes that eventually the deep issues that are the source of the pain we all experience will rise to the surface of consciousness. During centering prayer, when the trivial, day-to-day thoughts are cleared away, and a clean space is created within our heads, the core issues crawl from the unconscious into this rarely empty conscious state. It can be very difficult when these carefully tucked-away experiences come into consciousness and the peace that meditators seek in their solitude is shaken. At this time, Keating counsels the practitioner of centering prayer to let go of the thoughts. There is no need to dwell on them, but the fact that they have arisen, and been recognized, and then allowed to drift away, can be very healing. Keating likens the practice to psychotherapy, with centering prayer providing the opportunity for repressed thoughts to bubble to the surface, receive the brief attention of the meditator, accept the blessing of God, and be released.

A similar process can take place while running. Instead of simply allowing a jumble of random thoughts to occupy your mind during a run, or instead of directing your mind to the shopping list for the evening's menu or the composition of a memo that needs writing, the mind can be emptied of thoughts and allowed to rest. Random thoughts will arise just as they occur during centering prayer. Many of these thoughts will be trivial and can be easily released. You may then return to a focus on the breath, or to the sound of your foot touching the ground. Eventually, however, painful thoughts will arise. The idea is to let go of those as well. There is no need to dwell on them, analyze them, or understand them. Simply release the thoughts and return your attention to the breath. There is no one-shot cure here. The source of the pain will arise again, perhaps during the same run, perhaps not until years later, but each time the treatment is the same. Recognize the thought that has arisen, allow it to receive God's blessing, and let it go.

February 11, 2000—Running with Incessant Thoughts
  For reasons that escape me, yesterday's run on the Shoal Creek Trail was difficult. I never had the energy and strength that moved me the previous Monday or Saturday. Sometimes the mystery of running is completely beyond my understanding. I am weakening in my resolve to give up the relationship with Donna. Is it the need for sexual companionship? Or is it jealousy, or fear that I am making a mistake? It is a confusing time. She has taken her kids to Big Bend this weekend and I hope all is well. Learning of her trip to Switzerland affected me in an unexpected way. I immediately wondered if her former lover, "the count," had taken her there. Probably her

friend Karen paid for her to come, but immediately I had to deal with the green monster.

The run itself was permeated with thoughts of Donna. The jealousy I was feeling was reminiscent of the many miles I ran years ago when I ran with the heartache of losing my wife. Thoughts that I did not want to have flooded my brain. Emotions that I wished to feel no more crept inside me. Efforts to redirect my focus to my breath and to the physical sense of place proved futile. Even stretching after the run, a time in which I usually am most present to the divine, offered no escape from my troubled thoughts. I can only take this to mean that I am not finished with the issue.

When the cacophony of exterior noise is silence, we sadly find out that there is a roar of noise inside. We are pulled apart by conflicts, painful memories, overwhelming desires, and a barrage of extraneous thoughts. Now, when the outside world is still, we are forced to face the inner turmoil.

STEPHEN ROSSETTI

Running silences the exterior noise, but provides a place where the interior noise can be heard. It is impossible to silence the interior noise; it must be heard. Yet it is enough to allow the litany of voices to cry out. There is no need to dwell on any voice. The silence you find between each voice is the object of your search. And it is the constant return to silence, a willingness to turn away from the demands of each voice, that strengthens the connection with the Divine Voice. Spiritual muscles are being used that perhaps have never been exercised. We are accustomed to answering the call of worldly concerns. Turning away from that call, even for just the time it takes for a run in the park, requires training.

Internal vs. External Focus

There seems to be a clear division between an internal and an external focus when engaged in running meditation. In contemplative prayer, I spend many hours sitting, focusing on my breath, a mantra, or a holy word—attempting to create an empty space for God to explore. I generally sit alone, with my eyes closed, in a quiet place, in dim light or in the shadows of a day beginning or ending, without a telephone, radio, or television; minimizing the distractions that might pull me away from the silence I seek.

It is possible to take this approach when running, despite the compelling nature of external stimuli. Rather than closing your eyes, rest them on a distant object—without concentrating on it or even thinking about it. In sitting meditation, Buddhists typically lower their eyelids without closing them entirely, allowing the line of sight to rest on an object a few feet ahead, but not concentrating on the object. I've read that this is done to avoid the tendency to fall asleep, which can happen when meditating with the eyes fully closed.

It is not possible, necessary, or even desirable to completely shut out external stimuli, but as you begin to develop your practice, you may want to lessen that stimuli, perhaps by running on a less-crowded trail or on a trail farther removed from street noise. Once again the role of intentionality comes into play. If it is your intention to run and not focus on the externals, it can be done. The breath becomes of paramount importance. Perhaps you will choose to pay attention only to your breathing. Or you may decide to focus on a mantra that can be synchronized with the rhythm of your breath or running pace. In any case, the focus is on the internal, an approach that comes close to simulating the experience of a sitting meditation.

Focus on the Void

Part of the visual focus on the run that is particularly effective is the development of concentration on the negative image, the void. Try adopting the Buddhist Distant Mountain Gaze. When running, the object of this gaze must change as you round bends and encounter new vistas. Since new scenes appear, one must regularly change the object of the focus. Early in my running practice I preferred to focus on an object that was distinct, not hazy. I chose to focus on bridges, buildings, towers, or rock ledges. Even distant trees seemed too fuzzy. A sharp, distinct object in the distance seemed to provide the clarity, the definition I required. Later, as my practice developed, I avoided a focus on a particular object and concentrated my vision on the space between objects. The space formed by the crook of a tree became a perfect focal point. Focusing on the space framed by other objects provided a leap forward in meditation. Emptying the head of unneeded chatter was more easily accomplished if the object of the focus was nothingness rather than simply another object contributing to the clutter in the mind.

Finding God in the Stillness

I had been asked to lead a Christian education class on contemplation during Lent. After my Saturday hill run, while I was cooling down with a short walk down the street in front of my house, I was considering the nature of contemplation. I think of contemplation in the sense that it is used in *lectio divina*, a medieval monastic meditative reading of scripture involving stillness and listening with the ear of the heart. I can think of no way to really contemplate God, to contemplate the Unknowable, except to still my mind, to empty it and allow room for God to enter. Walking down the street Saturday morning, I imagined God in the gaps, in the space between the branches of trees, in between lines of poetry, in the pauses between activities.

December 2, 1996—Focus of Vision/Focus on the Field

Running with an awareness of my breath is not always easy for me, but today was different. Distractions still occurred—thoughts of work, plans for the evening, problems with the kids—all of these things intruded on my focus, but today external thoughts were less intrusive and I was able to readily regain an awareness of the present.

I often run with my eyes focused on a distant object, and I had been aware of the usefulness of a focus on the space between objects. Today the significance of this focus on the void was realized. I was running the Shoal Creek Trail, having spent forty-five minutes concentrating on breathing alone. It was dusk and I became aware of the light. The powerful effect of attention to the light was a discovery I had made a few weeks ago. This evening, as I looked ahead to a point where the trail made a sharp bend to the left, I could see a clearing in the trees and the brightness of the light from the setting sun reflecting on the bushes at the side of the trail. I kept my focus on this for the few minutes it took me to reach the bend. I then shifted the focus of my vision to the space formed by the crook in the branches of a distant tree at the next turn in the trail. I maintained as a focal point the field, rather than the object in the field. This made sense from a practical standpoint. My meditation was not interrupted by contemplation of the object of my vision. I had a focus, but not a focus that could overwhelm my attention to breathing.

Symbolically this made even more sense. The focus of my line of sight was a void, an absence, an emptiness. With my eyes I was concentrating on the nothingness that I sought with my heart. This seemed much more compatible with my aim to create a space for God to dwell.

If you try running with this kind of Distant Mountain Gaze, you may find that the perceived target that has occupied your sight for some distance and that appeared distinct from three hundred yards away evaporates as you approach it. You may have been focusing, for example, on a patch of sky whose perfect symmetry from a distance slowly falls apart as you see that the branch forming half of an arch was growing on a tree twenty yards ahead of the branch on the corresponding side of the arch. Or sides of the framed bit of blue were bushes and boulders scattered some distance from one another. What you find is that the goal that seemed attainable is now elusive. You may arrive at a portion of the goal and realize that it is incomplete. You move through the goal, noticing pieces of the objective as you pass by them. As the target falls apart around you, it becomes apparent how meaningless that goal has become. They are merely devices, tools, aids to keep us moving and focused. Another ethereal aim is likely to appear on the trail ahead. The importance lies in the journey, the run and the movement along the trail.

A God-Shaped Hole

In his book *The Meditative Mind,* Daniel Goldman says, "All meditative systems are either One or Zero—union with God or emptiness. The path to the One is through concentration on Him, to the Zero is insight into the voidness of one's mind." This seems a false dichotomy to me. Most Buddhists would not label this emptiness as God. And most theists would not refer to God as emptiness. However, I believe the two concepts are one and the same. It is the clearing of the mind that allows room for the Transcendent. God makes his presence clearly known in the void. In much the same way, God appears in people's lives when loss occurs. The loss of a job, a divorce, the death of a friend or family member, ailing health—all create emptiness. Life's circumstances create a void, and room for God is made. As the psychiatrist Gerald May has written, "Everyone has a God-shaped hole." We can attempt to fill that hole with all of the world's wonders and distractions, or we can strive to keep it empty, remaining as a place for God to reside. It is one of life's wondrous paradoxes that it is in the emptiness that we discover that life is not barren.

Running in Silence, Apophaticism

Thomas Merton says in his *Contemplative Prayer*: "He waits on the Word of God in silence, and when he is 'answered,' it is not so much by a word that bursts into his silence. It is by his silence itself suddenly, inexplicably revealing itself to him as a word of great power, full of the voice of God." Stephen Rossetti, in an explanation of what he calls the "pure gold of silence," suggests that this means that God's message is not merely found in the silence, that silence is not just the medium, but is the message itself.

The truth of this observation is endlessly revealed in the quest to find God in silence. Running the trails in silence, listening for God's voice, and hearing only your breath can eventually lead to the realization that God speaks in the silence itself. A deeper understanding of this reality can be gained through a simple exercise—a variation on the exercise for the second quarter of a run described on page 4. Use the sound of your footsteps as a mantra, a focal point to prevent your thoughts from jumping from one idea to the next. Assuming that you have acquired a good deal of practice focusing your attention directly on the sound of each step, I recommend trying this next exercise. This time, instead of focusing on the sound of each foot landing on the earth, focus on the silence existing between each step. There is an ephemeral moment during the stride when both feet are off the ground, the moment when the weight of your body is suspended between steps—a time when you are flying. This silence is admittedly brief. However, it is its brevity, its elusiveness that makes it such a worthy goal. It is the nothingness of running. It is the void. It is what takes place in the midst of the action of running. And it is in this empty space where God can be found most readily.

It has been my experience that, with concentrated focus on the silence between steps, the apparent duration of this moment in time is lengthened. It feels as if the sound of steps fades into the background while the silence of the stillness between the steps moves to the foreground. Extend the "hang time," the amount of time you are flying as you run, when neither foot is touching the ground. It may be helpful to physically extend this time as you increase your awareness of its presence. For a period of time, extend your stride and stretch the hang time.

December 1998—Falling Asleep While Running

Earlier today as I was heading home from my Saturday-morning hill run, I glanced up at a hillside park that looks down on the steep tree-lined streets that make up my route through the hills west of the Balconies fault line. The park, in fact, sits directly atop the fault and towers above the flat prairie to the east and the Texas hill country to the west. A quick loop through the small park, about a mile into the run, has been a part of my route for several years, giving me a small taste of rugged hill climbing. The uneven terrain helps to strengthen my ankles.

Gazing up at the park from the streets below, I could not remember if I had earlier made the run through its quarter mile of rocky trails. It was only after several moments of reflection that I could vaguely recall running through the park. I realized that I had virtually slept through that part of the run. Despite all my intentions to be present to my physical surroundings and to my breathing, I had almost no recollection of a significant part of the course. I had lost awareness. Early in a run I sometimes allow my mind to wander. Thoughts of the week's activities or of life's concerns move through my consciousness. If I am running for an hour or more, I often permit my mind to aimlessly move through these thoughts for about fifteen minutes. Just how aimlessly I had today allowed my thoughts to wander was pointed out by my being almost completely unaware of my presence on the rough trail.

It is not that unusual for me to completely forget what my run is about. I can start off with the best of intentions, and all falls away. I run unconsciously, allowing my mind to drift aimlessly from one topic to another with no resolution, while hanging on to spiteful thoughts. I lose track of where I physically am, how I feel, or how the elements feel around me. My aim, when this happens, is not to be too hard on myself, to understand that this too is part of the process. These long periods of mindlessness also play a purpose—if only as a reminder that the link with the self requires careful husbandry, constant tending. The weeds of thoughtlessness will crop up in the most fertile of newly tilled soil. Only if the soil were sterile—barren—would no weeds arise. It is through the act of weeding that a bountiful harvest can be gathered. Perhaps better said—the weeding is the harvest.

March 18, 2000—Running When Preoccupied with Troubles

After not having run for almost a week, I found the time to run yesterday afternoon. I was so drawn to the run by that point that I can't imagine doing anything else. God compelled me to run with the same insistence that I am drawn to the Eucharist and to Morning Prayer. The day had been very stressful. The workday had been challenging, it was the day of my ex-wife's wedding, I had learned of the impending death of my friend Dave, the effort to buy a new truck had been frustrating, and I hadn't prepared well for my evening class. As I ran, all of these concerns swam about my mind and left me with a sense of uneasiness that I rarely feel at this stage of my life. Each time I became aware of a thought, I let it go and returned to my breath and to the run. I was able to focus on the present only a brief time before my mind wandered to one of the events of the day. Still, the need to quiet my mind and allow space for the Divine was the more powerful urge, and each mundane thought was washed away by the rhythm of the run. I ran for an hour in the hills and never reached the level of consciousness that enabled me to rest completely in God's presence. The events of the day had occupied my thoughts enough that my usual strong sense of *self had been overtaken. How easy it is for the contemplative to stray from the path. On the run, God provided comfort and consolation. Yet because the day had ill-prepared me for an encounter with God at a higher level, I was only able to receive the nourishment of infant's milk. I was not ready to receive the meat of the more mature sojourner toward God. On this day, I received what I needed and for that I am grateful.*

This experience is much like that of the devoted churchgoer who finds solace in repeating the words of the liturgy even though she may feel dry spiritually. Running works much the same way. God may or may not appear, but going through the motions of running can take you to the place where his presence has been felt in the past. That alone is comforting and healing.

When the Practice of Running Meditation Becomes Stale

Spiritual journeys of all kind inevitably become difficult. It may be that for some time the practice of running meditation will be very fulfilling, that the level of awareness achieved while running will become higher, that you experience a richness in the running experience never felt before. You have a strong sense of yourself and of your place in the environment around you. You may complete your runs with a powerful sense of peace and gratitude. You begin to look in the eyes of runners you meet with love and compassion. All seems well.

Then slowly, over time, you lose interest in the process. The runs seem less rewarding spiritually. It becomes harder to focus on your breath or on a mantra. Distractions seem overwhelming. Thoughts of the day keep bombarding your consciousness. The peace that once lingered after the run has evaporated.

St. John of the Cross calls this "the dark night of the soul." Father Keating says that this is time when the "false self" is slipping away and that a sense of pain and alienation arises. In truth, this time when separation from God seems most acute actually comes from God. You are undergoing a time of purification of the false self. It is time for another stage in your spiritual development. You are being forced to find God, not in the mantras, the mudras, and the faces of strangers, but in the longing for God itself. The comfortable places where glimpses of God were possible are swept away and replaced by emptiness, the place where we can always find God at home.

So what do you do at this stage? It all seems stale, useless, like all the miles are for nothing. Chalk it up to progress. It means that you are getting somewhere. It also means that the practice is getting harder. It is difficult to persevere when the freshness of the experience has worn away. When the newness of the spiritual encounter is like young love, little effort is required to carry on. You eventually reach a stage where the practices of running meditation become familiar and lack the spark they once had. The answer is to persevere. Perseverance requires faith that the path you have chosen has reached another plateau. Climbing to a higher plateau means that more effort is required to reach that higher plane. Be aware that it is in this seemingly unrewarding quest that the opportunity for spiritual growth is most promising.

February 19, 1999—Post-Marathon Depression

It has now been five days since the marathon and since I have last run. The soreness is almost gone and I wouldn't have any trouble running today if my schedule permitted. I may run a few miles today or tomorrow. I would like to do that. I am beginning to feel a little anxious, in need of the energy expenditure a run provides. I also feel a little depressed. I think that it can be attributed to all of the preparation for a run, the buildup, and then suddenly, it is over. I have nothing left to train for. Once again, I am left with the conclusion that it is not the goal, but the effort to get there that is the essence of the journey. I suspect that even if I had won the marathon, I would still feel somewhat let down.

I am also growing very unhappy with a turn my career has

taken. *The work itself is too easy. Now that the goal of the marathon is behind me, the lack of challenge in my work looms large. My real challenge is determining how I can provide for my family and move in the direction of my call to God.*

In conversation with a fellow runner today, I learned that there is a widely recognized ailment known as post-marathon depression—PMD. I guess that I am not surprised to learn that such a phenomenon exists, since I so clearly felt its effect last week. This week, I am better, and have some perspective on the issue. It is of some comfort to know that I am not alone in experiencing the symptoms. The important matter is to not ignore the depression and to not avoid its effects without learning what I can from the experience.

Last week I went through a period of doubting my self-worth, feeling like a complete failure, feeling hopeless. The reality of my situation is that I have faced a great deal of failure, and may fail again—in the economic sense that most of society measures success and failure. Yet I can objectively see that I am building a relationship with a beautiful, loving woman, have two wonderful children, am healthy, own a pleasure-giving sailboat, have a few very close friends, am seriously writing daily. More to the point, this relatively brief and mild sense of depression compelled me to examine my place in life and my goals. The introspective period, though filled with self-doubt, anger with God, and tears, left me rededicated to my spiritual quest, and with an explicit plan of action. The post-marathon depression left me with the feeling that I had received a gift that was painful to receive but greatly beneficial.

At times things can seem so bad that they are beyond hope. It is not necessary to hope. Hope, in fact, can often get in the way of acceptance and full participation in the painful challenges of the present. For those who are beyond hope the breath offers relief from hopelessness. Hopelessness points the way. If you find yourself gasping for air, breathing shallowly, eyes darting in every direction—stop and breathe deeply. Better yet, start moving and breathing until you reach a place where hope is no longer necessary. "Abandon hope, ye *who enter here" (Dante Alighieri,* The Inferno) *marks not only the passage through the gates of hell but through the gates of heaven as well. Run, breathe, and abandon thoughts of hopes gone awry. Don't be so quick to replace the old hopes with new ones. Relish the hopelessness and return to the breath. One way to think of the breathing process while running is breathing in God and exhaling extraneous thoughts. You are allowing the thoughts arising from your head to move through your body and be expelled through your breath.*

Another runner, in speaking of the post-marathon blues, suggested finding a new goal, another marathon, and another reason to train. This is a typical reaction to loss. Find a new lover to replace the old one. I suggest that you allow time to absorb these losses, to live for a while in the empty spaces that remain after the loss. God's presence can be detected all over this barren territory.

It is during times such as these that I understand more fully what the novelist Gail Godwin speaks of as a "religion ache" or a "spiritual ache" (NPR's Fresh Air, *February 1, 1999 interview). She refers to it as a feeling that you are in companionship with something else, a yearning, a connection-making thing that says if you stop and pay attention, you will find a pattern. We are better able to perceive this pattern when we are empty. When we are truly empty, we hunger deeply and are less likely to be satisfied with any nourishment less sustaining than God's love.*

A Kind of Death

The void that is created by running, particularly long-distance running, is a kind of death. Throughout our lives, we are practicing for our death—rehearsing for the time when we face the empty space that is filled by God's eternal presence. The endurance run can be an opportunity to die before you die—a chance to rehearse death. During the course of the long run, one faces joy and sorrow, pleasure and pain, agony and relief, boredom and excitement, and the opportunity to have it all permeated with an experience of God. Just as in the larger arena we call life, the running life allows you to know each of these experiences without becoming any of them. The structure of the running prayer presents the opportunity to taste each of the emotions that are encountered in the sitting, standing, and walking world and then spit them out in favor of savoring the wine of God's presence.

I once heard Father Keating quote St. Anthony: "The only perfect prayer is when you don't know you are praying." I think this happens when prayer is at a level of intercourse that requires no conscious acknowledgment of the process as prayer. Consciousness of the present is complete, embracing, and without need of direction from us. We have relinquished control of the prayer to God.

Running is my meditation, mind flush, cosmic telephone, mood elevator
and spiritual communion.

LORRAINE MOLLER

When I run, I feel His pleasure.

OLYMPIAN ERIC LIDDELL IN *CHARIOTS OF FIRE*

I t is possible to live a life of complete devotion to God and never
experience God in a direct, mystical way. I have the deepest respect
for those whose spiritual practice does not provide them along the
way with the rewards of direct encounter with the Divine, yet whose
love for God is so great that they continue their practice, in faithful
devotion. Generally, my practice is also one of quiet devotion accompanied by a sense of God's presence—usually subtle, barely perceptible, but at the same time, unmistakable. However, I must also
count myself among those whom God recognizes to be stubborn,
unresponsive, and so lacking in faith that an occasional breathtaking,

unambiguous, and explicit encounter with the Transcendent is required to redirect my attention. I am like the disciple Thomas, whose doubts led Christ to reveal the wounds he received on the cross, so that Thomas might touch the scars with his own hands. This chapter symbolically contains the revelation of Christ's wounds. Described herein are encounters with the Divine that stand apart from my usual experiences on the running trail. Each of these experiences so profoundly altered the course of my life that I have chosen to separate them from the other, more typical and ultimately more sustaining, periods of quiet communion with the Transcendent. This chapter is about those times in which the Divine has spoken so clearly that, as inattentive as we can sometimes be, the source of the message is unmistakable.

Baseball from the Sky

I was still running from the pain. I had not yet realized that running could take me toward the Transcendent. I knew only that while I ran, the ache I felt in my heart would somehow lessen, become submerged in the swirl of effort, motion, and beauty of an afternoon run. I usually ran on the hike-and-bike trail that loops around and occasionally bridges the blue-green waters of Austin's Town Lake. As the name implies, this is an urban lake that is circled by an urban trail, but it is nonetheless an escape from the city. In fact, the sense of escape the trail offers is heightened by the proximity of the city streets. The downtown skyline is visible much of the way and traffic can always be heard. The city's presence is constant. The trail parallels streets and sidewalks, where only moments before, the runners had probably maneuvered their own vehicles through congested traffic. Looking to one side, the runner sees the city; looking to the other, he sees the shoreline and the serenity of the water. The lake is fed primarily by the Colorado River, but made holy by the flowing waters of Barton Creek, emanating from the city's spiritual center,

Barton Springs. When running around the lake, there is an automatic shift of orientation, away from the city and toward the water, away from the secular and toward the sacred.

As with most who ran that day, my shift in consciousness took place without my awareness of the change. I knew only that when I ran, I felt better. I didn't question why. Then the baseball fell from the sky. I was crossing the Congress Avenue Bridge. The bridge is expansive, bordered on both edges with a wide sidewalk. The bridge was unusually quiet, with cars visible only in the distance. The ball landed at my feet; a half step faster and it would have landed on my head. It had fallen from directly above. I stopped and looked around me. No one was near. One car receded in the distance. Another approached some fifty yards away. The ball had fallen from the sky. I picked it up and examined it. It was a very old baseball, not just well used. It was worn from time, not play. The seams were high, the leather was genuine horsehide, and it had the smell and feel of a ball that might have felt the sting of bats held by Gehrig or Ruth or DiMaggio. My first impulse was to hurl the ball over the railing and into the water below. It had appeared from nowhere and it seemed fitting to return it to nowhere. Instead I held the ball in my hand and resumed my run. I was certainly surprised to have a baseball fall from the sky, but my life had been topsy-turvy for so long that I wasn't completely astounded. I had grown to expect the unexpected. Ruling out baseball-bombing aircraft, I concluded that it must have fallen through one of Stephen Hawking's wormholes, the tunnels through which the renowned physicist believes it possible to move through time. I enjoyed holding the ball in my hand. I liked its feel and the sense it gave me of a connection with something historically significant—something bigger than myself. As I ran I occasionally tossed the ball into the air, contemplating the curious nature of the incident. I crossed the bridge and made my way back down to the trail. I continued running along the south shore of the lake, passing a large hotel and eventually running under the South 1st Street Bridge. I had run a half mile from the point of receiving the ball. As I passed by Auditorium Shores, a green expanse often used for concerts and fairs, I noticed from the corner of my eye a man appearing to be about my age playing baseball with a young boy.

The boy, though he held a very small bat, swung it awkwardly. As I drew closer, I could see that the boy seemed to be afflicted with a muscular disease—I guessed cerebral palsy—which had left him thin, weak, and lacking coordination. It was a struggle for him to even bring the tiny bat across his body, but he did so with a smile and a look of determination. I thought of my own son, close to this boy's age, but strong, fit, and agile. I shuddered. My eyes shifted back to the man I took to be the boy's father. He reached to the ground and picked up a few pebbles. Standing only a few feet in front of his son, he began tossing the pebbles across an imaginary home plate. Each time the father threw a pebble, the boy swung, always too low and always too late.

As I ran past, the father turned and looked at me over his left shoulder. His glance seemed that of a pitcher holding a runner on first. I looked down at the ball I had been carrying. The man held up his hand and, without a moment's hesitation, I threw him the ball. The man caught the ball, turned back toward his son, and resumed his game. The father offered no thanks, no acknowledgment of my offering. His attitude was one of acceptance, of recognition of all being as it should be. I was meant to provide him with a ball so that he could teach his son.

I resumed my run without looking back. I knew that this moment was theirs and that my role in this event was complete. As I ran down the trail I tried to figure out what this curious incident meant. It was easily the strangest occurrence I had ever witnessed. As I reflected on its meaning, then and over the next few days, I concluded that the message I had received was about the importance of baseball in my life. I had always been a fan and was even more so now that my son had shown both an interest and an aptitude for the game. I resolved to pay attention to baseball and be aware of the importance it might play in my life. Indeed, baseball has kept my son and me close over the years. I coached his teams a number of times and have thrown him more pitches and hit him more ground balls than I could ever count. More important, when we have had conflicts and found it difficult to talk, we could always have a catch. Throwing the ball back and forth between us, the lines of communication slowly open up. The rhythm of the throw and the catch, the repeated sound of the ball landing in the pocket of the glove, becomes a mantra. The shared mantra frees our minds from the troubling thoughts that separate us. Slowly we can begin to talk, usually beginning with baseball, but eventually about ourselves.

I have continued to ponder the meaning of the baseball from the sky over the years. I realized that its significance changes over time—that it has taken on the status of myth—and like myth, its meaning is subject to interpretation by those who encounter the legend. Later I began to see the story as a parable about the importance of running in my life. Indeed, running has become very important; in fact it has become a critical part of my spiritual practice. Still later, I understood the baseball myth as a story of giving back what I have received. The baseball was a gift that fell to me. It was grace in its purest form. I was able to pass on that gift of grace, almost immediately, to the place it belonged.

When I talk with my son, Nate, about the kind of listening prayer I do, his response is a skeptical, "What does God tell you?" It's a perfectly reasonable question. If I'm spending all this time listening to God, what does he have to say, and how does he say it? When God speaks, he doesn't always throw baseballs from the sky. Usually the voice of God is barely audible, or veiled in silence . . . but not always. At times the voice of God is thunderous and instantly recognizable, if only we listen.

Running as Re-Creation

When I first began practicing running meditation, I did not immediately experience the level of quiet I had come to know in sitting meditation. Eventually, I found that while the silence I felt in running meditation was of a different quality than in sitting meditation, it was no less profound. I remember asking God to help me to find the time to run and to explore this world of running with me. The idea of exploring uncharted waters with God as my fellow adventurer remains a thrilling notion. It assumes that God can learn, that God is also in the process of becoming, and that he is a dynamic God. Just as the image of God can be seen to transform through the pages of the Old Testament, and change radically with the New Testament, God is still changing. Perhaps it is not just that our conception of God changes, but that he and the way he relates to us changes as well.

Further developing this line of thinking it seemed that running was not only an uncultivated avenue of worship for me, but for God as well. Could God and I both be feeling our way along, learning how this kind of interaction works? It may not be merely a process of discovery, but of creation—with God as my co-creator. Why should we assume that God's role as a creator is over? Or that God is not capable of creating new ways to relate to man? As man evolves, different forms of worship, of prayer, of communication with God, are possible. Running was not a widespread recreational human activity, certainly in the West, until fairly recent times. Perhaps in earlier times, even God did not recognize it as an opportunity for communion. Here, in this activity primarily thought of as simple recreation, lies the possibility of re-creation—creating, with God, a different way of relating.

The process of discovery is a thrilling aspect of learning about prayer and running. Communion with God through meditation is a developed practice accompanied by thousands of years of experience chronicled in countless documents. The beginner can turn to numerous resources to help understand the practice and its methods. Running meditation, while relying on the wisdom of a related body of thought, is an exploration of an avenue to God that, as far as I know, few have trod. The runner embarking on this path can expect surprises, missteps, and perhaps great leaps toward a personal understanding of God.

September 9, 1999—Chance Encounters on the Trail

I was moving at a fairly decent pace down the Shoal Creek Trail when I heard footsteps coming up quickly behind me. I am seldom passed on this trail. Most of the faster runners run on Town Lake. In comparison with the Town Lake trail, the Shoal Creek Trail is rocky, not as scenic and not as popular with the running community. I heard the footsteps run up to within a few feet of me and then slow down. I glanced over my shoulder and saw a black male runner, breathing heavily and sweating profusely. He had now dropped off my pace, slowing to a near walk. A few minutes later, I heard the same running footsteps approaching. This time he ran up even with me and, between breaths, I heard him say with complete sincerity, "Hey, thanks a lot." I then realized that he had been using my methodical pace and me as a marker to measure his progress while sprinting in intervals. He could almost as effectively have picked out a distant tree and sprinted toward it. Instead, he chose me and thanked me for just being there. Oddly, I felt appreciated and pleased that I could help him, even though I did nothing more than I was already doing as part of my afternoon run.

I often feel that small incidents like this seem more significant when I am running than they would have had they happened at other times. Although I saw his face for only a moment, and he spoke only a few words, I remember him clearly and I can still hear his voice. Why did such a small interaction seem so meaningful? I have found that along with a heightened sense of awareness while running, I am also more receptive to all that I encounter.

I met the man on the trail again a few days later. He nodded and said hello as we passed. The sense of wisdom in his eyes created a noble impression. His smile was kinder than those usually received along the trail. I felt that he had seen and understood much. After that day I never saw him again, but in our brief encounter I glimpsed a bit of his essence, and of my own as well.

April 5, 1999—God's Presence in the Shallower Levels of Consciousness

This evening's run, an easy five miles on the Shoal Creek Trail, was a run that began with my will diminished. I had no desire to run, even though it was a beautiful day, relatively cool, and dry. I was feeling discouraged about work and seemed to have little energy. I had eaten too much at lunch and I was feeling heavy and slow. The run was fairly difficult and I struggled to gain a sense of self. Eventually, with my concerns over work weighing heavily on my heart, I resorted to asking verbally, in the form of a chant, for God's help. I was clearly operating at a lower level of consciousness, but God seemed willing to meet me there. I wasn't where I wanted to be on the spiritual path, but I sensed that God was still present.

April 22, 1999—Grace

I attended the noonday Eucharist at the Episcopal Seminary today. It is a vibrant and thoroughly involving service. I always sense the presence of the Holy Spirit among the seminarians. In the sermon, given by a local parish priest, reference was made to the relatively few number of times that she had clearly heard the voice of God speak in a direct manner. The month before, working in her garden, experiencing angst over the separation of a parishioner from her flock, she heard God's voice in the renewal of spring. I silently rejoiced and thanked God for the times I hear his voice.

I am beginning to understand more about why I am having this love affair with running. It is making sense in connection with the rest of my life. In the difficult years, I viewed running as an escape.

I was in such agony then that even while running, I was haunted by terrifying thoughts, fears, and visions of what my life had become. Perhaps running was an escape, but it was also God reaching out to me in a unique way.

Running in the Pecos Wilderness

A few years ago I traveled with my thirteen-year-old son, Nate, my nine-year-old daughter, Lillian, and our Australian shepherd pup, Tyke, to the Pecos Wilderness Area of New Mexico. We spent the first night at Iron Gate, a campground positioned at a major trailhead. The next morning we hiked up numerous switchbacks, through pine forests, across the sunny and windswept grasses of the treeless meadow known as Pecos Baldy, and continued on in the late afternoon toward the rugged knoll called Truchas Peak. Lillian had hiked strongly all day, carrying her small load of clothes and sleeping gear. As the day wore on, I could see that she was tiring and I offered to carry her pack. She gratefully accepted the offer and was soon bounding down the trail with a lightness of foot that characterizes her. She asked if she might take Tyke and walk ahead of her brother and me. I sympathized with her desire to be alone with her dog, having spent much of my childhood in such understanding company, so I agreed, taking pleasure in the independence she was showing in unfamiliar and challenging terrain.

Within a few short minutes, she and the dog were out of sight. I quickly became uncomfortable with her absence. I know the Pecos area well, having visited there for more than twenty-years, hiking its miles of rugged trails. Until that moment I had never felt remotely fearful, nor seriously considered the dangers that could lie behind every bend in the trail. I called for Lillian. I called for Tyke. There was no answer. There were no forks in the trail and it was plainly marked, so I didn't fear that she might have accidentally veered off the path, but my gnawing apprehension was that Tyke might have chased a rabbit or squirrel into the dense forest that surrounds the trail, and that Lillian might have headed after him.

Nate and I picked up our pace, calling for Lillian, whistling and calling for Tyke. We grew more and more concerned. Ten, twenty, eventually thirty very anxious minutes passed and there was still no sign of them. We bounded ahead, moving as quickly as our packs would allow us, continually calling Lillian's name and visually sweeping side to side, looking through the now-very-threatening forest, searching for a sign that they had left the trail. Evening was quickly approaching and even though it was midsummer, the nights are cold here in the lower Rockies, and without her pack, Lillian had no sleeping bag.

At this point I grew very concerned. Lillian was a small child and normally not too adventurous. I had a difficult time imagining her little body crawling over the numerous large tree trunks that had fallen over the trail or climbing up to unlatch a locked gate that crossed the trail at one point. I decided that she must have left the trail and that I should ditch my pack and retrace my steps. I instructed Nate to continue walking up the trail, calling out to Lillian and Tyke, in case we simply had not caught up with them yet.

After a hard look and firm instructions to my son, I turned around and started jogging back from where we had come. The surrounding forest, normally a place of refuge for me, now seemed ominous and threatening. I ran as quickly as I could while still keeping an eye out for any sign of Lillian or Tyke. I called constantly, "Lillian, Tyke! Here boy!" and then I whistled for Tyke, over and over again. I listened intently as I ran, hoping to hear Lillian's small voice amidst the sound of the wind moving through the trees. Adrenalin was pumping through my veins; every sense was keenly focused on finding my daughter.

Suddenly, I was almost knocked to the ground by a hard blow to the back of my head. It had taken me completely by surprise and I had no idea what had hit me until I looked up into the sky, just a few feet in front of me. The impact was the result of a dive-bombing attack from a very large hawk, now slowly flapping her wings and about to land in the branches of a pine tree fifty feet away and above me. She stayed on her perch only long enough to turn around, face my direction, push off from the branch, and drop through the air flying straight toward me. I was dazed from the impact of the bird, but instinctively reached to the ground for a stick to protect myself. As I lifted the stick above my head and whirled it around threateningly, the hawk continued its dive toward me. Only at the last moment, amid my shouts and the waving stick, did the hawk finally relent from her attack, pull up from the dive, and glide over to a waiting branch in a large tree behind me.

I fully expected her to take another dive at my head. I had already wheeled around to face her and, still brandishing the stick, we had a face-off. She began to scream at me and I was certain that if I were to relax my posture, she would resume her attack. I had no time or interest in doing battle with this bird; my beloved daughter was missing and my only concern was to find her. Still, I was aware that the top of my head was bleeding from the impact of either beak or talons. I ran on, continuing to wave the stick over my head and occasionally glancing over my shoulder to make sure that the still-shrieking hawk did not decide to launch another assault.

The nature of my run through the forest had changed dramatically. At first, in my search for Lillian, I was concerned and aware of an ominous sense of foreboding, but now I felt outright fearful. I ran with awareness that very real dangers existed and that my daughter was vulnerable to those dangers. I could feel my heart pounding in my chest. I resumed my watchful run, calling Lillian's name and listening hopefully for a response, still brandishing the stick in case I needed to fend off another onslaught from the hawk.

I lost track of time. I reached the point at which Lillian had lithely trotted ahead with Tyke jumping along at her side. I paused for a moment to be sure that this was indeed the place where I had last seen her. I ran perhaps a half mile farther up the trail in case she had veered off the path while Nate and I passed by her and she had, in turn, retraced steps searching for us. My calls were not returned and there was no sign of her.

Now deeply fearful, I turned around and began a faster run in the direction of my son, and, I hoped, my daughter. Still calling, looking, listening, I could see that twilight was not far away. The sun had dropped behind distant Truchas Peak and a chill was already hanging in the mountain air. I passed the location of the hawk attack, but saw no sign of the bird. I ran and called and listened until, finally, I could hear my son in the distance calling me. I raced toward him and could hear his footsteps approaching me around the next bend in the trail. Much to my relief, his first words were, "I found her. She's okay." Nate had encountered her on the trail, happily skipping along with Tyke, reveling in her independence. Her brother had quickly curtailed that freedom. Nate insisted that she sit on a log beside the trail and stay there until he returned with me. When we caught up with her, she was sitting most unhappily on the log where a horde of horseflies had found her and reduced her to tears. We quickly left the flies behind and moved on to higher and happier ground.

I look for meaning in such experiences. Typically, my first response is to attach a literal interpretation to events. In this case, for a time I became very protective of my daughter. I began to see the world as a more threatening place for her, filled with dangers that had never seemed threatening to me before. At this stage in my life, when I reflect on the story, I usually think about issues of awareness and consciousness while running. I had not before, nor since, run so far in a state of near panic. At the same time, I was as present to the situation as I have ever been. Every sense of my body was attuned to the physical environment. I was searching, with all my powers of observation, for my precious little girl.

The Dalai Lama, when asked how he could maintain such peace and composure after having seen the decimation of his people and homeland and after having been driven from Tibet to India replied, "Surely you do not expect me to lose my serenity?" I am beginning to understand how, even in the worst of circumstances, or perhaps especially in the worst of circumstances, it is possible to remain present.

I still search for understanding of the attack from the hawk. I have always treated wildlife with respect as the primary occupants of the land, where I am only a visitor. I felt betrayed and misunderstood by the hawk. My guess is that the hawk had young nesting in the trees nearby and regarded my running and yelling as an unusual threat. I recall that I felt that I had confronted evil—evil lurking in a place and in a creature that I held in high regard. Despite the attack, I now feel a kinship with the hawk, imagining that both of us were trying to protect our offspring. The story remains enigmatic and, like most personal myths, reveals its meaning over time, changing as I change.

Mountain Running

During the late summer of 1999, I spent a few days with the nuns and monks at the Olivetan Benedictine Monastery in Pecos, New Mexico. Since college days, a quarter of a century earlier, I had been driving past this monastery on the way to the high country of the Pecos Wilderness Area. Even in those youthful times, when the religious life had little appeal for me, I had been curious about the monastery. I had wondered what took place behind the monastery's adobe walls and if its inhabitants sensed the presence of God there, as clearly as I identified a sense of the holy in the rugged beauty of the natural world surrounding the enclave. Over the years, the mountains and streams of the Upper Pecos became a spiritual homeland for me. The drive from Austin, through the parched plains of West Texas, became a pilgrimage leading to a wilderness sanctuary where I found solitude and a connection with feelings for which I had no name.

As I grew older, my acceptance of the Divine Presence within the established church was rekindled. That summer, as I planned a northern New Mexico retreat, my curiosity about the monastery grew stronger and I telephoned to inquire about their guest policy. When I rang I was still uncertain whether my soul most required the freedom and solitude of the wilderness or the spirit of community found within this ancient Benedictine order. After first connecting with a recorded voice, letting me know that the monks were most likely in prayer, I eventually spoke with Father Bob. The gentle, welcoming voice of Father Bob, assuring me that they had plenty of room, was all the persuasion I needed to convince me that my time would be best spent living a few days of balance and order according to the Rule of St. Benedict.

Lying at the southernmost end of the thousand-mile-long Rocky Mountain system, the Sangre de Cristo Range offers majestic mountain views, isolated trails, conifer and aspen forests, flower-filled meadows, abundant wildlife, and clear, sparkling streams. To me, however, the biggest attraction of the lower Pecos high country is the opportunity it offers to escape from the sweltering summer heat of central Texas. The cool crispness of the air, in contrast to the heat and humidity of summer in Austin, sent the first signal to my body that my soul would soon be uplifted.

I awoke early on my first full day at the monastery so that I could attend Lauds, the first service of the day, at six A.M. A Eucharist service followed at 6:45. Breakfast, with fellow retreatants and a few members of the monastic community, was served afterward. Although the evening before I had made a few inquiries about trails leading from the monastery (to which Patrick, a rather portly English monk, who became a good friend, replied he was "not much of a hiker"), it was at breakfast that an energetic nun advised me to cross the river, climb the steps leading to the cross, and continue walking until I reached the fence line. She assured me that if I then followed the trail to the right, it would lead to an abandoned logging road that would take me on to the main system of trails running throughout the Santa Fe National Forest. I set off about nine in the morning. At home in August, the sun at this hour would have already made a morning run unpleasant. Here, the crisp, cool air was energizing. After crossing the narrow footbridge spanning the Pecos River behind the monastery, I bounded up the steps leading to the cliffside cross. I discovered that there was not only the single cross visible from the monastery, but that the Stations of the Cross, the symbolic representation of Christ's Passion, typically enacted during Holy Week, had been set up across the mountain's edge. I followed the nun's directions, as best I could. It was necessary to choose my steps carefully as I made my way up an ill-defined trail of shifting limestone, sandstone, and shale. I am accustomed to trail running and I was expecting, even anticipating, the forced attention to the present that comes with running an unfamiliar path. The initial climb was steep, and the higher altitudes should have made my breathing more labored, but the exhilaration I felt running in the midst of such beauty made the obstacles of thin air and steep slopes insignificant. Eventually, I did reach a wider trail and just as I entered this lane, perhaps twenty-five yards ahead of me, a large mountain lion exited the path. She wore a tawny, light honey–colored summer coat. When I happened upon her, the brush alongside the trail already hid her head. I caught only a glimpse of her heavily muscled shoulders and flanks as she slowly, but deliberately, moved out of sight. Without glimpsing her eyes, I knew that she had seen me, just as she sensed all that was around her. I was torn between the impulse to charge ahead and try to get another glance at her and the instincts of caution that urged me to retreat. As it was, I resumed my steady running pace, allowing my heart to calm, and looked deeply into the surrounding forest for another glimpse of her confident, graceful body. I saw her again only with my mind's eye, but retained within me something of the instinctive animal awareness that she practices to perfection each moment of her day.

After a while, the trail became indistinct again and I grew concerned that on my return trip I might not recognize the way that I had come. I decided to mark the uncertain forks in the trail. Each time I came to an intersection, I picked up two sticks and laid one on top of the other, placing them squarely in the middle of the proper pathway home. The trails continued to weave in and out of one another. Heavy midsummer rains had obscured some of them and created new shallow gullies reminiscent of older pathways created by man and wildlife. I would look back over my shoulder at each juncture and if the correct choice were unclear, I would lay down another set of small branches. Eventually, when the myriad of choices became too confusing, I halted my journey outward and turned around, heading back toward the monastery.

My run had eventually taken me into a deep valley and as I began running up the gradual incline leading homeward, I felt my muscles engage, creating the same sensation one feels when downshifting a powerful automobile. I enjoy the extra effort of mindfulness it takes to run uphill and, for a moment, I remembered and tried to emulate the grace of the mountain lion I had seen earlier. Eventually, I came to the first ambiguous crossroad with my casually placed sticks marking the chosen path. As I passed by the sticks and glanced down at them, I realized that I had unconsciously placed the sticks in the form of a cross, with the head of the cross marking the way home. I continued along the trail, encountering a cross at each doubtful intersection. Whenever the path homeward was unclear, I found another cross marking the way. I felt that the seemingly accidental configuration of sticks into a series of crosses had meaning far beyond their role as trail markers. I followed this array of crosses back to my starting point on the cliff overlooking the monastic grounds. Here were the Stations of the Cross I had noticed earlier. Now, however, I realized that my morning run had been a pilgrimage. Each intersection along the way had been a visit to a station of the cross. My awareness of the sense in which I shared in Christ's Passion had been a gradual unfolding, and not fully realized until the journey had ended. I understood, in a new way, how Christ's journey led him ultimately to the cross and how the cross marked the way to resurrection.

Perhaps this is the nature of our spiritual journey. With our own hands we carelessly mark our course, unaware of the guidance we receive at each uncertain crossroad. With any luck, we eventually realize that God has been there for us all along, guiding the way.

I made my way down the face of the cliff, but instead of immediately crossing the footbridge, I started running along the cliffside trail paralleling the river. I followed the steep and narrow trail upstream until it reached a point where vegetation had almost obscured the path and I was compelled to turn around. I then crossed the bridge and headed up the easier path on the opposite side of the river. I began to move more swiftly, no longer restrained by the necessity of focusing intently on the placement of each foot. The sound and sight of the river flowing alongside me renewed my energy. I moved in ecstasy. The trail continued to follow the river for perhaps a mile, occasionally diverging from the river's course, and then snaking back into alignment with the water's flow. The river was occasionally out of sight, but the sound of the water coursing downstream remained present. Eventually, when the trail met the main road, I turned back toward the monastery.

I reached a neglected campground appointed with an assortment of concrete picnic tables and benches—all leaning in various directions. I picked the table that seemed least likely to topple over and used it to begin stretching. Despite the cooler-than-Texas temperatures, after ninety minutes of running I was hot and soaked with sweat. The sound of the rapidly flowing cold waters of the Pecos River invited me. I abandoned my stretching and renewed my run with an easy sprint a quarter of a mile upstream. I came upon a bend in the river where the water was deep enough for a plunge. I removed my singlet, shoes, and socks and carefully waded into the icy mountain water. When I reached midstream, I braced my body against the force of the swiftly moving current and dunked my head beneath the surface. It was difficult to avoid being swept downstream, but I managed to submerge my entire body a couple of times before the water's chill crept into my bones. The baptism complete, I struggled to the shore.

I warmed in the sun at the water's edge, standing still and straight, naturally assuming the yoga mountain pose or *tadasana*. I stretched for a few moments more while the moisture dried from my body. Facing the stream, with the midmorning sun at my back, I found a comfortable place to cross my legs, sit among the smooth, broad, river-worn stones, and rest in God's peace.

I passed the remainder of the day in the pleasant company of the monastic community and retired early. Despite a fitful night's sleep, when I awoke the next morning, I found that I could not resist the beckoning of the Rocky Mountains' higher elevations. The prayer, the run along the river, the fellowship with the monks, had nourished me and filled me with joy. Still, the spirit of God has always touched me, even when I felt untouchable, in the high mountains of the Sangre de Cristo range. My aim was to combine the joy and spiritual connections I now experience while running with the sense of the sacred, which I have felt for so many years in the splendor of the mountains. As soon as I arrived at the trailhead, I feared that my pilgrimage would be ill fated. After driving for forty-five minutes on the narrow, winding road leading to Jack's Creek Campground, I discovered that I had left my running shoes in my room at the monastery. After chastising myself for the lack of presence of mind, I decided that a run in the high country was important enough to make an extra round-trip to the monastery to retrieve my shoes.

Almost two hours later, my feet were shod and I stood, once again, at the trailhead. Jack's Creek Campground stands at an elevation of 8,850 feet. The first two and a half miles of the trip calls for a climb of 1,050 feet. I had anticipated that the climb would be steep. I had not given much thought to the fact that the air would be much thinner than at the sea-level elevations where I normally ran. However, especially after the extra driving time, I was eager to run and I charged up the side of the first mountain. Within a quarter of a mile, I was gasping for breath, my lungs were burning, and I feared that I had severely miscalculated my abilities. I thought of the Mexican marathoners who train in the high altitudes of mountains outside of Mexico City. I pushed myself until I had to slow to a walk. I breathed deeply, but the air seemed to contain little of the life-giving oxygen I craved. I stopped for a few moments and took in breath after breath of the thin mountain air. Eventually, I began to breathe more easily and I renewed my ascent. This time, however, I made my way up the mountainside at a slower, steadier pace. Even at the slower pace, I realized that I would not be able to run the entire distance. I would have to occasionally slow to a walk to regain my breath. At first I was disappointed, but after a while, I settled into a pattern of alternating gentle uphill running with brisk walking, being careful not to reach the level of oxygen depletion I had reached in my initial assault on the mountain.

Despite the effort it took, the two-and-a-half-mile climb seemed to pass relatively quickly. As I neared the first summit I caught glimpses of the Pecos River Valley through the trees. I grew excited and when I finally broke into a clearing and the entire valley was revealed, I could hardly restrain my tears. I paused for a few moments to take in the view, then returned to the trail.

At the end of that initial two and one-half-mile climb, I knew that I would be able to make the rest of the nine-mile trip with relative ease. The hardest part was clearly behind me. Trail riders, who prefer to navigate the steep slopes on horseback, often use this particular trail. Unfortunately, the horses are very hard on the trails, leaving them badly worn and almost impassable in places. Running on a trail in this kind of condition requires a level of consciousness completely different from the "zoned out" mentality it is possible to maintain when running on an easy trail or on a track. It is necessary to choose the placement of each step. The ruts, the rocks, the roots, all lie in wait. Rattlesnakes present a constant danger and it requires vigilance to avoid accidentally startling one.

The next run across the meadows and through the forests descending to Jack's Creek was glorious. The sky had opened up above, and the distant mountaintops of Pecos Baldy and Truchas Peak stood majestically in the distance. When I reached my destination, I was eager to quench my thirst from the clear spring-fed stream. Kneeling on one knee, I reached into a shallow pool at the base of a small waterfall, scooped up the chilled water with a cupped hand, and brought the water to my mouth. While drinking, I kept a watchful eye on the surrounding forest. Some primordial instinct takes over when I drink from a mountain stream, encouraging me to stay alert to possible danger while enjoying the pleasure of a simple drink of water. I recall childhood memories of similar scenes, but I also have the sense that I have practiced awareness beside mountain streams in times long, long past. I took a few moments to absorb a sense of place and to feel a connection with the countless sentient beings that had quenched their thirst in this same spot. As I caught my breath I watched the Divine wind move through the aspen trees. In the distant treetops I saw the wind gather its force in the midst of the shimmering leaves. This rippling succession of wafer-shaped ornaments moved steadily toward me, until the quivering chorus of leaves surrounded me for only an instant and passed through the forest.

The return trip began with a brief incline, but soon turned into a downhill run for almost the entire homeward journey. The joy of a downhill run, after climbing for so long, was almost overwhelming, but in this setting required extra caution. In many places the soil had eroded badly, exposing the hazardous rocks that had rested beneath the earth's surface for millions of years, while in other places the trail had become a deep rut with steep, concave sides. Swift downhill running required landing on one side of the rutted trail and then rebounding off the opposite side, taking care to avoid landing on a sharp rock or twisting an ankle in a crevice, while keeping an eye on the trail ahead as well. Far from allowing this consciousness of immediate danger to consume all my awareness, I could also sense every movement of the aspen leaves, reach out to touch the leathery trunks of the ponderosa pines, hear the disturbed caws of the crows and the cackle of the wood peckers. Each sight, sound, and touch permeated my being. It was "Indian Running" at its finest.

As I neared the end of the descent, I noticed a pain beginning to build in the base of my spine. The constant jolt from the landing of each foot during this long downhill run was beginning to take its toll. At first I regarded the pain as only a small price to pay for such a lesson in awareness. Then I realized that the pain itself was another lesson. Consciously considering the pain and comparing it with the ache that was developing in my knees, I knew that if I regarded it as another experience of my senses, it would have no more control over my well-being than the rustle of the aspen leaves.

At the trip's highest point, I had reached an elevation of 10,550 feet before turning around. I had run for just under two hours, traveled nine miles, and journeyed into the heart of God.

Friend, our closeness is this:
anywhere you put your foot, feel me
in the firmness under you.

RUMI

Should his concentration falter, should his mind wander to the next hole,
the next set, the next inning, he will be undone . . . And the saint, for all
his talk of heaven and the hereafter, knows that everywhere is right here,
that all of time is right now, and that every man exists in the person in
front of him.

GEORGE SHEEHAN

When You Cook . . . Cook!

An Ancient Buddhist admonition states that "When you cook . . .
cook!" This simple directive is at the heart of my spiritual discipline,
attempting to be present to the task at hand, to avoid distractions,
and to maintain a singular focus. I have attempted this in an age in
which "multitasking" is a highly prized skill. Accolades go out to
those who can simultaneously juggle conference calls, multiple pro-
jects, and current knowledge of office politics. Students can't do their
homework without the radio blaring and family meals routinely take
place in front of the television. Input can be so constant and so

overlapping that thoughtful concentration on a single task has become a rarity. Since we find it difficult to focus on only a single task, the notion of doing nothing, emptying a space in one's head in order to allow room for the Divine, is a completely foreign idea.

How, then, can I be critical of the lack of focus that results when trying to accomplish multiple tasks at one time and still advocate combining running and meditation? The answer to this question lies in the observation that running, practiced as described herein, is actually a form of meditation itself, not a separate task that can be practiced in combination with meditation. The run, undertaken with an intention to focus on its transcendent dimension and practiced in a way that heightens the runner's awareness of the present becomes an experience closely akin to sitting meditation. Concentration improves, stress levels drop, and a sense of peace often prevails. Since you are exercising vigorously, the cardiovascular system benefits as well. Physical fitness is a bonus, not the primary motivation. In this case, two separate purposes can be achieved at the same time without one detracting from another. The primary aim, the intention to move closer to an understanding of God, is not in conflict with a desire for physical fitness. In fact, each goal can be enhanced by the presence of the other activity. Just as running can lead you to a greater realization of your spiritual being, you are likely to be a better runner because of your spiritual approach to running.

It is also useful to recognize that it is nearly impossible to separate ourselves from a culture that expects us to accomplish a great deal. The ability to juggle a variety of tasks is rewarded. Combining running and prayer enables one to accomplish two highly laudable goals at one time. A major cause of tension is the constant pressure we have to do more than we are able. Parents struggle between the demands of children, spouses, jobs, and friends. Couples try to find time to devote to each other and to their own, individual pursuits. Knowing that one is engaged in an activity that is beneficial on several fronts can make it easier to accept that what you are doing now is what you should be doing. Running meditation reduces the tension resulting from the perceived need to be two places at once, by allowing you to accomplish two goals at one time.

Clarity of Thought

In Chapter 2, "Emptying the Mind," I mentioned first becoming aware of the connection that exists between the ability to focus attention and engagement in repetitive physical exercise. In the summer of 1974, I bicycled alone from Kalispell, Montana, just south of the Canadian border, to my parents' home in north-central Texas. My clearest memory of the trip was of its timelessness. Traveling down deserted back roads as much as I could, stopping to rest in small towns, and cycling for about a hundred miles each day, I obviously had a great deal of time to think. I did not practice formal meditation at the time. My carefree existence at the age of twenty-three had not alerted me to the benefits of meditation. Nonetheless, the rhythm of the road, the meandering of my thoughts, and the endless motion of my legs gave me a clarity of thought that I had not known until then. The themes that captured my imagination were many and varied—and sometimes very different from my musings twenty-five-years later. However, the focus of attention I was able to devote to topics I chose to explore is something I envy today. With few distractions, my attention stayed focused on the topic of the hour or even the day. Subsequent reflection on this capacity to keep my thoughts on a single concept, a skill that has eluded me since that summer, has led me to the conclusion that the repetitive physical activity of cycling contributed greatly to my ability to concentrate. It was as if my mind, body, and spirit were all brought to bear on the issue at hand. The recognition of this phenomenon has contributed to a search for a similar clarity of focus through running. This time, however, not in a problem-solving mode, but in a quest for a connection with God.

Running Downhill in Awareness

I love to run in the hills. Hill running provides a rigorous workout. Different muscles are used when you churn up hill or glide downhill, giving a few muscles a break from the repetition. The physical effect of running uphill is much like the effect of a fast sprint. The cardiovascular benefits are tremendous and leg muscles gain strength in a way not possible when running only on flat surfaces. Running downhill, on the other hand, like running on a precarious surface, forces the runner to focus completely on the run. It takes some practice in order to be comfortable with running quickly downhill. You have to abandon some of the natural fear of falling that arises when you allow gravity to propel you down the hill, but the result can be an almost effortless, floating kind of run. Lean your body slightly forward, allowing your feet to make contact with the running surface in a natural heel-to-toe progression. Resist the urge to lean backward and land flatfooted. Eventually you will gain confidence in your ability to run downhill without the fear of falling; a heightened awareness of the downhill run will remain.

Running down a steep incline requires that you pay attention to speed, foot placement, the trail surface, and all other variables that might cause you to go tumbling down the hill, head over heels. An occasional run that contains an element of small potential threat to physical well-being can force the runner to a level of awareness that he may not have experienced previously. Repeated exposure to a situation with mandatory heightened awareness makes it easier to voluntarily enter into a similar state in less hazardous conditions.

Attention to the Trail

I remember an almost flawless six-mile run on the Shoal Creek Trail. The near-perfection was not a result of the weather (which was ideal), the state of the trail (atrocious), or my physical condition (not bad). The exceptional quality of the run was a result of the need to focus on the poorly maintained trail, which was only partially visible in the twilight. Recognizing that I needed to pay close attention to my footing, I made the best of the situation. I dropped the mantra I had been chanting and shifted my attention solely to my breath and toward every aspect of the linkage between my feet and the trail. I noticed the trail surface, listening to the varying sounds my shoes made as they landed on soft earth, gravel, or rocky ground. I noted whether I was stepping lightly or landing hard, whether the sound of my steps moved in rapid staccato, or fell in distantly spaced intervals. I looked up the trail to see if an incline awaited me, anticipating the tightening in my thighs that told me I was climbing uphill. I watched the placement of each step, nimbly moving around the larger stones in the path, avoiding the ruts, and seeking a safe place to land each foot. All the while, I consciously breathed, not necessarily synchronizing breath with step (the terrain was too uncertain for that), but always aware of the interplay between breath and step. The difficulty of the path held my attention as closely as a mantra. I had no resentment of the difficulty, no desire to have the trail repaired, and no thought about the conditions other than their effect on the run. The immediacy of attention was cleansing. The wholeness, the simplicity, the peace that results when the clamoring chorus of competing thoughts is finally stilled elevates the spirit.

At this point, I reached a level of awareness that usually evades me. I realized that awareness of the present and the emptying of the head of extraneous thoughts were one and the same. It is only through a complete focus on the present that the head can be emptied. It is in this emptiness that God and creative powers reside. Some runners, I understand, use their running time to do shopping lists, write memos, or solve technical problems. Physiologically, this is not a very good time for such tasks. The flow of highly oxygenated blood to the brain while exercising seems to reduce the ability to work with numbers or perform other left-brain functions. More important, it does not allow the runner to take advantage of this ideal opportunity to contact the source of creation. It bears repeating that when attention is shifted away from worldly concerns, a void is created, and God rushes in. Prayerful communion is possible in a way that may have never been available before.

Always being careful to maintain the lifeline of attention to the immediacy of the breath, truly creative direction can be implanted. There is no need to seek divine inspiration. Focus on the respiration and the inspiration will follow.

November 5, 1998—Uncertain Footing

It was the week before elections, and a major bond issue included money to maintain and upgrade city parks. A long-time conspiracy theorist who still remembers the words of Abby Hoffman, "Just because you're paranoid doesn't mean they aren't out to get you," I suspected that the city had allowed the trails to fall into such a state of disrepair in order to secure the votes of the running and walking community. Whether or not the conspiracy theory was true, the neglect of the trails had made them susceptible to the torrential downpours we had received and they were badly damaged and, in some areas, quite dangerous.

The sun was setting earlier, at 5:40 on this day, and the tips of the lengthening shadows danced at my feet. The combination of the slippery, uneven surface, and the lack of visibility compelled me to focus my attention on the trail just a few feet in front of me. If I was to avoid injury, I had to pay attention to the position of each footfall. The enforced concentration on the present moment was a blessing in disguise. Distracting thoughts were few and brief. I simply breathed and carefully watched each step I took. I was continually brought back to the present by the urgent need to attend to my safety.

February 11, 1999—Running with Abandon

An unwillingness to release control over the run was made apparent to me on the short three-mile tapering run I made yesterday in preparation for the marathon. I feared injury on this last week of training, so I ran cautiously. I was afraid to run too fast. On the downhill sections, I failed to run with the abandon that usually propels me past more cautious runners. Crossing the rocky creek bed I slowed to a walk and stepped gingerly around the boulders. I failed to listen properly to the trail. I ran with fear and without joy. I am convinced that running with apprehension sets up expectations of failure and makes it more likely that accidents will happen. Fortunately, I wasn't injured, but the overcautious approach to running was dangerous and unfulfilling.

I am not arguing that danger on the trail should be ignored. In fact, I would argue just the opposite. Hazardous conditions demand the level of awareness that I urge runners to maintain throughout the run. Pay attention to loose footing, protruding rocks, and slippery surfaces in the same way you notice a smooth trail surface, the shade of an overhanging tree, or a following breeze. Run with awareness of danger, but run fearlessly.

Heightened Sensitivity

I have realized that over the past few years of running and meditating I have become more conscious of subtle differences in the way I feel and have grown more sensitive to variations in the external environment. I attribute this change to a heightened awareness of both my surroundings and the physical environment's effect on my mind and body. For example, I have developed an intolerance for the quantities of caffeine that are present, even in decaffeinated coffee. I know how much sleep I need—seven hours. If I have more or less, I do not operate at optimal level. I am aware of a difference in mood as a result of lack of sunshine. I must carefully monitor doses and types of medications because their impact can be pronounced. I do not think that it is simply that I am more affected by these subtle differences in my environment than I once was. I believe that these kinds of external forces have always had an impact on my physical and mental well-being. The difference is that now I am more in tune with what these forces are. I now am very conscious of how variations in the type of foods I eat, and the times I eat them, affect how I feel and my performance when I run. My diet, in preparation for last Sunday's eighteen-mile run, seemed appropriate and well timed. As a result, I felt strong and well nourished throughout most of the run. A small container of Gu, an easily absorbed high-energy food, toward the end of the run, provided me with the boost I needed.

The challenge of running long distances compels the runner to pay close attention to all the variables that might have an effect on his performance. The long run is difficult enough that even seemingly small factors can limit or improve performance. Nothing can safely be ignored. The factors that can effect the run—the wind, temperature, running surface, fellow runners, attitude, training, diet, age—are virtually endless. The important point here, however, is how this heightened awareness of the factors affecting the quality of the run can extend well beyond running. An overall awareness of the physical environment, and how it affects your sense of well-being, can easily follow. You will find that as you begin to pay more attention to the things that affect how you run, you will also begin to notice all the things that impact how you live.

Awareness of the Body

An awareness of the body comes very naturally when running. The sensations of breathing, the tensing and releasing of the muscles, the contact between the soles of your feet and the earth's surface, the stimulated portals of pain and pleasure, all direct consciousness toward the body and away from the cerebral. This natural tendency to focus attention on the immediacy of the body's impressions is a very positive step toward praying in the present. Because of the body's natural recognition of the moment, the attention of the mind is shifted away from yesterday's trials and tomorrow's worries and toward what is happening now. It is in this present moment that we find God. The body, rather than the mind, is your natural ally in the quest to find God in the present.

Novice Runner's Desire Not to Think About Running

I was explaining to a good friend how I was collecting my thoughts on running and meditation. Her response was that she wished she could focus her attention on something besides the physical act of running. She wished to escape from her awareness of running. She wanted distraction. When the two of us met a friend at the grocery store, it was apparent that he had just returned from a hard run. In conversation, the two of them commiserated about how much they hated running. I, personally, do not understand why people who hate to run continue with it, but they often do. I suppose it helps them get into shape, but spiritual progress seems unlikely.

My friend expressed envy toward those people who spend their running time composing memos, planning the weekend, or solving problems left over from the workday. I suspect, however, that she is in a more fortunate position than she realizes. She is present to her task. Even if she finds it unpleasant, arduous, and even painful, she is present to the run. That is more than I can often say about myself. My advice to her was to stop trying to escape, but to embrace the act of running—even the pain. I urged her to concentrate on those breaths she was having difficulty getting, to remember that God is breath, to absorb the tiredness in her legs, to experience the pain fully, to be aware of all the discomforts without trying to avoid them.

The Touch of God

Anthony De Mello's *Sadhana: A Way to God* contains a number of beautiful exercises designed to create a sense of awareness. The instructions provided in his chapter "The Touch of God" are the inspiration for the following exercise designed to cultivate awareness while running:

Focus your awareness on every sensation in your body. Examine each sensation one at a time, bringing your attention to each subtle pressure, pain, and bit of resistance your body feels. As your attention moves from one impression to another, know that each feeling is the result of a biochemical reaction resulting from the action of God. Consciously make the link between each sensation and the presence of God. Experience each of the body's perceptions as a manifestation of the Divine. Begin at your feet. Feel the snugness of the tightly laced shoe. Notice the pressure of even the smallest stone as the sensation passes through the sole of your shoe. Feel the warmth that surrounds your feet and know that all these perceptions come from God. Carry this exercise from your feet up through your body to the top of your head. Feel the touch of God in each sensation, whether it is pleasurable or painful.

You Are the Run

We are continually engaged in the process of becoming. Running mindfully can provide a powerful recognition of that process. Who and what we are in a given moment is defined by the context of that moment. The people, the places, the physical conditions that surround us, shape our being. As Rabbi David Cooper explains in his book *God Is a Verb* God can be more accurately described as a process than a being. Attempts to name God, to describe God, are inadequate to describe what is an interactive process: God-ing. Likewise, it would be more precise to say that I am Roger-ing than to say that I am Roger. What Roger-ing is can be more accurately understood by noting what I am actually doing—writing, talking on the phone, helping my children with homework, or sailing. This is never truer than when I am running. When I run, I "am" running. In other words, when I run, I become running. All that I was before the run, and all that I will be again when the run is complete, is of secondary importance. For the moment, I am the run, and nothing more.

An awareness that the self is in the process of being created constantly, and that we play a role in that creative process, can be a transforming realization. Hold this notion in your heart as you run. Remain conscious of how who you are is being created as you run. Are you running with the grace of a gazelle or plodding along with shuffling feet? Take note of your form. If your stamina does not allow you to run with the posture and carriage you wish to assume, then run in shorter intervals, allowing breaks to catch your breath. Are you feeling mean-spirited or angry? Run with a slight smile on your face (even one that doesn't come easily) and look with kindness into the eyes of those you meet. Always run with the form of the God-filled person you are in the process of becoming.

Recognize that the elements in the surrounding environment are more than obstacles, encouragement, or scenery. The temperature of the air, a head wind, a following breeze, a steep incline, a gentle downhill slope, the shade of a tree-lined path, or the oppressive heat of the noonday sun do not merely deplete or restore our energy; they become a part of the transformation that takes place with every run. The hot sun beating down may cause you to slow your pace without it being viewed as the enemy. For the conscious runner, the sun, the wind, and the rain are as much a part of the run as the length of your stride and your attention to breathing. The sun is not to be cursed anymore than the shade is to be praised. They are elements contributing to the wholeness of the running state—the complete sense of being. All that you encounter is an aspect of the run and a part of what you are becoming.

Awareness Training

Yesterday's run on the Shoal Creek Trail was a difficult one, not because of the physical challenge, but because of the distress I was

feeling over a serious development at work. It was a struggle to re-
main present to the run. Still, it was a battle worth engagement.
Over and over again I found my mind moving back to the problem
and away from awareness of the present. Over and over again, I
attempted to bring my mind back. Never for long did my mind
stray, and never for long did it remain fully conscious. This was in-
deed a workout; it was training as surely as the deliberate covering
of miles before a race is training. I was trying to be present under
challenging circumstances.

When I returned home to the kids, the challenge remained. I had
spent the previous hour preparing to remain present to them. The
trials from work still tried to occupy my mind and when they did, I
breathed and tried to move my attention toward showing love to my
children. I had practiced this very act on the trail, attempting to love
strangers I met, when my mind moved me toward absorption with
my own problems.

In *God Is a Verb,* Rabbi David Cooper speaks of the balance that
must be created by intention and awareness. He observes that good
intentions are not enough to ensure a positive outcome. Intentions
must be coupled with a heightened level of awareness. Elevated consciousness enables our positive intentions to be realized. Running
provides a forum in which to practice this combination of intention
and awareness. Begin the run with a clear declaration of your intention to commune with God. Other goals may be realized on the run,
but be certain of the primary objective of union with the Divine.
Once the run has begun, the declared intention is released. Focus
attention on the present. Focus on the run, on becoming one with
the run. Do this by being aware of all that surrounds you, all sensory
stimuli, and how your physical nature experiences what is being felt.
Listen for God in your breath.

Staying Mindful

A few years ago an interviewer asked Thich Nhat Hahn, the noted Vietnamese poet, scholar, and peace activist, considered by many to be a "Living Buddha," about his experiences as a monk living in war-torn South Vietnam in the sixties. He spoke of fleeing flames and bullets and bombs and how it is possible to stay aware even under horrific conditions. The questions were about how he could practice mindfulness with such extreme violence all around him. His response was that, "It is possible to run mindfully. If I get lost in panic and fear I cannot run mindfully." Even though this kindly monk was running for his life, he was able to maintain an inner calmness. Surely if it is possible to run mindfully through the chaos of gunfire and exploding bombs, it is possible for us to run on a busy hike and bike trail with peace and a heightened sense of awareness.

August 20, 1999—Light and Dark
   This week has been less of a struggle. I feel that I have made a small journey upward on the spiraling path to remain present in the midst of adversity. During the weeks prior to this one, my heart ached and I was consumed with waves of melancholy. I could feel the sadness move in and out of my heart as I strove to remain conscious both to the pain and to the healing power of love. I have been granted a respite from the struggle this week. Little has changed (always the promise of money next week) in my circumstances; I've simply learned something of how to live better in the midst of uncertainty.
   This running in the sunlight and shade, the rich imagery of light and darkness, was not lost on my imagination as I traversed equally mixed territory in my life beyond the running trail. As I ran, using all the senses that God gave me, I was aware of the contrast of light and dark. Yet, at the same time, I was not consumed by the dimness of the shadows or overcome by the brightness of the sunlight. I

simply moved in their midst, felt them fully, and continued on my journey with an acute awareness of the light. I held fast to the knowledge that shadows do not exist without the light. And so it was during these weeks of both uncertainty and happiness. Over the weekend I had enjoyed a splendid game of chess with my son and gone on a midnight sail under a dark sky occasionally illuminated with late summer's Perseus meteor shower. These joys were interlaced with disappointment over prospective work and lingering regret over past failure. Moving through the darkness of those moments was far more difficult than passing through the shadowland of the running trail. The experience of intimate awareness of the physical passage through sunlight and shadow gave me the insight I needed to see that my passage through life's shadows was not so different. I found comfort in the recognition that my soul existed apart from the light and dark through which I passed. A recognition that the divine light is the source of the shadows themselves allowed me to see that these elements of darkness exist so that I might experience them and learn from them. I am compelled to offer thanks to God that life is not all "sweetness and light," and for allowing me to move beyond the shallow understanding that I would have if I knew only bright days.

August 9, 1999—Conveying Presence

Today's run along the Shoal Creek Trail was hot but very satisfying. As I ran, I kept my eyes on the trail, just a few feet in front of me. I looked at nothing in particular. I simply held my gaze on the ground ahead as I moved steadily forward. I breathed purposefully, concentrating on each respiration, and allowing a rhythm to form in time with the sound of my footsteps. Just moments before applying my senses and my being to this trinity of breath, sight, and sound, my thoughts had been occupied with the past. A sense of melancholy that had enveloped me last week began to wash over me again. Quite deliberately, I shifted my attention to the present— to my breath, to the sound of my steps, and to seeing only the trail passing beneath my feet. I held this focus for some time. Eventually,

I heard the sound of another runner approaching. I continued to hold my gaze on the ground until the runner was only a few feet in front of me. I looked up, smiled, and found my glance and smile returned. I regained and then held my original focus until a few minutes later another runner appeared. Again, I did not look up until he was almost upon me. At that moment, I looked into his eyes, smiled, and again received a smile in return. I think that if I attempt to make eye contact too early, people tend to avert their gaze, whereas if I hold my attention to the trail until the last moment, I am more likely to make a linkage. I then have the opportunity to connect, offer a blessing, and return to, in fact never abandon, my closely held consciousness.

This conscious interweaving of attention to the internal with attention to the external is excellent mindfulness practice. Use your breath to hold on to an awareness of the Divine Presence. Keeping that awareness uppermost in your consciousness, you then let go of that single focus on the breath just long enough for you to smile at an oncoming stranger. In this moment you transmit your awareness of the Divine into the consciousness of someone you have never met. Each time this conscious shift from the internal to the external is made, you become more proficient at living a mindful life.

Running with a deliberate awareness of the senses is a practice that lies firmly within the Tantric tradition of Buddhist forms of meditation. Both the southern and Zen branches of Buddhism strive to eliminate the impact of the physical senses on meditation, ultimately hoping to achieve a higher level of awareness in the midst of silence. Tantric Buddhism, practiced principally by the Tibetans, is differentiated most clearly from other forms of Buddhism by the belief that Nirvana, or enlightenment, can be achieved in a single lifetime rather than through a series of reincarnations. Attaining enlightenment in one life is considered possible through this utilization of the physical senses rather than through an avoidance of their influence on consciousness. Tantric Buddhists enlist the senses of sound, movement, and sight to propel the seeker of enlightenment forward on his journey. The senses are seen not as distractions, but as aids to the achievement of Nirvana. As part of a meditation practice, Tantric Buddhists refer to sound as a *mantra*, movement as a *mudra*, and sight as a *mandala*. In running meditation, we also rely on mantras, mudras, and mandalas (and occasionally taste and smell as well) to assist in our effort to attain a heightened level of awareness.

December 5, 1998—The Senses
   As I ran this morning, I practiced the usual "Toward the One" chant and used the Distant Mountain Gaze—focusing my consciousness on my breath, and my vision on a void in the distance. This centering of vision provides a point of reference for your eyes without creating another distraction, since you are focusing on the emptiness between objects, rather than the object itself.

As is usually the case, sights, sounds, and other sensations intrude on your attention to your breath. There is something of a paradox here. Meditation of this sort heightens your overall sense of awareness. Yet you are constantly bringing your awareness back to a single component—breathing. I suggest that you embrace this paradox—run in it. Be attentive to the colors in a single leaf that has fallen at your feet, the sound of a squirrel rustling in the leaves of the branches above, the faint ringing of church bells miles away, or subtle shifts in the wind's direction. Although it seems impossible to restrict your awareness solely to your breathing with so much going on around you, the good news is that there is no need to even try to shut out awareness of other sensations. Remember that this is a practice. You are practicing returning to your breath after taking note of sensations. At the same time you are practicing nonattachment, letting go of each wondrous sensation as you run past it.

We are slaves to visual stimuli. Things we see have an enormous impact on our thinking—the visual sense directs our thoughts more powerfully than the other senses. Therefore it is recommended in sitting meditation to close, or nearly close, your eyes, and in running meditation to create a kind of visual restriction by focusing on the space between objects. Your peripheral vision alone will provide you with an abundance of distractions, and the opportunity to practice returning to your breath.

The other senses—hearing, taste, smell, and touch—all continue to provide stimuli and potential disruptions to your focus on breathing. Treat each of these senses as conduits of opportunities to remind you of your breath. Acknowledge each sound, taste, smell, and feeling that moves across your consciousness, but remain unattached to them. You cannot stop them from arising, nor should you, but you can resist dwelling on them.

Occasionally, I feel it necessary to remind the reader that this is as much a book about living as it is about running. Few things that I have to say about running and prayer apply only to the act of rapidly putting one foot in front of another. We face distractions of all kinds in our lives—distractions that take us away from the recognition that we are creatures made in God's image. Our mission is to live in this world, surrounded by the world's material distractions, and develop an awareness of the spiritual dimension. Each of our experiences, monumental or mundane—the death of a friend an argument with a spouse, the graduation of a child, the smell of a rose, or the sound of a saxophone—present chances to return to the spiritual world that is our natural home. As adults living in the Western world in the third millennium, we do not so readily abide in that spiritual homeland. It is our task to recognize that the way each of us experiences the world is an avenue that takes us to the spiritual realm and, at the same time, enables us to be fully human participants in a temporal society.

October 14, 1997—Listening
   A wonderful run today—sunny, cool, the trail packed with runners, walkers, and cyclists. My meditation for the day was based on

the sense of hearing. I focused on hearing everything as I ran. I heard so much that I wished I had brought an audio recorder with me so that I could record it all. I listened to the sound of my feet on the path, breathing (mine, other runners', dogs'), traffic (not just the hum of traffic, but the individual braking sounds, exhaust pipes, and accelerating engines), birds, dogs splashing in the water, friends and acquaintances calling my name, laughter, talking, the wind in the leaves, the beep, beep, beep of a construction vehicle in reverse. . . . What does this have to do with prayer? Everything. Prayer is about a connection with all there is—awareness, a consciousness of all things, a union with all things, a union with God. Awareness of God's presence is not about holding on to an image of a distant ruler sitting on a throne in heaven. We find God in the midst of creation, by listening. But creation is vast and overwhelming, so where can we begin? We start with an awareness of the breath—the breath alone, then branching out from that to an awareness of the things that the other senses bring us. Can we know all things—become aware of all that surrounds us? No, but we may be able to fully grasp at least some of the things around us. By focusing on one sense at a time, we are able to practice awareness without being overwhelmed by all the data that the senses provide. We learn about God one small step at a time.

August 19, 1999—Running in the Shadows

The tree-lined Shoal Creek Trail, between six and seven on an August evening, is bathed in a mixture of light and shade. This trail offers a retreat from the still oppressive summer sun. Seeking shade, I usually choose to run on a portion of the trail where the leaves and branches of the oak and cedar trees are the densest and thus provide me with the most protection from the Texas sun. Yet even in the midst of the most abundant foliage, sunlight filters through the branches and dances on the trail, on the tree trunks along the trail's eastern edge, and on the cavernous faces of the over-

hanging cliffs. I was drawn to this mixture of sun and shadow and shifted the focus of my attention away from the mantra I had been reciting and onto this visual feast of light and dark. The interplay of light and shadow became the dominant feature in the landscape, while every other aspect of the scene faded into the background. I watched the fingers of light fold around the outline of branch-shaped shadows, while the actual branches from which the profiles arose were not revealed. As I moved from sunlight to shadow, I felt the presence and the absence of the sun's rays on my skin. And in the grottolike areas of the trail, where direct sunlight rarely penetrates, I could sense the cool, damp, musty smell of air emanating from crevices plunging deep into the earth. In the sunny portions of the trail I could feel the difference in the temperature of the air as I drew it into my nostrils.

September 13, 1999—Running from the Darkness to the Light
   Saturday was the first day of my first seminary class. I was thrilled, but I did not want the morning class to prevent me from continuing with my Saturday-morning-hill-run routine so I chose to get up earlier than usual and run before class. I generally choose not to run so early in the mornings. My body is stiff and achy when I first wake up. I also lack the desire to run. My preference is to move into the day slowly: shower, meditate, take a cup of tea to my study, and then begin writing. After working all day, sitting most of the time, my limbs yearn to be pressed into action. Early in the morning my body doesn't want to be pushed. Consequently, when I run on Saturday mornings, I arise a little later than usual and move about the house for about forty-five minutes before running out the door.
   Despite my reluctance to break with my established pattern of moving slowly in the morning (and I recognize the benefits of diverging from a stale routine), I got up early enough to run. It was still very dark when I walked out the door. I paused for a moment

to take in the night sky. Venus was shining brightly and the few stars that were visible in the spaces between scattered clouds were almost as brilliant. I breathed deeply, bowed toward the rusty iron cross reigning over my patio garden, asked for God's blessings on the day, and walked mindfully down the sidewalk leading to the street. I began running slowly, but despite my pace, muscles throughout my body ached. In particular, I felt a pain in my lower back. I've slept on a mattress on the floor for many years and I wondered if it was time for me to give my aging body more comfort. I began to breathe methodically and to be aware of my breathing. I picked up the pace slightly, conscious of the importance of maintaining proper form. The aches and pains diminished and, within a few minutes, ceased altogether.

Although it is mid-September, the days are still very hot. It was a relief to run at a time before the energy-sapping heat slows the pace. I felt little tiredness. I marveled at how the darkness still prevailed, but noticed how the sky was beginning to lighten. The darkness changes to light so slowly that we only notice the change after it happens. On my run, I watched the night turn to day. I focused my attention on the disappearance of stars and the creation of still-faint shadows. I listened to the diminishing sounds of the morning dove and the rising sound of the city's traffic. Streetlamps were extinguished. I awakened with the city.

January 19, 2000—Sacrament of the Present Moment
    Yesterday's run was a fast seven miles on the Shoal Creek Trail. I felt energetic enough to run intervals along the way. Running faster was a delightful change from the slower routine I had settled into. The change in pace awakened my consciousness, enabling me to sense God's presence in a way that corresponded to the effort I was expending, the pattern in which I was breathing, and the rapidity with which the scenery passed. I ran hard, walked, and ran slowly as I recovered from the sprints. Each way of moving—and of being—

brought with it an opportunity to relate to God in a different way. It was a way of experiencing Jean-Pierre de Caussade's Sacrament of the Present Moment. De Caussade urges us to accept whatever method of communicating grace God chooses. He says that, "What he ordains for us each moment is what is most holy, best, and most divine for us. Whether contemplation, meditation, prayer, inward silence, intuition, quietude, or activity are what we wish for ourselves, the best is God's purpose for us at the present moment."

Born Again

Running, like most physical exercise, is usually refreshing. Even though you are expending energy and, if you press hard, may be temporarily winded and in need of a brief recovery period, the overall effect is a replenishment of the body's sense of well-being. If you are tired and sleepy before the run, you are likely to find that the run has awakened your body and your mind. You are renewed by the run. This sense of renewal is at the core of why running can be an important tool in the development of spirit. Each run can be used to awaken the runner to the presence of the Divine. In her very accessible books on Buddhist practices, Sylvia Boorstein speaks of her desire to be an "awakened Jew"—to move through life with the awareness of the present emphasized by the teachers of Zen Buddhism. We can be awakened Jews, Christians, Muslims, Buddhists, and Hindus. Practicing running and living in this awakened state, rather than detracting from our individual religions, makes us far better practitioners of our faith.

Those who profess to be "born again" Christians seem to have missed this point. The statement usually implies that at some time in the born-again Christian's past he had an experience of Christ entering his life and, along with that entrance, of accepting Christ's presence. Surely, a once-in-a-lifetime experience of this sort is not sufficient to propel one into the open doors of heaven. This rebirth must happen repeatedly, in fact, constantly. God's grace is present for us at all times; it is up to the individual to awaken to that presence—to be reborn—over and over again. We sleepwalk through most of our lives. Waking up is our lifelong endeavor. The meditative runner is fortunate enough to have found a way that refreshes his body and renews his spirit—enabling him to be born again with every run.

breath and chant: aids to mindfulness

The breath that does not repeat the name of God is a wasted breath.

KABIR

We are street people. Our Sisters walk the streets and they pray as they walk. Sometimes they tell me how much time it took to reach a place, they tell me how many rosaries they said—three rosaries, four rosaries. They walk so rapidly that in Calcutta they are called "the racing Sisters."

MOTHER TERESA

Breath is usually expressed in Greek as *pneuma*, which can also mean air, wind, or spirit. In Hebrew *ruah* is translated as breath, but it can also mean creative energy or life-giving force. An awareness of the breath as spirit, of our capacity to bring the Divine into our being as we take oxygen into our lungs, is critical to understanding how running can become prayer.

Although we can voluntarily alter our breathing patterns, breathing is usually an involuntary reflex. Typically, we breathe without being conscious of it at all. The body recognizes the need for oxygen and we automatically take a breath. Yet it is possible to be aware of your breath and exercise control over the breathing pattern.

This kind of conscious control over breath allows you to practice a deliberate, mindful influence over what is usually a mechanical process. This awareness of breath can bring you to an overall awareness of the present. Another likely consequence of this kind of practice is an improved ability to control other kinds of, usually involuntary, responses. Outbursts of temper, expressions of frustration, feelings of anxiety or insecurity generally arise without a conscious willing of them to occur. Breathing typically occurs naturally, but the same awakening of connections that lead to awareness of the breath can lead to an awareness of all our actions. If we are to express anger or dissatisfaction of any kind, it is possible to do so consciously, not as an unconscious reaction to external stimuli. Just as we learn to watch ourselves breathe as we run, we can learn to watch ourselves choose how to act. Instead of relinquishing control over our actions to our emotions, a heightened sense of awareness makes it possible to act without simply reacting to an emotional state.

When you are running, you naturally breathe louder, deeper, and more frequently than when you are at rest. If your breathing remained shallow while running, you would likely hyperventilate or, at the very least, struggle to the point of exhaustion. Developing a focus, an awareness of the breath, can be fairly easily accomplished while running. This same awareness of breathing can be extended into the daily routine. The experiences of anxiety, frustration, and anger act on the body in much the same way that running does—increasing our heart rate, sending adrenalin pumping, causing us to sweat, but if our bodies react in this way and we continue to breathe shallowly, the effect would be much the same as running and not breathing deeply. We grow weaker, we think less clearly, and we react instead of acting consciously Deeper, more conscious breathing restores balance and equilibrium. Developing the practice of awareness of breath can have an impact one's ability to read the physical indicators of the onset of fear, anxiety, and anger. Once we have learned to recognize when we are fearful, anxious, or angry, we can use a consciously controlled breathing pattern to bring our emotions into perspective.

In sitting meditation, focus on the breath plays a paramount role. This is also true with running meditation. However, with regard to breath, runners experience a considerable advantage over traditional sitting meditation. Breathing is a much more pronounced activity when running than when sitting. In sitting, meditation respirations slow to an almost imperceptible level. Stillness and quiet are necessary for proper attention to be paid to the breath. When sitting, the sensations are subtle. When running, it is almost impossible to avoid awareness of the breath. You can hear the sound of deep breathing echoing in your ears. Your expanding and contracting lungs cause your chest to rise and fall. Your speed, the terrain, the elevation, and your body's fitness all affect the respiration rate. Changes in the rate help bring your awareness back to the breath. Attention to the breath flows naturally from the run.

An Exercise: Counting Breaths

A good way to begin the practice of focusing on breathing while running is to rely on a method of focusing on the breath commonly practiced in *zazen,* the traditional Zen Buddhist sitting meditation. Try counting the breaths in groups of ten. Begin the count on the first exhalation by mentally counting "one." There is no need to count the inhalations; simply count each exhalation, one by one, until you reach ten. At that point, begin again at one and count to ten, over and over again. Continue breathing and counting breaths until the run is completed.

It is important to remember that the focus should be on the breathing, not on the counting; that is an easy trap in which to fall. The numbers are not important. They are tools to help you avoid distractions, but be careful not to allow the tool itself to take you away from the breath. If your imagination takes you away from the breath, take no notice of it. Simply return your attention to your breathing.

When you are breathing, you are taking in oxygen. This oxygen not only provides fuel for your body, but it feeds the spirit that flames within you. Conscious breathing provides the fuel to feed your spiritual growth. You are providing nourishment to the Divine that is always present within. The spirit, if it is to flourish, must be fed. An awareness of the role that breath plays while running heightens our awareness of the Divine Presence. Listening is the key. Listen to the sound of your breath.

Chants and Mantras

Mantras and chants have been used for thousands of years by many different religions for a variety of purposes. Mantra is usually thought of as a Hindu or Buddhist devotional incantation, the repetition of a word or phrase aimed at the suspension of thought. Among Christian and Islamic traditions, chants, in which words with irregular rhythm are fitted together by singing several syllables with the same note, are meant to encourage an encounter with God. In both East and West, the rhythmic repetition of a single phrase is recognized as a means of transporting one to a higher spiritual plane. Herein, I tend to use *chant* and *mantra* interchangeably, regarding both as similar and valuable aids to mindfulness. When running, I typically use a mantra as a means of avoiding distraction. Ideally, I could focus and hold my attention solely on my breathing, but this is a very difficult undertaking. Using the chant or mantra as a reminder to return to the breath eases the task.

The rhythm of the run changes as the pace of the run and the breathing level fluctuate. The running pace and the breathing pattern can help determine the mantra selected and its rhythm. Early in the run, assuming that I begin the run slowly, I might select a mantra that is in keeping with the energetic but slightly restrained pace of a run that has just begun. At the end of a working day, I often feel like a tiger just released from its cage, and my impulse is to leap out of the cage of my automobile and plunge headlong into the forest. Practicing restraint allows me time to warm my muscles properly, retain energy for the long run ahead, and move thoughtfully into a suitable chant that reminds me of the purpose of the run. You will find that using a slower chant will help you practice the restraint necessary in the beginning of a run and aid in clearly establishing the run's intent.

When running with a mantra or chant, it is important to remember that the breathing pattern should not be altered to fit the chant. Rather, the rhythm of the chant should be changed to fit whatever breathing pattern develops naturally over the course of the run. The number of syllables uttered with each breath in, or each breath out, may vary as you breathe more or less rapidly. It may be easier to hold the syllables for a longer or shorter period of time with each inhalation or exhalation rather than vary the number of syllables said with each breath. The focus on the breath is the important thing. Seek God's presence—that "Oneness"—in the breath.

As you become attuned to your breathing, you will notice that occasionally your breathing pattern will be interrupted by an intermittent need to take a single very large breath or to perhaps not inhale for a beat and feel a need to swallow instead. Disruptions of this sort are to be expected and, in fact, are opportunities to heighten your awareness of breathing. After the interruption has passed, start the chant over again, remembering that the chant is merely a tool. The aim is the awareness of God's presence through the breath. There is no need for the words of the chant to be clearly audible. The recitation of the chant can be purely mental, or it might be only barely whispered.

A Selection of Chants and Mantras

The next few pages describe a number of chants and mantras that I have found useful in my exploration of running meditation. All but one has its origins in the Islamic and Christian traditions. Please do not feel bound by these selections. The actual words matter far less than the intention behind the words. I urge you to find phrases within your own tradition and experience that enable you to participate in prayerful exercise.

"Toward the One"

The Sufi teacher Pir Villayat Khan suggests the meditative practice of silently chanting "Toward the One" while breathing in and out. While Khan's advice is aimed at a sitting meditation, it can be readily adapted to running meditation. The technique is simple. Breathe in with one syllable of the mantra, breath out with the next, and repeat. The word "toward" points the runner forward and implies a goal or a direction—a purpose in running. The "One" you are running toward is God, but the runner is not simply heading in the direction of a separate being, but moving closer to a oneness with God. The "One" is both God and man. The goal you are running toward is a unity of God and man—a movement away from separation from the Divine and toward wholeness. Remember, it is not as if God is waiting at the finish line. Rather, each step takes the runner closer to a realization that God's presence—God's grace—is with us already, and we need only to pay attention to that presence.

October 1, 1998—Sufi Chant
   I went for a run on Shoal Creek yesterday. From the moment I touched the ground with my new running shoes I was chanting a Sufi chant "Toward the One." In truth, I had forgotten the exact chant, remembering it as "Toward the Oneness." At the onset, this chant seemed too New Age, but I stayed with it because of the forward momentum it gave me and because it seemed very easy to hang on to. I was able to keep the chant top of mind almost throughout the run.

"Elah, Elah, Elohim"

A frequently used Islamic chant, "Elah, Elah, Elohim," works very well when running. The words can be translated as, "There is no God but God" or as, "God of Gods, Lord of Lords." The absence of hard consonants in this chant allows the words to flow freely with the breath. The words seem to say themselves, rising naturally with each breath. I have found that the chant can be uttered silently while running when timed with the breath in the following pattern: El (inhale), ah (exhale), El (inhale), ah (exhale), El (inhale), o (exhale), hi (inhale), im (exhale).

This is a beautiful running chant. The specific translation of the words may be lost while running. However, the simple resonance of the chant sounds holy and worshipful.

"Leave Behind All You Have"

I first learned this chant as an accompaniment to a walking meditation we did in a spiritual formation class I took one evening at the Episcopal Seminary of the Southwest: "Leave behind all you have, / And come and follow me."

I practiced the walk and the chant the next morning. It was a cool morning, the first really cool morning of the fall season. It felt good to be outside at dawn, feeling as if I were following in the steps of the Divine. As a running chant, it works well with a smooth, even, steady run.

The Trisagion

I also first learned this chant as an accompaniment to a walking meditation. The words are those of a prayer known as the Trisagion: "Holy God, Holy and Mighty, Holy Immortal One, Have Mercy Upon Us."

I often use this chant when I am feeling reverent or worshipful. The words of praise for the Divine coupled with the recognition of our own need for mercy can be very powerful. The chant seems to impart a feeling of both power and humility. This isn't a sprinting chant. It works best when running on a flat, consistent surface, not requiring sporadic bursts of energy.

June 8, 1998—Trisagion

It was a hot, though breezy, run on Town Lake. From the beginning of my run I began to chant. As usual, my chanting was mental, using my breath to actually chant would deplete my oxygen supply, and draw unwanted attention to myself and to the spiritual aim of my run. (More likely, I would just be perceived as odd.) As I ran and chanted today, I very naturally fell into a rhythm linking the chant and my pace. This often happens, but today the chant brought buoyancy to my rather plodding step. The first thing I noticed was that I immediately passed the runner I had been following for half of a mile. He could have slowed down, but I am inclined to believe that my chanted, lighter step was also faster. It didn't really take any more effort to run this way; it simply required consciousness and actualization of my desire to step a little lighter, land less heavily on my heals, and roll my step through my entire foot, ending the contact between my foot and the ground at my instep through my toes. I was aware of a slight kick at the end of each stride, keeping time with the "Holy God, Holy and Mighty" cadence. Linking the exaggerated high stride with the chant had the effect of consciously linking the spiritual with the physical—the essence of what I am trying to achieve.

September 28, 1998—More Trisagion

I ran again on Sunday morning instead of going to church. I readied myself for the run, meditating on the patio before leaving the house for Town Lake. The trail around the lake is crowded on Sundays. I hope they all find God there. Some do. Some find only pain. Others find friends, or at least hope to. All are searching for something. Most seem lonely.

The run yesterday was the beginning of my Sunday distance runs. It was only seven and a half miles, very little more than a usual run around Town Lake, but it is the beginning. I will shortly begin adding a mile a week until I have reached twenty-two to twenty-three miles, two weeks before the marathon. It was not easy yesterday, the heat at midday was still very oppressive, and I think the bagel I ate before the run was not a good idea.

I began the run chanting the Trisagion out loud. This wasn't planned. It was simply a spontaneous expression of joy at being where I was. I am generally too inhibited to make such an outward display of my inward feelings, but no one was nearby, and I didn't think about it. It just happened. In the past I had found the Trisagion to be too slow to properly accompany a fast run, so I attempted to switch to my one-breath-per-syllable Jesus Prayer. Despite my efforts to remain with the Jesus Prayer, I kept returning to the Trisagion, eventually landing on a ratio of breath to words that flowed smoothly and didn't require excessive concentration. I carried the chant with me throughout most of the run.

The pleasing discovery of the morning was how long the chant remained with me after the run. I held the chant in my heart while stretching, walking to the car, and when driving home. Most vividly, I remember the walk to the car. My breath had slowed down, but my heart was still beating at a pace faster than usually occurs when I am just walking. My stride was very deliberate and my posture erect. I could not avoid smiling slightly. I was experiencing the rewards of running and by continuing the chant and remaining focused on my breath I was prolonging the joy. This is how I want to always walk—to always live. Running, meditating, allows me to chip away at the times when I am not present. If I can remain present to God while running and praying and increase the amount of time I intentionally seek God's presence, the times that I forget my purpose will diminish.

September 2, 1998—Lord Have Mercy, Christ Have Mercy

I ran on the Shoal Creek Trail this evening. Early in the run I attempted to use the remembered sound of the beach as a mantra, wanting to synchronize the breaking waves with the rhythm of my breathing. Luckily, I attempted the exercise for only a short time before I realized why it was not working; it should have been obvious. An awareness of the present is necessary in meditating. My effort to link my breathing with an experience outside the present moment was taking me away from the place where God exists most perceptibly. Anything that takes you away from that awareness is defeating the purpose.

The mantra that I settled on was not very different from the pattern used in the ribald chants that marching Marines practice in basic training. (Admittedly, the actual words in the Marine chants might be somewhat different.) Here a four-syllable chant works well—two syllables said silently as you inhale, and two syllables silently recited as you exhale. The chant I used was: "Lord have (inhale), Mercy (exhale) Christ have (inhale) Mercy (exhale)." Used as a part of the Episcopal liturgy, these two simple phrases are spoken slowly. As a running chant, they are spoken in more of a rapid, staccato fashion.

The Jesus Prayer

In its complete form, the Jesus Prayer reads, "Lord Jesus Christ, only son of God, have mercy upon me, a sinner." It is the fundamental spiritual practice of hesychasm, a tradition of prayer in the Eastern Orthodox Church. The aim is to have some form of this prayer on your lips and in your heart at all times—a response to the ultimate goal of "prayer without ceasing."

When you are running, your breathing pattern varies considerably, depending on the intensity of the run, your personal fitness, variations in the terrain, and speed. Part of the beauty of the Jesus Prayer is the way it lends itself to such changes. The complete form of the prayer is too lengthy to be useful as a running chant. It can be readily shortened to "Jesus Christ—Have Mercy," or "Christ—Have Mercy," or, simply, "Je—sus." Again, the words are only vehicles enabling you to pay attention to breathing, and ultimately to allow you to be more receptive to God's grace. The pattern of breathing and chanting that I typically use is as follows: "Je—sus (inhale), Christ—have (exhale), Mer—cy (inhale), On—me (exhale)."

One day, while sitting and praying the Jesus Prayer, I attempted to use the rhythm and cadence that I normally use when running and chanting the Jesus Prayer. It seemed very slow. I had to unnaturally stretch the syllables so that the time it took to say the word fit more closely with the time it took to inhale or exhale. Since we breathe much more rapidly when running, a one-syllable chant with each inspiration and with each expiration works quite well. When sitting, it seems more natural to repeat several syllables with each inhalation or exhalation. Some chants work better in a running meditation and others work better while sitting; furthermore, a chant that works well for a long slower run may not be the most natural chant to use on a fast run, or when running in the hills. Let your breathing dictate the phrasing of the chant. Don't try to force the chant to unnaturally fit your breathing.

However, don't assume that a phrasing that works while sitting won't work while running. A chanting pace that initially seems unnatural may in fact heighten your mindfulness. You may become acutely aware of how slowly and carefully you are saying the prayer. A very deliberate slowing or speeding of the chant allows you to experience it in a different way. The experience is akin to attaching different melodies to the liturgy at different times and different places. The practice of singing the liturgy changes according to the differences in the manner in which it is sung.

July 30, 1999—Christ Consciousness
    Two days ago I found myself in a deep state of depression. I was
so low that I e-mailed my friend Gary a "poor pitiful me" letter.
That helped, but a hard run on Town Lake, a swim at Barton

Springs, an evening in the presence of my daughter, and, probably most significantly, the remembrance of the Jesus Prayer brought me back to consciousness. I've been rereading Franny and Zooey, the short J. D. Salinger novel dealing with the Jesus Prayer. The part that has held the most significance for me is Zooey telling his sister, Franny, that the only reason to pray the Jesus Prayer is, "to endow the person who says it with Christ-consciousness." In their conversation, Zooey urges Franny to understand the importance of Jesus, noting that Jesus was picked for the task because he alone knew that we are carrying the "Kingdom of Heaven around inside of us." We don't pray so that our lives will be filled with "dolls and saints" and so that hardship will be removed; we pray to realize the kingdom of God that lies within. That is why Christ is worth following. As the incarnation of God on earth, his is the most literal example we have of the realization of God in man. His visit to earth was to let us know that we can follow his example, if we open our eyes.

I have been using the Jesus Prayer not constantly but much of the time the past few days. It has enabled me to cope with my financial woes and the negative energy that friends might bring with them, and to listen to my associates with attention. I prayed the prayer when I ran, worked with weights, did sitting meditation, drove the car, among other activities. I can see that it helps at various stages; when feeling low, the prayer can help you regain your sense of self. The sense of well-being is elevated to a point where consciousness can be raised.

During Wednesday's run I prayed the Jesus Prayer for the first half of the run. I was feeling far too depressed to think of elevation "Toward the One." Then, without a conscious decision to switch chants, "Toward the One" took the Jesus Prayer's place. My initial impulse was to resist the change, but then I knew that this was right. I realized that I had received the "mercy" that would allow me to move closer to God's presence.

Weight Training

While weight lifting last week, I incorporated, really for the first time, a chant into the exercises. It was during the time when I was still feeling especially low and the Jesus Prayer felt appropriate. I breathed and chanted with a similar pattern I had adopted with running, beginning with an inhalation. As is generally recommended with weight training, the exertion, pushing or pulling the weight, is synchronized with the exhalation. The pattern I use is as follows: "Je (inhale), sus (exhale), Christ (inhale), have (exhale), mer (inhale), cy (exhale), on (inhale), me (exhale)."

Before beginning each exercise, count the number of exhalations that are involved in the chant (in this case there are four). With each weight-lifting set, recite the chant as many times as you need to give you the number of repetitions you would normally do within a set.

There is no reason this could not become a normal part of a weight-lifting routine. I found that, especially in the troubling time I was experiencing last week, I needed all the conscious breathing time available to me—whatever I was doing. In the past, I often used weight lifting as a time to listen to the radio. However, particularly during difficult times, weight training can clearly be used as another opportunity to purposely connect with the prayerful breathing.

The Prayer of the Heart

In the classic Russian Orthodox introduction to the use of the Jesus Prayer, *The Way of a Pilgrim,* a blind man teaches the pilgrim how to pray the "Prayer of the Heart." In this prayer one learns to listen attentively to the beating of the heart, synchronizing the timing of the breath and the recitation of the Jesus Prayer with the heartbeat. In a sitting meditation, I have been unable to actually hear or feel the beating of my heart in my chest. However, attentiveness to the beating of your heart while breathing may bring you to greater depths of prayer. Likewise, I have been unable to actually hear the beating of my heart while running. After I have stopped, at the end of a rapid run, I can certainly feel my heart beating. And if I stop running for a moment in the midst of a run, I can easily feel my pulse with my fingers. I think the key to incorporating the Prayer of the Heart to running meditation is cultivating an awareness of the heartbeat. Becoming aware of my pulse rate enabled me to time the chanting of the Jesus Prayer with my heart rate. An abbreviated Jesus Prayer was synchronized with the beating of my heart, with each beat corresponding to a syllable in the prayer. The rate at which I chanted of course varied with my pace and how far I had run.

It worked well to establish the synchronization of heartbeats, breathing, and chant before starting the run. It established the intention, set the tone for the run as well as determining how the chant would be said. I use the term *said* loosely. It would be unwise to actually verbalize the chant while running. It is difficult to speak constantly while running at a substantial pace. Saying the chant is, at most, only mouthing the words. The portion of the prayer that is said while exhaling may become more audible, but obviously very little sound is produced while you are inhaling. The pattern that I settled on is meant only as an example. Just as the words chosen for a chant are far less important than the attention they bring to breathing, the cadence, the rhythm, and how the words fit into breathing patterns is of little consequence. Choose a pattern that works for you. Alter the rhythm of the chant as your breathing patterns change. Allow natural rhythms to take over. Your intention is to be aware of your breathing and to link that with an awareness of your beating heart.

When you have finished your run, maintain an awareness of the breath and heart, through the Jesus Prayer. Continue with the prayer through the stretching exercises. Be aware of your slowing respirations and heart rate and slow down the prayer in the same fashion. Carry the prayer with you as long as you can.

July 30, 1999—The Trinity

I ran on Town Lake this morning—unusual for a Saturday. I saw several people I knew. It was kind of nice, although the run itself was difficult. I think I am not yet used to the summer heat. Most of the run I chanted the Jesus Prayer. Midway through the run I tried a new mantra, "Fa-ther, Son-and, Ho-ly, Spir-it." This is in four phrases like the shortened version of the Jesus Prayer, but recognizes the Trinity in a way that has been absent from my spiritual practice. I breathed in on one syllable and out on the next. For a short time I timed my breathing with the sound and feel of my feet touching the earth. I need the rhythmic serenity of a run on the beach—soon. I had a small fight with Nate this morning, but despite the fact that it wasn't a huge disagreement, it left me feeling deflated. I went to sleep last night thinking how much I loved him, and how painful it is to have us estranged.

November 9, 1998—James Brown and "I Feel Good!"

Yesterday's run was a fast eleven-mile run on Shoal Creek and Town Lake. The sky was overcast, the temperature was about sixty-five degrees, and I felt a remarkable lightness of being. I attribute the lightness partially to a recent lack of conflict with Donna. The deeper cause, however, is a result of Saturday's mystical experience praying with my friend Robert. The surrender of the body that I felt was so profound that I have carried the sensation with me for two days now. My step is lighter, my attachment to secular concerns diminished. It was a memorable experience that I carry with me still.

The lightness carried through to my run. I felt good. So good, in fact, that no chant I had ever learned was able to break through the refrain of thanksgiving that I learned many years ago from a man whose preoccupation with the condition of the soul is legendary—Mr.

James Brown. "I feel good—so good—I got you" echoed in my
brain. At first I resisted it. Tunes from popular and sacred music of-
ten arise in my head and I usually let them go. Yesterday I em-
braced the chant. It was such a delightful counterpoint, a celebration
of the closeness to God that I had experienced the day before, that it
demanded release. James Brown ran beside me most of the journey.

Mudra

Within the Buddhist and Hindu traditions, mudra usually refers to
the signs or gestures of the hands that accompany the recitation of
mantras, or to the use of the hands in dance and ritual. In tantric
meditation the practitioner, by creating the mudra with his own
hands, brings the presence of Divine Power into his own body.
Among Buddhists, the symbolic hand movements of the mudra, coupled with the mantra, are meant to elicit states of mind in harmony
with those of Buddhas and Bodhisattvas.

The use of hand gestures as symbolic representations of Divine
Power is evident not only within Buddhist and Hindu practices, but
can also be seen in religious imagery and practice throughout the
world. Among Christians, the placing of palms together with fingers
pointing upward is a common prayerful gesture, whose symbolism
is shared with the Buddhist mudra of worship. The use of the hand
in offering blessings, making the sign of the cross, the laying on of
hands in ordination, and the use of the hands to anoint or baptize
are all highly ritualized gestures similar to mudras. When making a
prayer of petition, Muslims hold their hands in front of their bodies,
with palms facing upward. After making the request, the palms are
rubbed on the face. The ancient Hebrews and Egyptians clapped
their hands in praise. The Sioux raised their arms with palms facing
the divine spirit and then lowered them to the earth. Mudras are
intended to strengthen the mystical connection with the Divine, particularly when used in combination with a mantra, by engaging the
body in the meditation practice.

In her book *The Spirited Walker,* Carolyn Scott Kortge suggests a mudra-type exercise that can be used to strengthen the habit of mindfulness while walking. I have found that a variation on her suggestion works very well as an accompaniment to running meditation. Kortge links the practice to the stepping, but, as might be expected, I prefer to synchronize the finger and thumb motion of the mudra to the breath and to a chant.

The mantra I usually use is the four-syllable Sufi chant I mentioned earlier: "Toward the One." Each syllable is mentally pronounced as you exhale. If you try this particular linkage of breath to syllable while sitting, the timing seems a bit off; however, when running, and therefore breathing more rapidly and deeply, it flows quite nicely. On the first exhale, "To," touch the thumb of each hand to the forefinger. On the second exhale, "ward," touch the thumb to the middle finger. On the third exhale, "the," touch the thumb to the ring finger. Finally, while exhaling "One," touch the thumb to the little finger. Immediately begin the chant and its accompanying finger movements again. Repeat the pattern over and over as you run. I am usually able to stay with this combination of breathing, mantra, and mudra with minimal distractions for much of my hour run. There is less opportunity for extraneous thoughts to enter into your mind when you are so fully occupied with the three-part practice. Other four-syllable chants can work just as well. Think of the practice as using the prayer beads that God has provided.

Over lunch recently, a friend described his experience running with the "Toward the One" chant and the mudra. He, as I might have expected from this creative friend, made the chant his own by doing his personal version—alternately tapping forefinger and middle finger to the thumb while chanting. He also timed the chant with steps, particularly with the forward movement of his left leg. Interestingly, he found it irritating that, after tiring of the chant, he could not stop it from rolling on in his head. I should have suggested that he drop the chant and focus only on the breath. His musical ability probably enables him to easily invent a wide range of complex chanting and rhythmic patterns (both audible and physical). He may be able to focus on the breath alone, without the aid of a mantra. If so, consciousness of a pattern (now presumably breathing alone) persisting after the run would become a highly desirable condition, not an irritant.

Ali Darwish, an Egyptian Sufi teacher, has recognized the coincidence that "when one says 'Allah' your tongue goes up toward heaven and you come back." This mudra of the tongue can be used as yet another way to direct your thoughts to the present while sitting, walking, or running. Simply raise your tongue to the roof of your mouth and lower it back down, in time with your breathing. The repeated expression of *Allah,* a name for God that has always seemed to me more of a sigh than a label for the Divine, may indeed point you toward heaven. Initially, I had some difficulty moving my tongue in a way that did not interfere with the mouth breathing that happens after I become winded. However, with a little practice I was able to breathe easily and still perform the mudra.

Chotki

In the summer of 1996, I spent a few days at a Russian Orthodox monastery located in the heart of the Texas Hill Country. It was an austere, parched environment. The weather was hot, the accommodations were spartan, and the monks were not particularly welcoming. The monks gather for prayer several times over the course of the day and, except for occasionally bowing to touch the floor, stand throughout each service. A vigil was held one evening during which the monks stood in their heavy robes and chanted throughout most of the still-warm night. I was told that, "Russians have legs of iron." I noticed that each of the monks carried with them a slender, carefully knotted, black rope. I later learned that this was a prayer rope, or *chotki*—similar in purpose to Catholic rosary beads. The *chotki* is used throughout the Eastern Orthodox faith as a way of tracking the recitation of the Jesus Prayer. While I was at the monastery, I bought a *chotki* that was made by monks living on an island off the coast of Greece.

November 21, 1998—Chotki *vs. Chant*

   I ran again today using the mudra in combination with the "Toward the One" chant and breathing. This is an excellent three-part practice. As usual, I had carried the chotki *with me on the Saturday hill run. A quarter of the way into the run I put the* chotki *in my pocket and began to use my fingers to count prayers in much the same way that prayer beads are used. Occupying my hands, focusing on breathing, and fending off extraneous thoughts by chanting has produced a stillness, an openness, a receptiveness to creativity that is very satisfying. Instead of the chatter or the endless mulling over of events, or being stuck in a way of thinking that has long since proven to be unproductive, I am able to clear my mind of the clutter and be open to creativity—and thus to the source of creation.*

   I like the sequence of touching the thumb to the little finger and ending with thumb to forefinger while chanting "One." This seems fitting. Another advantage to using the finger count over the chotki *(in addition to always having fingers with you) is the balanced feel that results from using both hands in the exercise. There is a total involvement of all parts of the mind and body in the exercise. It becomes a prayer of the lungs, hands, and legs—not merely a prayer of the tongue.*

For many years now the *chotki* has been a companion on my early-Saturday-morning run in the hills. It seems too ostentatious for runs on the crowded hike and bike trails on Town Lake or even the less populated Shoal Creek Trail. I prefer to carry it in private. The prayer rope has proven to be a very effective means of bringing me back to my breath, to the mantra, and to the present. Sometimes, as the monks would have intended the *chotki* to be used, I recite some form of the Jesus Prayer. The rhythm has begun to permeate much of my life. For a while the prayer rope hung from my rearview mirror. ("I don't care if it rains or freezes, long as I've got my plastic Jeezes, riding on the dashboard of my car.") Hanging an object of adoration from my rearview mirror felt a little foreign to me and my kids gave me a hard time about it, so it now rests on the coat rack by my front door. As I enter my home, the *chotki* hangs as a visible symbol, a physical reminder, of the importance of remaining present to God.

6

> Think that you're gliding out from the face of a cliff
> Like an eagle. Think you're walking
> Like a tiger walks by himself in the forest.
> You're most handsome when you're after food.
> RUMI

In contrast to the runs described earlier, in "Emptying the Mind," which involve an apophatic approach—a belief that human categories are incapable of conceptualizing God—the types of runs described here are characteristic of the cataphatic approach to God. Cataphatic language or theology involves a positive conception of the divine experience. There is an underlying assumption that God can be conceived in concrete terms, that the Transcendent is in some sense "knowable." To refer to God as "holy" or "love" or "truth," or even to refer to God at all, is indicative of a measure of cataphaticism. This path requires the creative use of the imagination. Since the nature of God has not been revealed fully to man, it is essential, in order to conceive of God, to engage the personal imagination. The image one holds of the Divine can be visualized in countless ways. For example, the Trinity provides Christians with three different conceptions of the nature of the Transcendent. God is pictured as the Father, the Son, or the Holy Spirit. Each divine image is distinct and carries with it characteristics and connotations shared by the consciousness of the Christian community and held in the minds of individual believers.

I am inclined to believe that our conception of God is so limited and misses the mark so badly, that God must be laughing at our futile attempts to comprehend him. Yet just as Mark Twain was reluctant to join any organization that would accept him as a member, I would be unlikely to worship a God that I could understand. God is so much bigger than we can possibly imagine.

Having said that, it is essential to recognize that humans cannot avoid attributing human characteristics to the Divine. We imagine God to be our friend, our savior, our father, our mother, or our tormentor. I do the same, even though experience tells me I find God most readily in silence and my intellect tells me that a god worth worshiping must be far grander than anything my anthropomorphizing brain can conceive. My answer to this dilemma is to recognize that all the ways I conceive of God are wrong, but to use each of these inadequate musings on the nature of the Divine to bring me closer to the Truth. What follows are examples of how, in my running life, I have used the creative imagination to allow the presence of God to become a more substantive feature of my existence. These images give me something to hang on to—something tangible to grasp when my apophatic theology fails me.

Running in the Presence of God

The Practice of the Presence of God is a small book written more than three hundred years ago by a monk known as Brother Lawrence. It was Brother Lawrence's practice to remain aware of the presence of God throughout each activity of the day. Brother Lawrence's practice involved placing himself constantly in the presence of God through an act of the imagination. As Robin Mass puts it in an article on recollection in the Carmelite tradition, "he saw himself constantly before the gaze of the Almighty." For Brother Lawrence, every activity, whether working in the kitchen or praying, became opportunities to rest in God's presence. The runner can adopt this practice. Simply imagine that God is with you constantly on the run. It matters little how you conceive of God. Take whatever conception of God you have, and allow that image of God to accompany you on the trail. Or, imagine that you are as Brother Lawrence, "constantly before the gaze of the Almighty."

Are You Running With Me, Jesus?

This is a variation of another Anthony De Mello prayer practice. As you run, imagine that Jesus is at your side, running along with you. Imagine how Jesus would look with kindness into the faces of all whom the two of you meet. Imagine how He would find good in everyone you encounter. Look for good in everyone. Look for good within yourself.

A Typical Cataphatic Run

Late in the summer of 2000, I spent a week at the Alta Retreat Center in western Wyoming, in a beautiful valley just below the foothills of the Teton Range. The focus of the retreat was centering prayer, a method of praying that teaches reliance on a "holy word" to keep one's focus from shifting toward random thoughts and toward listening to God's silence. We typically prayed several hours each day while sitting, using the holy word to guide us back from wandering thoughts and roaming imaginations. This kind of prayer is an example of the apophatic approach. In this approach to prayer, the senses are stilled, the mind is less engaged, and one simply rests in silence.

One morning late in the week, the retreat director suggested that I skip one of the prayer sessions and take a run along a nearby country lane. I welcomed the idea, having come across the perfect spot to run when I had taken a bike ride earlier in the week. The road ran parallel to the mountain range. The view from the west of the Tetons, I am told, is not as spectacular as the view from the east. This may be so, but the majestic range, reigned over by the craggy Grand Teton, was a magnificent sight to a boy more accustomed to the gentle rises of the Texas Hill Country. The wheat harvests were just beginning in this half of the state and the wheat fields in the valley separating me from the mountains were flaming gold. The fields of grain alternated with patches of green alfalfa creating a color palate no earthly designer could have imagined. The farmhouses, here inevitably log cabins, dotted the landscape. The rugged mountain range served as an untamed backdrop to the domesticated tranquility of the valley's farming endeavors. As I ran, I passed huge stacks of alfalfa hay, propped up on each end by two-by-fours to prevent shifting bales from tumbling out of the carefully configured formation of evenly stacked rectangles. A young boy on a tractor passed me, moving so slowly up the narrow lane that his speed exceeded mine only by a scant one to two miles per hour. A coyote crossed the road in front of me, pausing to glance in my direction before hurrying to the cover of a waiting stand of hardwood trees. At almost the same moment, an orange-tailed hawk left her perch in a tree beside me and flew to the next largest tree ahead. When I reached her new vantage point, she flew farther on, now determined to avoid new intrusions on her territory. I delighted in the sight of two mares, one nursing her newborn foal, the other watching her young colt run and kick its heels skyward. I passed a barn with the rich, earth smell of decaying manure.

Running on this country lane, I deliberately chose to make use of all of my senses. I didn't want to miss a thing. Having spent many hours in silence during the previous few days, I longed to experience God in a broader context, to be open to knowledge of God in the way that he is presented in nature. This was a purely cataphatic run. Just as with my sitting meditations, I chose not to follow random thoughts, but here I did not pursue silencing the mind. Rather, I focused my attention on whatever presented itself to me in that particular moment of my existence. Running in a new place, I usually have no other choice. I am interested in what fresh sensation awaits me around each bend in the road. Though less rehearsed, it is no less an experience of God's presence than the unfolding of the liturgy in a worship service. God speaks directly through each sight, sound, and smell.

October 13, 1998—The St. Francis Run

I ran on the Shoal Creek Trail yesterday evening from Temple Beth Israel on 38th Street to Town Lake and back. It occurred to me how the kind of running prayer I am able to successfully pray is too often dependent on my state of mind or on the events that surround my life. Yesterday, all was well in my life. There were few major problems. I felt at peace. On a day like yesterday, I mostly felt joy and thankfulness. I had ample love to share, so I offered it to every runner I met. As runners approached, I looked at them directly, appraised the extent of their pain, and offered them God's relief. Some looked up at me; most did not. All received a smile and a blessing. I greeted those who returned my gaze. I am aware that with this kind of practice, the blessing reflects back onto me. I am the real beneficiary. By offering God's love, I receive it.

It is important, however, not to offer these blessings with the expectation of receiving anything in return. Your smile will go largely unnoticed. Your greeting may not be returned. It matters not. This is practice in giving, in offering unrequited love. It is a simple enough matter to offer a blessing to a stranger on the running trail. Chances are, this person has done nothing to hurt you, is not in competition

with you, and wants nothing from you. Still, it is good practice for
the daily encounters with those whom it is difficult to love or offer
God's blessings. The less challenging environment of the running
trail can enable you to become accustomed to this way of regarding
your fellow human beings.

It is less difficult to engage in this practice when you are in a joy-
ful and thankful state. You have something to give. The next stage
is to try the practice when you think you have less to give—to share
love and joy when you, yourself, are in pain and in need of love
yourself. When you run, keep in mind the prayer attributed to St.
Francis:

> *Grant that we may not so much seek to be consoled as to console;*
> *to be understood as to understand; to be loved as to love.*

The Mother Teresa Run

Just as Mother Teresa saw Christ in the face of everyone she met, it
is possible to conduct a run that models her behavior. As you run,
maintaining the practiced smile of the contemplative runner, offer a
blessing to everyone you meet. If possible, catch their eyes and offer
the blessings with your gaze. If they do not return the look, it is just
as well. Extend a silent *namaste,* shalom, or peace. Send positive
energy, ask that the force be with them, or simply wish them good
luck. In some way make a connection, based on love, with each
person you encounter. At times this is automatic; other times it is
more difficult. On the running trail you are likely to encounter all
manner of human beings—the young, the old, the thin, the fat, the
rich, the poor. . . . I find it easy to pray for the homeless. So often
the wild-eyed, unshaven street people bring Jesus to mind. This is
just the sort of disguise I would expect Christ to adopt. I often quite
purposely seek contact with their eyes so that I might peer into their
soul, seeking the Christly presence within. It's more difficult to find
the eyes of the chattering, bejeweled, and distracted sorority girls

who also run the trail. God lives just as surely in their hearts, but their young lives have usually not yet provided them with the measure of difficulty that would cause them to ask for God's presence.

This is an excellent practice for the newly initiated contemplative runner—perhaps on the first time out. If the trail is crowded, it is one prayer after another. As I did this today, I realized that I had never offered so many blessings individually to so many strangers.

It is easy to offer prayers to the moms and babies, to the emaciated old man who continues to run when he looks like he can barely walk, to the lonely face that seems to need a smile and a prayer, but everyone merits God's love and we are asked, as Christians, to be the conveyor of that love. One of the most moving photographs this past week (I'm writing this one week after the deaths of Princess Diana and Mother Teresa) was that of Mother Teresa and Princess Di on the streets of Calcutta. Mother Teresa offered God's love to the richest and the poorest, without judgment.

Continue the eye contact and the prayerful blessing as you grow tired and the run becomes more difficult. This is more good practice for life. Finally, as you near the end of the run, when breathing, running erect, and focusing your sweat-filled eyes are not easy, gently return your attention to your breath. You may find that a loving connection with those you meet persists long after the run has ended.

Looking for the Divinity in All You Meet

Practice seeing the divine essence in everyone you meet on the trail. This is similar to the Mother Teresa run, but instead of offering a blessing to everyone, look for the divinity within him or her. Regard each person you meet as a son or daughter of God, as the Christ or as the Buddha. Look into their eyes. Receive their unspoken blessings. This is a blessing not just from God, but also from others. Ask for a blessing and practice receiving it. Enjoy the feeling of being blessed. Carry it with you when you run. You will run lighter.

September 24, 1997—Running in Thankfulness

Today was the first day of fall-like weather. Perfect for running. I was feeling very low today, having talked with Donna until midnight and then tossing and turning the remainder of the night. I decided to try a Steindl-Rast run, inspired by the teachings of the Benedictine monk Brother David Steindl-Rast, whose spiritual practice centered on gratitude. My aim was to run in a spirit of thankfulness. I did not feel at all thankful before the run, but running in this manner proved far easier than I expected. It was as if the absence of thankfulness created a void that was waiting to be filled if only I paid attention. I thanked God for the cool air, the lake, and the sun. Seeing a train pass, I thought of my dad and the forty years he spent running locomotives. I thanked God for him and his ever-present smell of diesel fuel. I rested in a spirit of thankfulness the entire run, focusing at first on the present physical gifts I was receiving and then allowing my mind to drift to other graces I had received. The run restored me. The spirit remains with me still. Thank God for all you encounter on the trail, even the pain.

Polishing the Lamp of the Heart

The Sufi mystic Wali Ali described a meditation that he calls "a holy war against those enemies within ourselves, against hatred and jealousy and greed." This prayer is very similar to the Greek Orthodox Prayer of the Heart, which is described in detail in the "Breath and Chant" chapter. Called Polishing the Lamp of the Heart, the practice requires the same close attention to breathing and the same simultaneous awareness of the heart as the Prayer of the Heart. The difference is that rather than attempting to synchronize the breath with the heartbeat, the idea is to use the breath to "massage" the heart. As your lungs fill with air, imagine the breath gently touching and caressing the heart. The breath is used to comfort the heart, easing the pent-up emotions and pain residing there. The feelings lying at the surface of the heart are first released, and then eventually the deeper, more heartfelt emotions may rise to the surface. Release them through this gentle massaging action of the breath in contact with the heart. Be aware of each breath and the movement it creates in the center of the chest, caressing the heart.

A prayer of Polishing the Lamp of the Heart can be very helpful when the heart is aching, in need of a soothing massage. I remember one day in particular, in early October of 1998, when I first tried using this prayer as a running meditation. I had begun my morning hill run with the "Toward the One" chant, remembering it incorrectly as "Forward to the One." At first, this seemed like a song the Chinese might have intoned during the Cultural Revolution as they marched each morning to the rice fields. I stayed with the chant, nonetheless, for most of the run, until the troubles I had experienced the night before with my son became too much for me. I felt wounded by the rift that had developed between us, and I was preoccupied with the memory of our disagreement. I decided to try the Sufi practice of Polishing the Lamp of the Heart while I ran. I first paid close attention to my breath, and then visualized my heart being massaged by my breath. As my lungs filled with air, I imagined them swelling and drawing closer to the heart, gently massaging, offering comfort to my heart.

I was three-quarters of the way through my run. I could see my expanded lungs caressing my heart—soothing my heart, caring for my heart. Almost immediately, the pain I was feeling from the bitter words my son had uttered the evening before sprang to the surface. On this day in my life, I had a variety of concerns: work, my role in the church, seeking a loving relationship with Donna, friends who are very ill—all affecting me deeply. Yet as my breath was massaging my heart, the concern that was causing me the most grief would not stay submerged. Thoughts of the troubled relationship with my son were unavoidable.

As I ran, I allowed the thoughts to linger, to receive God's blessing through the breath. I dwelt with the thoughts for a moment longer than I would have usually allowed extraneous thoughts to remain. And then I let them go. The change in my state of mind was dramatic enough to send chills through my body. The burden I was carrying was lifted to such a degree that I felt lightened and I ran much faster. I returned to my breath, and then to the Jesus Prayer and, after a mile or two more, to my home. Upon arriving home I awakened my son, fed him, and took him to the ballpark for his Saturday-morning baseball game. His attitude was somewhat surly, but tolerable. The fierce anger of the night before had subsided. By the late afternoon the wounds had healed and we were father and son again.

That same afternoon I met with a friend who was dying of cancer. Robert Hopper, a noted scholar in the field of communications, as well as an accomplished folksinger, shared a song with me that he had written about his father. The song was filled with rich images of his childhood impressions of his father. I was deeply moved. We often prayed together and I was eager to share with him my running experience with the Polishing the Lamp of the Heart prayer I had practiced earlier in the day. After explaining to Robert how the prayer worked, he demonstrated an eagerness to try it. We began by simply focusing our attention on our breathing and then onto the image of the breath massaging the heart. Almost immediately, I felt a flood of emotion. Images of my father came to mind and I felt as if I was in the presence of both my father and my son. I was overwhelmed with a sense of love for both of them. One tear after another streamed from behind my closed eyelids. I felt a tremendous sense of relief. Once again, as with the Morning Prayer run, I chose not to part with the images I had received as readily as I usually dispense with the thoughts that creep into my consciousness during prayer. I could tell that healing was taking place—that I had brought a concern of mine to God's presence, and that I was the beneficiary of God's grace. Eventually I let go of the images and returned to breathing. I opened my eyes, wiped away the tears, and shared the experience with Robert.

September 27, 1998—The Nail and the Cross

In the middle of my Saturday-morning hill run, I noticed a sixteen-penny rusted nail lying on the pavement a few feet ahead of me. I slowed down just enough to scoop it up. I was in the midst of congratulating myself for a simple act of good citizenship—saving the unaware motorist from a possible flat tire—when my attention was redirected to the nail. There was nothing particularly unusual about finding the nail. A good deal of home building and remodeling was going on in the area; it was to be expected that an occasional errant nail would find its way to the neighborhood streets. Its rustiness indicated that it apparently had lain in the street, or at least out in the weather, for some time. The rust was the only obvious similarity between this nail and the nails that I imagined were used to hang Christ on the cross. Nonetheless, as I held the nail in my hand, the image of the crucified Christ came into my heart. Ordinarily, a stray nail would have remained just a nail—nothing more. When I run, however, rain becomes baptism, a stranger's smile becomes a saint's blessing, a gentle breeze is provided by God's breath, shade from the sun is a sign of Divine compassion, a nail is a symbol of the martyr's sacrifice, and each step brings me closer in communion with God.

Rather than toss the nail into the next roadside trash can, I held it in my hand, felt its rough texture, pressed the point against the flesh of my palm, and ran on. I made no effort to visualize the Passion of Christ, or to solidify a connection between the object I carried and its sacred imagery. It was enough to hold it and to return to my breathing. When my attention strayed from my breath, an awareness of the weight and feel of the nail reminded me of my goal and the breathing that would take me there. I carried the nail for mile after mile until, near the end of the run, I stopped long enough to place the nail in the soil of a neighbor's redwood planter, where I imagined it would eventually rust away in the damp earth.

November 8, 1999—Reversing Spacing

I met and prayed with my friend Robert yesterday afternoon. His condition is rapidly deteriorating. His liver is unable to perform one of its usual functions, removal of ammonia from the blood. As a result he tires very easily. He is so tired, in fact, that at times of the day his speech is very difficult to understand. When he called on the phone to confirm our meeting time, I failed to recognize his weakened voice. After speaking with him I felt that the Sufi prayer of Reversing Spacing as described by Reshad Feild would be of some help. The prayer involves focusing all attention on the center of the chest and slowly surrendering all of your senses to God. Instead of seeing, you imagine that you are being watched. Instead of hearing, you imagine that you are being heard. Instead of touching, you sense that you are being touched. Donna suggested that considering Robert's difficulty in communicating verbally I should add that instead of speaking, you should imagine that you are being spoken to. Instead of tasting, imagine that you are being tasted. (Reshad Feild adds, "So make yourself taste good.") Finally, instead of breathing, allow yourself to be breathed. Relinquish control of sensory perception to the Divine. Abandon your power to God, allowing yourself to trust completely.

The shared exercise proved to be both powerful and difficult for each of us. I knew that Robert was practicing for the day when he would relinquish, not just the power of speech that was abandoning him this day, but also all control over his senses to God. I understood, for the first time, the prophet Mohammed's admonition to "Die before dying." My own experience during the prayer was that of a complete fading away of my body. I existed, alongside Robert, as spirit, devoid of human flesh. I moved through the exercise slowly, being seen, being heard, being felt, tasted, and breathed. I recall that at one point the phone rang and the answering machine picked up a caller's voice. On one level I heard the ringing and the *voice, but the meditation was so deep that the phone call only served to heighten my awareness of the condition of surrender in which I found myself.*

Robert found the exercise difficult but cleansing. Despite the intensity of the man's faith and trust in God, he was not ready to turn loose of his earthly existence. He is a man who has loved and been loved by many, and God has been good to him. He is reluctant to turn away from the blessings he has received.

Reversing Spacing, a Failed Attempt

The reversing-spacing practice was so profound that I decided to attempt the same exercise while running. I moved through the prayer methodically, first attempting to imagine that I was being heard, listened to. I heard my breathing and the sound of the gravel path crunching beneath my feet. I tried to imagine myself being seen, but the visual display surrounding the trail held my attention. Besides, to be seen rather than to see seemed to require that I close my eyes— a highly impractical action while running. I found it difficult to imagine being tasted when the salty taste of sweat was constantly at my lips. Giving over my sense of touch was even more difficult when I felt so many sensations: the heavily worked muscles and tendons within my body; the sensitive areas of my skin, as they rubbed and chaffed against even the light fabric of my running clothes; my skin's reactions to the variations in temperature and humidity, light and dark of the fast-approaching evening. Ignoring the diversity of sensory input that surrounded me seemed to run directly counter to the awareness approach to prayerful running I had adopted. Eventually I came to the realization that what works in a sitting meditation may not be well suited for running meditation. Heightened awareness to that which surrounds me while running brings me into God's Presence. While sitting, external stimuli play a far less pronounced role. While running, the conscious recognition of the external stimuli can take you inward. However, an inward focus that ignores the sensory input of the present can be both physically dangerous and damaging to the goal of awareness.

Indian Running

As a child, I had often imagined that I was a young Indian brave. Summers and Saturdays were spent riding my Appaloosa pony along the creeks, through the woods, and down the country roads surrounding my family's small ranch. My father had insisted that I learn to ride bareback before I was given a saddle, and the lesson enabled me to appreciate the joy of clinging to my horse's sweating back with her girth clinched tightly between my knees. She would gallop at full speed while I lowered my head beside her neck, making my shirtless, sun-bronzed body less visible to the "white soldiers" who might be watching.

A few short decades later, this same image of myself as the Indian brave has returned. I had been reading from Peter Nabokov's 1981 book, *Indian Running,* an excellent and comprehensive study of the nature of running among Native American Indian tribes. Nabokov makes little attempt to generalize about the characteristics of running he observed among the various American Indian tribes. However, there does seem to be a common thread woven through the Indian approach to running that seems to be shared by these varied cultures. The running Indian experiences a unique level of connection with the physical elements surrounding him. The kinship with the land, the sky, the sun is so direct, so physically felt that the separateness is gone. The Native American Indian runner seems at one with the natural environment surrounding him. Looking at this experience, as an urbanite of the second and third millennia, I long for this Oneness. I wish to know what it is like to feel such a bond with the physical world that I become a part of it.

During the second half of my run along Shoal Creek yesterday, I consciously tried to allow my spirit to meld with that of the earth, wind, and sky surrounding me. My attempts were through the channels of awareness—implementing the methods of awareness training that had been a part of my running for several years. I heard the crunch of the gravel beneath my feet, I felt the gentle breeze, I saw the lengthening shadows surrounding me—I sensed these elements deeply, I breathed them into my body, but they were not a part of my being. I remained separate from all that I sensed.

Nearing the end of the run, my efforts seemed futile, overly ambitious, even silly. My thoughts drifted to the image of the Navajo runner about whom I had been reading. I had an image in my mind of how he ran—erect, dignified, alert, his feet only lightly touching the ground, single-minded in his purpose. Instantly, I became the Navajo. The Oneness that I imagined the Indian felt became much more comprehensible. I breathed in a different way, my stride lengthened; my foot touched the earth with lightness. I was no longer running through an urban park, but was traversing the plains with an urgent mission. Fulfillment of that mission was dependent on an awareness of all that went on around me and the benevolence of the spirits that inhabited each of those elements.

On a hill run yesterday, I again imagined that I was an Indian runner, as had happened, unintentionally, on the Shoal Creek Trail last week. It had been fairly easy on the rugged path along Shoal Creek, where city sights and noises are a distant backdrop. It was more of a stretch to picture myself wearing the moccasins of an Indian runner when I was traveling down the well-paved streets of a fashionable West Austin neighborhood. Still, I retained the notion and I found myself assuming the posture of a stealthy, fleet-footed brave. As the manner in which I carried myself changed, my attitude changed, and I noticed a heightened level of awareness. The advice I once received from a friend to "act as if you have already received" proved valid. I ran as one who is connected with Creation—and it became so.

It may be that primitive man was more directly connected to the Creator. He lived in the midst of an abundance of sensory impressions of God's power and love. It was an existence confined to the natural world, but with an intuitive grasp, if not an intellectual understanding, of his place in the spiritual world that surrounded him. As we have distanced ourselves from the natural world, we more easily lose sight of the spiritual. Special steps must be taken to reestablish that connection. Therefore, we build sanctuaries, holy places where the presence of God can be felt. We create elaborate rituals through which we can sense God's presence in a way that can be naturally felt in the forest or desert. When I run, I find it easier to establish that connection in places far removed from the impact of civilization. Unfortunately, I don't live in such a place, so I have learned how to find God where I am. As we congregate in urban centers, the chance to go where man in the preponderance of his evolutionary years found God, are lessened. Our challenge is to continue to find the Spirit in all creation, not just amidst nature. How to find God when we run on the high school track, or in city streets, as readily as five hundred miles away in the desert is our challenge. Yet this is the challenge that will lead us into more complete communion with God. How do we locate God in the less God-friendly environments? Our quest is to find God amidst hostility, at work, at play, not just at church on Sunday morning, but wherever we find ourselves. The spiritual path runs through varied terrain, and God lurks around every corner.

Alexander M. Stephen has described how Hopi chiefs would run great distances in wide circles, gathering the attention of the "cloud chiefs" and then on succeeding days, travel in smaller and smaller radii, bringing the clouds to the area where the rain was sought. This was running with the intent of establishing a link between the Hopi's needs and the providence of the spirit world—"sympathetic magic," as anthropologists call it.

Nabokov describes a more typical "participatory dimension" to the interplay of Indian running and the spirit world. He notes that "running meant joining in the motion which is at the heart of life itself." He describes how "everything from the Navajo settlement pattern to healing rituals contains the motif of ceaseless motion." For the Navajo, and other Native American Indians, "running could be a link between worlds, a way of communicating with timeless spirits and powers."

My own experience with running has much in kind with the Navajo notion of how the very motion of running creates a natural linkage with the life forces that surround us. When I run, I seldom engage in prayers of supplication. I am unlikely to directly ask the spirit world for assistance. However, like the Navajo, I may sometimes be seeking to influence the spirit world by bringing the motion of my own body into synchronization with the motion of the universe. If this happens, it largely occurs outside the realm of my consciousness. Usually, I simply run in the present, in tune with the world that surrounds me.

Nabokov cites Aristotle's definition of motion as the "mode in which the future belongs to the present . . . the joint presence of potentiality and actuality." The runner is bringing the future into the present in a direct physical way. This occurs in the most literal way as the runner views the path ahead and, simultaneously, negotiates the path beneath his feet. The future has relevance, not as an abstract forecast, or as a vision to be hoped for or feared, but only as it effects an immediate touching down of the foot to the earth. The future brings us into the present in a more direct sense than usually occurs. We move physically into the future, and the future flows into the present.

I wish to experience God in every way possible during running. I have relied on chants, awareness exercises, prayer ropes, counting breaths—all manner of aids from a variety of religions. The practice of running, as done by Native American Indians, was first a practical consideration. It was the method used to convey messages from one place to another. Foot travel was the fastest method of delivery. Still on a practical level, running was a prayer of petition—a way of asking God to bring rain clouds to the parched earth or running to "strengthen the sun." On a deeper level, the Indian runner becomes one with the running, with the physical elements that surround the run—the wind, the clouds, and the sun. It is not that the runner simply runs like the wind, drifts like the clouds, or burns like the sun; the Indian runner becomes these elements.

The mythology and ritual of the Zuni tribe in New Mexico is filled with allusions to running—particularly kick-stick racing. The highly ritualized practice of running while kicking a stick provides a way of focusing attention, engaging both mind and body. The anthropologist Alfred Kroeber noted that he had never heard from a Zuni the least reference to a historical event (Nabokov, 106). When running, the Zuni are so grounded in the present that the entire notion of history is a foreign concept. We tend to function in the past and in the future, with little regard for the present. Running consciously is one area in which living in the present is an attainable goal.

Among the Navajo, it is traditional for young boys to run early in the morning and start running to the west, following the direction of the sun's path. Nabokov quotes a Ramah Navajo as saying that he often begins running in the late afternoon, "Then I give myself a sort of challenge, running east away from the sun to try and outrun my shadow." Most of the runners I know run loops, so they are likely to run both in the direction of the sun's progress across the sky and also opposite the sun's progress. Pay attention to the direction you run the loop. If you typically run one direction, run the opposite way. Be aware of your run in relation to the sun. Are you chasing your shadow, or is your shadow chasing you?

Anthropologist Thomas Buckley, who studied the Yurok tribe of Northern California, equates the advanced style of running practiced by the Yurok with the meditation practices of Eastern mysticism. Privileged tribal youth were chosen to undergo elaborate running training called *hokep* that was designed to put the runner in touch with unseen elements in the world. Buckley referred to a running technique called skimming, which enables the runner to enter a state of consciousness that allows him to glide effortlessly over bushes covering the mountain slopes.

"True running," among the Yurok, was achieved by viewing the trail as a living entity capable of communicating directly with the runner. Runners were instructed to sing and talk to the trail and to view the trail as moving by itself underneath the runner's feet. Guidance from the trail could be received as the runner learned to trust and listen to the trail. Learning to trust the trail sometimes involved running swiftly along the trail with eyes closed.

The runner was taught to not interfere with the run, but to trust in the earth. Instead of merely being aware of how the feet feel when they strike against the earth, the Yurok focus on sensing the ground pushing up against the soles of the feet, propelling him along. The aspiring runner was also taught to visualize the air moving past him as a kind of rope that he could use to grasp with this hands to pull himself along.

The perceptual abilities of the running Yurok seem far beyond what most of us may be able to attain. It is relatively easy to focus attention on the elements of the run that have a direct impact on the body. The Yurok seemed to be able to extend the focus beyond their bodies and to allow the trail itself to speak to them, to direct them, to control the nature of the run. Relinquishment of control to the physical elements requires a level of awareness that is achieved only through much practice and the cultivation of a willingness to listen intently to the spirit of the run.

A Theocentric Run

Dr. Ellen F. Davis, in a series of lectures she offered in the fall of 1999, presents a picture of a universe in which all creation is capable of worshiping God. She reminded us of how, in the Psalms, the rivers clap and the oceans roar in praise of God. In response to these ideas I was prompted to try a God-centered run—a run in which

God would be honored by the voice of nature. I suggest that you undertake a run in which all elements of the natural world join you in your run. Experience the sound of the babbling brook, the rustle of the wind in the trees, the scent of the fruit trees blooming as praise to God. Join in with this chorus. Look, purposefully, for signs of God's creations, offering praise. Become one among the many voices of praise.

Running with the Oracle

The run can provide insight to unanswered questions, but as with the ancient Oracle, the answer often arrives in a riddle and truly emanates from the self. Even so, both the questions asked and the answers received can often become clearer in the run.

We often worry and fret over the issues confronting us. We might systematically list the pros and cons of taking alternative courses of action. We consult friends, family, or clergy. We pray fervently for answers. We look to our intellect. We ask our heart. And often life's great issues remain unsolved. Spiritual running provides a way for the answers to percolate to the top. It is likely that an inordinate amount of time has already been spent consciously considering the problem at hand. I suggest that through running you allow another level of being to grapple with the uncertainty. The unconscious is much more comfortable with inconsistencies, uncertainties, and paradox than the conscious mind. It makes sense to allow this part of your mind to take over. Depending on your religious orientation, you may know this practice as one of "giving it up to God" rather than consulting the Oracle. The label matters little. The efficacy of the practice is dependent on our willingness to relinquish the belief that we can find the answers on our own.

I have found it useful, in preparation for such a run, to deliberately acknowledge the purpose of the run. For me this is done with a simple, direct, verbal prayer—asking God for guidance. What follows is an intense period of listening. It is not necessary, indeed it is at cross-purposes with the objective, to continue thinking of the issue. The problem has been handed over to God and our task is to simply listen.

This listening is accomplished in the same way as with other exercises we have discussed. Bring your attention to the present, use a mantra, practice an awareness exercise, or focus on your breathing or the touch of your foot to the path. By letting go of the problem in this way you are allowing a new approach to develop that is outside of the structure in which you are holding the dilemma. The creative forces of the Divine can come into play without the limiting influence of our attention. At worst, you will feel some measure of relief from having spent the duration of the run not having to deal with your problem. At best, you may receive an answer. The reply is unlikely to be in the form that you expect, it may not be the answer you want, it may only be the answer for the time being, or it may lead you to understand that you are asking the wrong questions. Still, the work required to interpret the answer you do receive is likely to lead you in the right direction.

April 11, 1999—Running with the Angels

Following the example of Rabbi Cooper's Archangel Meditation, based on a traditional Jewish bedtime prayer for angelic protection, I chose my Saturday-morning hill run as the time to run with the angels. Until now, I had never really considered angels closely. In recent years, particularly in popular culture, the subject of angels has received a lot of attention. Probably because of the excessive hype, I had ignored the phenomenon. In this case, however, Rabbi Cooper's description of a meditation involving the angels hit a respondent chord within me, and I determined to see if the sitting meditation translated well to a running meditation.

I had run only a few blocks when the angel Michael joined me on my right-hand side. Michael, God's messenger, was cheerful and chatty. I asked questions of Michael and he, without hesitation, gave me the answers that I already knew to be true, but was reluctant to face. It was as if I was talking with a wise and trusted friend, or perhaps to an understanding therapist. I felt as if I was immediately understood. Moreover, not only was I understood, but the circumstances surrounding the choices to be made were understood as well. I had confidence in the advice. I was running and talking with a new, but immediately close, companion.

In a short while I heard the footsteps of Gabriel, the angel of God's strength, coming up behind us and taking his place at my left side. I immediately felt his power and knew that as he ran along beside me he was sharing his strength with me. The steep hills seemed less formidable, my legs more powerful. The two angels and I moved in perfect harmony. Our feet touched the ground at the same time. Our breathing was simultaneous. (I was appreciative of them relying on their feet to carry them along and not using their wings.) I knew that the strength Gabriel brought with him was available to not only help me physically through a challenging run, but through the emotional and spiritual challenges I face in other aspects of my life.

I then realized that running along behind us was the angel Raphael—God's healer. He was there to heal the aches and pains of running as well as the deeper psychological wounds that I carry with me. Raphael preferred to run in the background—present and available when needed to administer God's healing grace.

A few moments later, Uriel, the angel of God's light, came from behind and took his place in front of the pack. His light shined brightly, showing us the way. I felt sure that we could have run safely together on the darkest night. We continued the run, and the sense that I was surrounded by these four angels gained in intensity as we trotted along together. Raphael provided constant care, Gabriel's presence strengthened me, Uriel showed us the path, and Michael kept us in constant communication with God. The feeling of shared companionship was as real as any shared run I have experienced. I felt as if I was in the company of good friends.

Halfway through the run, as we made our way up Mountain

Climb Drive, conversation ceased. Together, we focused on our breathing and, together, this angelic choir chanted, "Toward the One." After we reached the top of the hill, we ran in silence. I listened to the sound of our breathing in unison, and the sound of our feet landing in perfect synchronization. I felt loved and cared for by each of these running angels. Finally, about a mile before I reached home, the angels peeled off one by one until I was alone again. They left so that I could rest in solitude with God. Running in God's presence, I no longer required the presence of His angels. Yet I was left with the clear sense that they would be there for me, waiting to appear when I needed their company.

The Outward Run and the Inward Run

For a recent run I considered it as consisting of two distinct parts—an outward run and an inward run. That is, a run away from home and a run toward home. I began the outward run with a very deliberate awareness exercise. Remembering the Rumi poem about the leonine walk, I ran with the awareness of a lion moving quickly down the trail—stalking prey, answering the cry of offspring, or being hunted. I adopted the same acute sense of awareness that I imagine an animal, whose reliance on the physical senses are the necessary basis of his survival, must have as it travels through hostile terrain. I listened carefully to the songs of each bird I encountered. I heard the rising and falling traffic noise, as well as the engine noise and squeaky brakes of individual automobiles. I noticed the sounds of the human voice—the animated chatter of the girls from the nearby sorority houses and the playful tone of the father pushing his giggling son in a running buggy. I smelled acrid exhaust fumes, the musty odor of the ancient grotto along the creek side, the heavily perfumed scent of passing runners, the dust lingering in the air from the newly constructed limestone embankment. I looked through the leaves at every turn, anticipating what might lie ahead. I noted the gathering clouds, the position of the sun, and read the emotions in every stranger's face. Although I moved quickly, I made each step cautiously, as if the urgency of my mission required that I suffer no harm.

It was a game—a bit of make believe. Yet it was a game that brought me completely to the present. Each bit of sensory information that I received was instantly examined for possible significance to the journey and then dropped. As I called each of the five senses into play, there was no room for lingering thoughts of the business day. The present, to be experienced fully, demanded my attention.

I continued this exercise until I reached the planned turn-around point on the trail. I stopped for a moment, sipped a drink of water, and started the return trip by walking for a few yards. My attention, which had moments before been darting from each sight, sound, or smell to the next, was suddenly, involuntarily, brought to bear solely on my breathing. All of the attentiveness of each of my senses, which I had directed outwardly to the infinite elements in my immediate surroundings, was suddenly concentrated in a funneling whirl of energy to my breath. It felt as if I had returned home. The heightened awareness that I had purposefully cultivated on the twenty-minute outward trip became, in a consolidated form, the tools for knowing only the breath.

On the return home, the run inward, I was able, with unusual ease, to hold my attention on my breath. I was still aware of the passing sights and sounds, but the journey had brought me an acuteness of perception that was best expended on the most immediate— the breath. The sound I now heard was the voice of my breath, accompanied only by the echo of my footsteps.

God Is Running Toward You

Just as Sufis are the "impatient ones," the believers who cannot wait until death to know God, the prayerful runner finds it inadequate to sit and wait for the Spirit to appear. It fits the runner's personality more to rise from a kneeling supplication and run toward God. What he finds is that God is running toward him at twice the speed.

Recall the vision of Mohammed, mentioned in an earlier chapter, of your taking a single step toward God and finding that God has advanced ten steps toward you. Hold this thought, this image, while running. As you take a single stride toward God, he is sprinting toward you. In order to draw closer to God, it is only necessary to move in his direction. Know that even if your run is aimless, God is still with you. If you wish to have God revealed to you, he is a cooperative partner in the endeavor, rushing toward you with every step you take. This recognition provides both comfort and a challenge. There is comfort in knowing that God is already with us, and challenge in the knowledge that the presence of the Divine can become more fully realized with each step. The reward is clearly obtainable when we accept that God wants contact with us as much as we seek it with him.

Your conception of God may make it difficult to imagine the Transcendent running down the hike and bike trail. If so, hold the image of Christ, Mohammad, Elijah, or a young Siddhartha running toward you. Envision him as you might, in robes or in running shorts, bearded or clean-shaven, but running from a great distance toward you with lightning speed, running to greet you with all the love, compassion, and forgiveness you seek. Allow him to run toward you for the duration of the run. Finish your run with a burst of speed. And imagine receiving a greeting from God's emissary that is akin to the greetings we see when a long-absent soldier returns to his wife waiting for him on the airport tarmac. Imagine the embrace of this God-being as you welcome him home.

a sense of place

> Talk to me not
> Of time and place;
> I owe I'm happy
> In the chase.
> SHAKESPEARE

> Now, here, you see, it takes all the running you can do, to keep in the
> same place. If you want to get somewhere else, you must run at least
> twice as fast as that!
> LEWIS CARROLL, *THROUGH THE LOOKING-GLASS*

One of the reasons I attend the church that I do, All Saints' Episcopal Church in Austin, Texas, is because of the sense that I have of God's presence there. Worship is held there in a very beautiful and old sanctuary. It is made holy by the years of prayers that have been offered to God within its walls. I feel much the same way about the places I regularly run. The trails have taken on a sense of the sacred because I have sanctified them with my prayer runs. I sometimes feel that I should remove my shoes because I know that I am running on "holy ground." I know the places on the trails where overhanging branches create a brush arbor and where God's presence can be felt as if one were in church. I notice the moments when the trail opens up to the sky and I am surrounded by the light of His mercy. The presence of the lakes and creeks along the trail bring to mind the waters of baptism and the miracle of transformation. With eyes closed, stretching after each run, I bow my head, experiencing fully a spirit of thankfulness for the blessing of the run. It is all a prayer and the trail can be as sacred as your prayers make it.

The virtues of taking the same path over and over again, getting to know the way with deeper insight, learning to see that same way with freshness, are myriad. But it is interesting, fun, and insightful to find renewal in yet untraveled places. When I start such a run, whether it is in the desert, in the forest, or in an unexplored city, I inevitably spend the first part of the run reveling in the new sights and sounds I have encountered. I never really feel like I know a place until I have run through it. On a run, I develop a kinship with an area that I never develop when viewing it from a car window. Concealed in an automobile, the sensory impressions are limited, but running through an area, one develops different levels of knowing, of noticing that which surrounds you.

I find running in a new place to be much like worshiping in a new setting. While there is a richness that can come from the familiarity of a particular style or place of worship, I have lately enjoyed experiencing the methods of worship practiced by various faiths in a variety of settings. In the same way, I have found that running in a different place brings with it a different set of experiences that can be known in the light of expanded awareness. Each new setting provides an opportunity to practice an enlightened way of sensing and of being, without the crutch of familiar places. Running in a new place stretches your capacity for spiritual running.

From the Body of Christ to the Father

I've always enjoyed the beach, and try to visit one every year. I've made frequent trips to Padre Island, but on a recent trip, I realized that I couldn't recall ever having been consciously aware of the meaning behind the name of this long slender island off Texas's southern coast. Most place names in South Texas seem to be of Spanish origin. But the names have become such a part of the ordinary lexicon that their original meaning is lost. For most Texans, *Padre* denotes brown sandy beaches, spring break, and a weekend getaway. Even non-Spanish speakers know, if they think about it, that *padre* means *father*. And, if they devoted a little more thought to it, would realize that the *father* referred to in its original meaning was a heavenly, rather than an earthly, father. While driving from Corpus Christi to Padre Island and again, when starting my run along that shoreline, the symbolism of the place names didn't escape me. I was fully aware that the arching causeway provided the link from the "body of Christ" to the "Father."

For me, it's the sand. Running on the beach is about many things, but the feel of the sand, the directness of the connection with the earth, running along the thin line that separates the sea from the land—no other running experience is comparable. I have written about the sensory stimulation that is present in many of the places that I have run and how, often, the sensory input is a distraction from the meditative dimension of running. On the beach, especially running alone on a quiet beach, all the sensory information takes you back to the Self.

Sand on the beach changes as the tide moves in and out and the waves crash onto the shore. The sand most distant from the water's edge is very soft and is a real chore to run on. It is almost impossible to maintain any kind of rhythm as your feet plunge deeply into it with each step. It's a struggle to pull your feet out of the cavity created with each churning step forward. Closer to the water, the sand can be very hard and crusty. Your feet pound against this sand, much like running on pavement. At the water's edge, all is perfect. Where the last remains of each crashing wave skitter in widely arching patterns toward the shore, the waiting dry sand absorbs the salty water and, for only a few moments, creates the perfect running surface. Its perfection can be grasped only when barefoot.

Along London Road

There are few, if any, similarities of place that come to mind when comparing a warm summer's day run on Padre Island to the unrelenting cold and dampness experienced during my runs in England. During those days, actually two years of living in England, I ran primarily to stay in shape. My most vivid memories are of running in Preston Park near our home in Brighton, in East Sussex. The weather was usually bad—rainy and cold—even during the summer months. Runners were rare. As a Texan living in England, I was already a novelty; as a runner I was more so. Few Brits understood my desire to don my running shoes and deliberately set out in the almost constant drizzle and fog. I typically left the side door of our flat at a run, moving quickly down the sidewalk along Florence Road to the bottom of the hill where it joined the London Road. The park was beautifully typical of the formal English parks scattered throughout the villages and cities of the country. Majestic elm trees guarded the park's borders, while its interior was adorned with manicured hedges, rosebushes, and in early spring's orderly succession, plantings of crocuses, daffodils, and tulips. At the north end of the park was Preston Manor, the stately legacy of a privileged family's almost forgotten dominance over a portion of the East Sussex countryside. Within the manor's grounds were a croquet lawn and the family cemetery (including the graveyard for generations of family terriers—"Here lies Tatters, not that it matters," or "Major, a true Scot." Below the remains of the Preston estate lay a cricket pitch, surrounded by a gracefully banked velodrome for bicycle racing. Rose gardens, bowling greens populated by ancient white-clad bowlers, teahouses, and the usual assortment of English follies—all had a place in this splendid park. I often walked in this park. Walking was the norm, and the norm was clearly what was expected. Yet, as runners know, walking doesn't satisfy when the need to run is there.

So, I ran endlessly in the park—around the cricket pitch, through the pet cemetery, amid the rose gardens, and past the bowlers. Although the sun must have occasionally shone while I ran, I have no recollection of it ever doing so. A blanket of fog rolling in from the English Channel usually enveloped the city. Often the fog became so heavy, so laden with moisture, that it was difficult to tell if it had actually started to rain. It didn't matter. I was always wet within five minutes of beginning a run. Perspiration mixed with drizzling rainwater can produce a dampness that is utterly complete, and so much wetter than any plunge in a pool. I was always hot and cold at the same time. After a time, my feet and hands were numb, while the vinyl windbreaker I wore kept the trunk of my body too warm. I peeled off layers and then put them back on. I ran with my hands in my pockets and then dangling at my sides.

The English, always too polite to take obvious notice of me, still quite clearly regarded me as insane. They walked in good weather and bad, but always appropriately dressed and with the requisite umbrella. They might run to catch a bus or train, but to run by choice, in a public park, in inclement weather, clearly made me suspect. The English usually keep their comments in reserve, though I do remember my upstairs neighbor, regarding my soaked countenance dripping on our shared garden path, commenting on my running with only a barely perceptible bit of sarcasm, "That certainly seems health-giving."

Running in My Youth

Looking back on my experience with running, I am curious about how and when I first began to receive the blessing of spiritual running. I ran as a teenager, but primarily to get in shape for the grueling two-a-day practices that awaited me at the beginning of the high school football season. Running seemed like punishment then and I remained largely unaware of the larger dimension it would eventually play in my life. I do remember that I alternated days of running wind sprints with days of running distances. On the distance run, I would cover about five miles, running on the dirt roads connecting the distant farmhouses in the rural area of the Cross Timbers region of Texas where I grew up. I knew these roads well, having traveled them countless times on horseback, in the school bus, or while exploring with my dog on foot.

I vividly remember the road's surface. Red sand was everywhere—sometimes piled so high that my shoes would almost disappear into it. Other places, where infrequent downpours of rain would create shallow rivers across the road, a washboard effect was created, although in my late-summer runs the last significant rainfall was likely to be a distant memory and the effect was less perceptible. As the road climbed the first hill about a mile from home, hard limestone had pushed its way to the road's surface. The road at the top of the hill was more frequently traveled and better maintained. It was covered with fine gravel and its smooth surface tempted drivers to travel much faster than on the lower section of road. As the pickup trucks roared past, I was left to breathe from suffocating clouds of white dust. The images remain vivid in my mind. But I knew nothing of how attention to these elements in my environment could be used to elevate my overall awareness of who I was and my place within the Divine scheme. I understood only that I could make it through the torture of Texas high school football practices if I prepared for it by running. Running was to be endured, not appreciated. Still, I must have been paying attention. The ease with which I can place myself back on the country roads I ran more than thirty years ago indicates that my senses were fully engaged, even then. I was paying attention to my physical environment, but the significance of that awareness would not occur to me until many years later. Nonetheless, the groundwork for a lifetime of running with a sense of God's presence was laid.

The Oblate Monastery

Almost twenty years later I began to recognize the effects, if not the reality, of God's presence while running. A job required me to be separated from my home and family for the first time. Everything I loved was in Austin, but my regular work schedule was four ten-hour days in San Antonio, seventy miles south of home. Typically, I spent two evenings a week in San Antonio. My boss and friend permitted me to stay in his usually unoccupied penthouse condominium while it was undergoing some renovation. The inhabitable parts were a modest bedroom and a bathroom, and a deck with a view that was wonderful. In the evenings I could watch the sunset, but more important, the view encompassed the Oblate Seminary grounds. I found a small opening in the fence behind the condos that allowed me to gain entrance to the Oblate property at a remote corner, and I soon found myself exploring the grounds of the monastery. I began to run along a short trail that wound through the woods and outlying buildings at the northwest edge of the grounds. Most of my run was spent thinking of the past, what I had lost, or planning for the future. At that time I had a dream of rebuilding my business, but in a different way. I wanted to work alone, to practice my craft in the Texas Hill Country, maybe on the shores of the Guadalupe River. I ran in the evenings, after normal hours for classes, so I saw few people. An occasional priest or nun might nod in my direction, but I think I communed with the dead more than the living. As I ran past the gravestones of former Oblate community members, I imagined their lives as monastics. Occasionally I stopped at the grotto. I thought it a curiosity at the time, but in fact, it was God calling to me in my despair. I ran on and on, not knowing, not even asking why I ran at this place, this holy ground. For almost a year, running in the Oblate grounds gave me a sense of comfort I couldn't find elsewhere in this foreign city. This small park was a womb, and inside this womb I was being nurtured and fed, prepared for a day when

I would be mature enough to enter a new world. That awakening to a new world was still over two years away and I had much growing to do until then. Among the Oblates, I was learning to run.

One doesn't have to traverse the grounds of an Oblate monastery to be running on "holy ground." We have the ability to make any place holy ground. In his book on prayer walking, Linus Mundy says that the word *contemplate* literally means *make a temple*. This is what we are doing when we introduce prayer to a place. We create a holy space. The space that we create is, in fact, more within ourselves than dependent on external factors. Even so, the creation of holy space, contemplating a place, creating a temple, is certainly easier in some places than others. Some places simply feel right. There is a "sense of place" about some running locations that make prayer more likely to happen. Traffic noise, busy streets, excessive pavement, bone-chilling wind—these can be obstacles to a prayerful run, but not insurmountable ones.

Manhattan

I recall a few years ago when I had the chance to leave the oppressive August heat of Texas behind, and enjoyed a few days of welcome relief in New York. Looking forward to running there, I planned it for the morning of my first full day. My run began at the Barbizon Hotel at Sixty-third and Lexington. It was raining lightly. Umbrellas were out, some people tarried under awnings, but most of the New Yorkers went about their business with little notice of the summer shower. I had seen the rain falling on the streets from my fifth-story corner room and couldn't wait to join the city waiting below my window.

I started running along Sixty-third Street toward Central Park. I ran past Park Avenue's apartments and flowered median, Madison Avenue's upscale stores, and came to Fifth Avenue, where I turned right and headed uptown. I remained along the park's perimeter, still captivated by the presence of the magnificent buildings standing guard at its edge. I began to make brief forays into the park's interior, my attention caught by a winding trail, an unusual structure, or simply my natural inclination toward grass and trees. Yet each time I went deeply inside the park, the city called me back, and I would turn and run a few blocks along the park's edges so that I could admire the architecture and the city's scurrying residents. Throughout the run I moved back and forth, between urban and pastoral, amazed at how both could so comfortably coexist in the heart of Manhattan. Along the way I noticed how I was drawn to each and how the contrast thrilled me. Yet I was aware of an unsettled feeling. I missed the solitude of the pastoral setting while I ran among the crowds and buildings. And then I wondered what architectural marvel or human antics I was missing while surrounded by nature's more subtle pleasures at the heart of the park. The lure of the city's energy, the vibrancy of this city like no other, kept me moving outward while the peace and serenity I experienced in the urban oasis of Central Park told me that this was the city's spiritual core. This was, I realize now, the reason for my quandary. I sought to connect with the spirit of the city and I could feel the tug of that spirit in many places.

As I moved at the pace of an everyday run, Manhattan's spirit was revealed to me. My senses were attuned to the sights, sounds, and smells that provide the clues to the essence of a place. I moved at a pace that allowed me to experience these sensations fully. My focus on breathing, rather than on old worries or future plans, opened a space for new sensations to enter into my consciousness. I could experience the city with the innocence of a child.

From my first run in Central Park, three years earlier, I remembered the trail that circled the reservoir at the park's center. The trail was being improved with a crushed-cinder surface that made a delightful crunch under foot and offered just the right resistance. I continued north, following winding trails and roads, generally heading uptown. Within Central Park there are many meandering paths, but there are a series of concentric trails: The outermost path is the city street, adjacent to the park is a wide sidewalk, within the park is a restricted-access paved road (meant primarily for bicyclists and runners). Within the paved road is a smaller dirt and gravel road, used by park vehicles and some pedestrians. Within that road lies a paved path—moving in the same winding way as the outer roads. Each of these paths lay deeper in the heart of the park. Each path offers the traveler a different experience—more urban or more pastoral, more or fewer people, a different type of running surface.

Running near the center of the park, I noticed a sign reading GREAT LAWN and was compelled by the name to move in that direction. Approaching from the north, I saw a beautiful green meadow containing soccer fields and four baseball diamonds. On the closest diamond, I could see that a baseball game was just beginning. It was a pickup game, but with a complete contingent of players on both sides and with at least some of the players in partial uniform. Both teams were speaking Spanish and appeared to be from Central America. They began to play with the joy of a Saturday morning, far removed from the drudgery of whatever labor occupied their long workdays far from home. Their baseball skills were limited, but their enthusiasm for the game was unbounded. I shared their passion for the game. Two weeks before, I had finished coaching my son's summer junior varsity team. I don't typically go too long without seeing some baseball, and withdrawal had set in. The thrill of the game found a ready home in my heart.

I noticed that the stout catcher wore a New York Yankees jersey— No. 2—fabulous shortstop Derek Jeter. That seemed a good choice, even for a catcher. Jeter was having a great season. I suspected that the catcher must be from Jeter's home country and that he was showing his loyalty. Then I noticed the pitcher. He, too, was wearing a Yankee's jersey. When he turned around to watch a line drive fly past the second baseman, I saw that the name on the back of his jersey read "Jeter." I looked at the first baseman's jersey—Yankees, No. 2—Jeter. I glanced at the guy playing second—Jeter. I realized that Jeter was also playing third and center field. The shortstop was wearing a light jacket over his jersey, but I strongly suspected that he, too, was a Jeter. Their entire team was made up of Derek Jeters. Jeter was probably the best shortstop in the game and I thought that these guys, pleased with the success of their fellow countryman, a compatriot who had made it big in Los Estados Unidos, were proudly displaying his name. I later learned that Jeter's father is black and his mother is Irish. My guess is the jerseys were on the discount rack at the sporting goods store.

Running on, I moved constantly in and out of the park—into the woods, through the meadows, and then back to where the city begins to encroach on the park's boundaries. It came to mind how, if the city's inhabitants left, the park's borders would expand, pushing beyond the surrounding sidewalks with grass and trees spreading into the streets. It is this borderland that offers intrigue—the land at the edge of light and dark, the civilized and the primitive, the exposed and the hidden.

I ran completely around the park, turning to head back only when the park's northern green edges turned into the brick and mortar of 110th Street. During this hot summer period in Texas, I had been limiting my runs to less than an hour, but on this day I ran for almost an hour before turning back in the direction of the hotel. There was so much to see and feel. It involved me so much, that I had to keep moving.

Running in unfamiliar places is a very different experience from running at home. If this is a meditation run, it is of a different sort. It is certainly an exercise in awareness, but maintaining that awareness, that sense of presence in my surroundings, requires no particular structure. It happens quite easily, naturally. I made no effort to chant internally, focus intentionally on my breathing, or concentrate on a distant image. I ran with a complete sense of where I was. This was not my first run in Central Park, but it was my first solitary run there and the first where I had run with such presence. I ran with openness, receptivity to my surroundings, not noticing everything about me—there was far too much to take in—but absorbing those sights and sounds and smells into my being. All that I sensed became a part of me.

A few times I was so drawn to the places I encountered at the park's interior that I had to stop. On the run home I came across the Delacorte Theater. This is the theater in the round where the Public Theatre performs the works of Shakespeare during the summer. The doors were open and I could view the stage crew preparing the set for the next week's performance. I love the serenity of an empty theater—anyplace, really, that has once contained throngs of people, when empty retains their silent collective voices, and I still hear them. At a theater the absent crowd's noises are added to the voices of the actors and they echo off of one another.

Ultimately, it was this void in the midst of plenty that gave this run meaning. It is the void that I seek on every run. Typically the empty space is created within my mind. Seeing the symbolic recreation of this emptiness within the heart of the city allowed me to understand it more clearly. At the same time, I became more acutely aware of the richness that exists within the void. It is within this nothingness that elements of the spirit thrive and are revealed. The true abundance can be found amidst the seemingly empty.

Big Bend

I hadn't expected to find the empty space favorable to a divine encounter in midtown Manhattan. Perhaps I unconsciously sought it out. A year or so later, I quite deliberately sought out a place to run where emptiness prevails and where solitude quite naturally leads to an encounter with the Transcendent. I decided to go for a long run in the rugged deserts of Big Bend National Park along the Mexican border in southwest Texas.

Why embark on such a physically difficult journey when the presence of God might be as easily recognized during a leisurely stroll in the neighborhood park? I can't resist the call to pilgrimage. I can take a walk in the park and find God, but the lure of the pilgrimage, with the foreknowledge of the difficulties involved and the singularity of the intentions behind the pilgrimage, seems my destiny. A run in the desert, in particular, ripe with the imagery of man's soulful search for God in a barren place, could not have been more perfect for me.

Ostensibly, the reason for the run was to cap the training I had been doing for the Austin Motorola Marathon to be held three weeks later. A twenty-two-mile run seemed an appropriate distance to end the training for the 26.2 miles I would face with the marathon. Typically, when I have neared the end of marathon training and the longer training runs are indeed longer, I begin to seek different places to run. I begin to look for a change of scenery, something different to do. At least these are the reasons I offered most others to explain why I chose to take a twenty-two-mile run in the desert. The truth is: This run is a pilgrimage. In a sense, every run I take has aspects of the journey to God, but the desert run is a very deliberate quest, an effort to find God in a setting where I have, in the past, found him most real.

Donna and I spent the first night of the trip at the Gage Hotel in Marathon, Texas. I slept fitfully, eagerly anticipating the run ahead. In the late evening a tremendous dust storm had blown into the Big Bend area. When we arrived about sunset, all was brown. Dust permeated our skin. I could taste it in my throat. I felt the grit between my teeth. The northwest wind was fierce and cold, causing travelers to scurry from their cars to the quiet of the hotel lobby. Our room was up the creaking stairs, at the end of the long hall, at the northwest corner of the old hotel. The walls of our room accepted the brunt of the windstorm. It was as if the corner of our room was the bow of a mighty ship, on a windward heading. A constant barrage of sand particles blasted against the windowpanes. The windows themselves shook and whistled throughout the night. In the night I dreamed that my legs were very tired and very heavy and that I would never be able to complete the run. I was relieved the next morning to find that my legs were in fact rested and strong.

I breakfasted well on fruit, granola, tea, and bagels toasted in the flames of the lobby fireplace. We drove south toward the park, both of us noticing the lingering cold, the persistent wind, the cloud cover, and the bleakness of the landscape. Our shared comments, however, were only of the absence of the dust that had been so pervasive the evening before. Donna, aware of how important the run was to me, would do nothing to dissuade me from my mission.

We turned off the main road leading into the park headquarters and headed two miles up a gravel road called Dagger Flat, named for the dagger-shaped leaves of a variety of yucca plant plentiful in the area. We soon reached the intersection with Old Ore Road—as the name implies, the remains of a long-since-abandoned mining route. I had chosen this particular road for a number of reasons— its remoteness, its desert setting on the edge of mountainous terrain, its length (26.4 miles, just beyond marathon distance), and the fact that it ended very near a much beloved natural hot springs on the shores of the Rio Grande.

Despite the absence of discouraging words, I could see in Donna's eyes that she was deeply worried. This was her first experience of Big Bend, and to the uninitiated, the seemingly endless landscape of this country is formidable. The cold and windy weather conditions, the difficulty of the task awaiting me, and the long road looming in the distance left her anxious about what lay ahead. I, too, found the cold and wind intimidating, but I am more comfortable in the territory. I felt at home in the emptiness of the place.

I stretched very little, dressing in the warm truck and began the run with no more ceremony than a quick kiss from Donna. My concern over the strength and chill of the wind was quickly alleviated when I actually started the run. The wind was strong, but at my back. I was a little cool, but I was dressed more warmly than usual and I could tell that even though the air temperature was unlikely to rise, I would quickly warm up. The road started out very straight, stretching perhaps a mile into the distance before curving out of sight. It was difficult to predict the path the road would take through the awaiting miles, but it became apparent very quickly that this portion of the desert was far from flat. Before I rounded the first bend, I turned and waved at Donna. She was inside the vehicle, but from the distance I waved, I could not see her. I imagined her anxious smile in return.

When I looked out on the long, lonely road ahead of me, I was struck by its seeming endlessness and its isolation. In the introduction to his *Essential Rumi*, Coleman Barks describes Rumi's poetry as containing "detailed directions on how to get to the Friend." The park service had published a map showing the way down the Old Ore Road, along with a description of the sights along the journey. They made no mention of the fact that God would be waiting at the end of the trip. If they had, they would have been wrong, because God's presence was made evident along the way through *zhikr*, the remembering that everything is God. God doesn't wait at the finish line. If you are waiting to see God in heaven, he won't be there. The realization of God comes in our remembering that he is constantly with us in all things and in all people. Our task is simply to recognize that fact and hold it with us.

The desert floor has a clear sense of sparseness. It is not empty, but neither is it cluttered. The prickly pear, the creosote plant, the Lechuguilla, Candelilla, and yucca—these are the predominant plants in this part of the Chihahuan desert. The scarcity of rainfall dictates that these plants are naturally spaced far apart, in a surprisingly consistent pattern. I have run in places where the vegetation is lush, where identifying the plants along the trail would be an endless task. Here, too, I noticed the plants and named them during the first part of the journey. I had just relearned the plants on the drive down and felt the need to address them by their proper names. After the initial introduction, familiarizing myself with my surroundings, I could begin to settle in to the business at hand, the reason for my run.

At the beginning of the run, I was fearful of what lay ahead. I had never been down this isolated road and I knew of no one who had run its distance. As the fear subsided I became awestruck by the beauty of the distant mountains—and less aware of the immediate physical hazards of the trail. But in only a few minutes, the road began to reflect the ruggedness of the landscape. In building an old road such as this, little effort was made to level the terrain it traversed. As I had seen from the map, the Old Ore Road only skirts the Dead Horse Mountains to the east. However, the geological events that produced the mountain range spilled over into the surrounding desert floor, leaving hills and valleys, draws, gulches, and washes. At times the footing was an even gravel surface. Other times, the depth of the ruts made it very difficult for a four-wheel drive vehicle to cross. I remember the feel of the flat limestone stretches, hard, but even and responsive. Other times the same limestone occurred at a fault line, and instead of the flat surface, I found myself running on the knifelike edges of the inverted limestone strata. At other places the occasional rain had turned the sand into a classic washboard surface. On occasion the remains of volcanic activity were felt in the pebble-sized ground lava, akin to perfect cinder running tracks. I would sometimes find myself bogged down in deep fine sand. Each surface I encountered brought me back to an awareness of place and being. For practical reasons I had to pay attention to the varied running surfaces I encountered. If I was to understand the essence of the run, attention to this same detail was required.

An hour into the run, I was so exhilarated by the physical manifestations of God's handiwork that my prayer became simple praise and thankfulness—a wordless appreciation of where I was. I felt the joy of a return home to a land of spiritual awakening. Two hours into the run, the euphoria had worn away, and I was left with a quieter sense of contentment, a resting in the arms of God. I was still feeling strong, but the steep uphill runs were growing more difficult. I was called more insistently back to the breath and back to each step on the rocky road. The immediacy of the experience came more clearly into being. The passage of time was very slow, marked more by the changing perspective of the distant Chisos

Mountains than by the digits on my running watch. When I started the run, the view of the Chisos range was of Panther and Pummel Peaks to the southwest. Gradually, as I moved toward the southeastern corner of the park, near the Rio Grande, the South Rim of Chisos Basin moved more into view. The change was almost imperceptible and I became aware of it because I had clearly noted how the mountains looked at the beginning of the run. It was as if the Chisos Mountains were the center of a giant clock and I was riding the tip of the hour hand as it traveled from twelve o'clock toward three. Time takes on a different meaning when riding on the hands of the clock.

At three hours, I was very tired. It took a great deal of effort to avoid shuffling down the road. Despite chanting in combination with breathing, I found that my focus was shifting toward the finish. I was ready for the encounter with exhaustion to end. I felt that I was losing the battle to remain present. The "remembering" came less frequently.

In the midst of each of these hourly snapshots of consciousness lay the gamut of possible emotions. Throughout it all, always in the background, was a call to consciousness. I experienced hardship, then moved back to my breath. I felt joy, and let that pass as well. Remaining conscious of the present, when I was very tired, was perhaps the most formidable challenge. As I grew weary, I was less tempted to enjoy the splendor of the distant surroundings, but I also found it more difficult to lightly place my feet on the uncertain ground. The natural tendency when tired is to plod along, mindlessly. Here, while nearing exhaustion, was an opportunity to practice a mindful focus on breathing, when simply taking the next breath and putting one foot in front of the other is all I could manage to do. How different this was from practicing paying attention to the breath at the beginning of the run. Then my senses were overwhelmed with the physical beauty of the created world. Earlier, awareness of breath had seemed incidental to the experience. At this point in the run, each breath brought salvation.

Although I wished to successfully complete the run, and never had any real doubt that I would, I focused very little on the end. My intention was to find God, not by completing a pilgrimage, but by *zhikr*, the remembering that everything is God. It is rare that I have such a length of time during which this remembrance is practiced with such intention. It is also rare to be in a setting where every encounter is directing me toward this knowledge.

On my first trip to this part of the world, in 1971, I was twenty years old—courageous, thoughtless, foolish, and hungry for experience. Because the shuttling of canoes and automobiles was required then, as part of the logistics of an extended float trip through the isolated lower canyons of Big Bend, it was necessary for my traveling companion and I to hitch a ride down a dusty back road with a rather grizzled pickup-driving rancher. I cast a glance across the brown wasteland and threw out the comment that this was "God-forsaken country." The rancher turned to me and said, "Son, this *is* God's country." Despite the foolishness of youth, after two days in the desert, I knew precisely what he meant.

The same sparseness that brought forth my ignorant comment so many years ago was my companion on this journey down Old Ore Road. Although it was a run from one geographical point to another, it was much more an inward journey. The inward journey was toward the creation of a void, the generation of space, of silence, where God's voice could be heard. The desert cooperated fully with its offering of near silence. Though the wind was incessant, it was at my back and, because it and I moved at the same speed, its passage was generally silent. Only at the hilltop peaks, where the wind lost direction and whirled around me, did its howl become part of the setting. At one point a strong gust blew through the branches of a large yucca plant, vigorously shaking its seedpods and causing me to jump at the rattlesnake-like reverberation. A rare bird might cry in the distance, but its call simply brought me home. The only other sound was that of my feet as they encountered the ground; this sound varied as the complexion of the earth's face changed from ruddy to smooth to pitted.

The desert has a distinct, albeit subtle, smell. The dominant smell in this part of the park is the sagelike aroma of the creosote bush. If you crumble the leaves between your fingers, it becomes quite pungent. Left alone to stand in the evenly spaced formation it naturally assumes, it's barely noticeable. Eventually smell is no longer apparent and only the light scent of dust stirred by the wind reaches olfactory awareness.

It is this dearth of sensory stimulation that makes the desert experience so important. Solitude is readily accessible. The limited nature of the sights, sounds, and smells in the desert allow the traveler to empty the soul without the interference of a multitude of distractions. The sensory stimuli that are present—the ever-watchful distant mountain peaks, the shifting winds, the changing footing, the uphill and downhill courses—are all intermittent calls to consciousness, to the remembering that all is God.

At just under three and a half hours, I could see that the rode continued to turn and climb in the distance and I grew discouraged. Just at that moment, I rounded a sharp bend and could see Donna's Explorer waiting two hundred yards ahead. The sight of the journey's end gave me enough energy to slightly accelerate the pace and end the journey with a hint of lightness.

Gatorade, an orange, and some almonds sustained me until we reached the hot springs. Yoga exercises and an hour-long soak in the springs revived me enough to take a short, slow walk later in the day through the splendor of nearby Boquillas Canyon.

Lurking within my soul has always been a desire for adventure. In my youth this desire was played out in wilderness trips, white water canoeing, cross-country cycling, and travel. As a young adult, this same need for adventure took the form of ventures in business, typically ill fated, but usually providing the thrill of the uncertain quest. At middle age, an adventurous spirit still dwells within me, but now the exciting element of the adventure is an opportunity to experience God's presence firsthand. Having tasted the mystical flesh of the Divine, nothing else thrills me so. It is also apparent that it is the quest itself, this acting on the burning desire to know God, that motivates me. The struggle, the seeking after God, this is the journey of a lifetime. I am truly a pilgrim and my aim is not simply the goal that lies at the end of the pilgrimage, but the adventure with God that attends every step of the journey.

When I returned from the trip to Big Bend and was asked about the run, I was uncertain how to best reply. To those who wouldn't understand, I was likely to offer a flippant answer. I would say that the run was "great" or "hard" or "beautiful." These replies were, at least on a superficial level, perfectly true. The twenty-two-mile run down the Old Ore Road in Big Bend was like life itself. The same can be said for almost every run I take. Every run contains elements of the "stuff of which life is made." All the worries, fears, distractions, hopes, regrets, pain, and joy that fill life are often played out over the course of an hour-long run. Running in Big Bend, a place where God's spirit abounds, the examples of God's handiwork are evident as both challenging obstacles and lofty displays of inspiration. I felt as if years of experience in dwelling in the Divine Presence were compressed into only a few hours. At times it was easy, exhilarating, joyous, and awe inspiring. Then I would emerge from a dry creek bed to find that the trail had become dangerous, worrisome, difficult, painful, and exhausting. Almost any adjective that could be used to describe the course of life could be used to describe how I felt during some part of the journey. The notion that one could compress many of the meaningful human reactions to life into a three and a half-hour run is a provocative thought. In a sense, this happens with every run. I tend to saddle each run with the complexities of my personal existence. And over the course of the run, these complexities are reduced to the simple matter of moving and breathing in God's presence. This reduction from the complex to the simple is, in reality, an expansion of consciousness—a realization that life's complexities can be conceived through these same simplifying lenses.

The light of mindfulness can illuminate all that seemed dark and troublesome.

Engagement in the practice of mindfulness is a lifelong endeavor. The serious practitioner awakens each morning with the intention of being mindful throughout the day. Most of us are immediately distracted and drift in and out of consciousness as the day progresses. During times set aside specifically for meditation, the level of awareness achieved is typically higher. Yet the average meditation session is twenty to thirty minutes—a small portion of the day. A running meditation, particularly one like the Big Bend run, allows an extended period of time devoted, in its entirety, to establishing a connection with prayer. As I have mentioned before, the running meditation is a step closer to those experiences faced in the average life, than a meditation on the Zafu pillow might present.

The Streets of Las Vegas

Three weeks after my experience running Old Ore Road, I was back in the desert. This time I found myself attending a trade show in Las Vegas, Nevada. I had spent the first day talking business to countless people inside a convention hall. In the evening I had made a halfhearted attempt to experience the nightlife of Vegas, but the incessant ringing of slot machines and the constant presence of cigarette smoke drove me back to my room. The next morning, determined to at least catch a glimpse of what Las Vegas was about, I decided to go for a run down Las Vegas Boulevard. I left the Stardust Hotel at seven A.M. and started running south, in the direction of most of the newer casinos. Treasure Island first caught my eye; straight out of Disneyland, it has a pirate ship that actually sinks during evening performances. There, I was thankful for the wooden planks that simulated the wharf surrounding the island's harbor. They provided me with a more cushioned running surface than the endless miles of concrete and asphalt that make up the city. Next door to

Treasure Island was another gargantuan replica—the Venetian Hotel's regularly erupting volcano. Again, I found a welcome escape from the concrete, glass, and steel, but it was through the falseness of this simulated volcano in the midst of an artificially created tropical paradise replete with waterfalls and, startlingly out of place, lush vegetation. I passed Caesar's Palace, with an appeal that was so irresistible I had to slow down to a trot and tour the inside of the place. I found plastic laminate Roman architecture, re-creations of ancient Rome's finest statuary, and faux everything. New York, New York, made me stop so that I could take it all in. It was as if a condensed, hollow version of the New York skyline had been transported to the desert, the Brooklyn Bridge placed in front of it, and the whole thing sanitized so that Middle America could experience the city without fear of being mugged.

Construction was going on everywhere. I saw a huge new casino under construction called Paris, certain to have the Eiffel Tower, Notre Dame, and a chance to stroll the Champs Elysees without the inconvenience of all those rude French-speaking Parisians and, across the street, an Italian Renaissance re-creation, soon to offer Italy without the fear or hope of having one's posterior pinched. On and on, Las Vegas offers the multitudes a chance to see the Seven Wonders of the World, and then some, without the inconvenience of jet lag.

Typically, during the first ten minutes of a run, my mind is a jumble of barely connected thoughts. Ideas, memories, and impressions race through my brain. But as I settle into the run, my thinking becomes less of a muddle; a certain clarity of mind develops. While I run, and focus my attention on breathing, the barrage of thoughts tends to lessen. Fewer thoughts, external to the run, impinge on my consciousness. Also, the time span between extraneous thoughts tends to lengthen, while the extraneous thoughts that remain become more coherent. In order to lessen the degree of interference from unwanted distractions, I generally try to run in a place where the external stimulation is at a minimum. The dirt and gravel trail, the trees and grass, the lake, all provide a minimalist backdrop, a land-scape without significant distractions.

As you might imagine, running in the heart of Las Vegas is a com-pletely different experience. Part of the process of acquainting myself with a new city includes going for a run through downtown. I've run through New York, Paris, London, Chicago, Los Angeles, and many others. Each city run had its own delights, difficulties, fascinations, and distractions. Running in Las Vegas is like running nowhere else. Run-ning from my hotel, seeing each casino for the first time, dashing in-side a few lobbies and gaming halls, I knew there was no hope of the outward-bound part of my run being more than a fleet-footed sight-seeing tour. After forty-five minutes of the impressions of Las Vegas whizzing past my field of vision, I longed for the nurturing of my spirit that usually takes place when I run. I decided to turn around, head back to the hotel, and begin running in my contemplative way.

I began by counting breaths. I had run far enough and then quick-ened my pace to a level where my breathing was rhythmic and fairly heavy. At this stage of a run, I am usually able to focus on my breathing rather clearly, without undue interference. Distractions are always present, and they continually move in and out of my con-sciousness. Usually these intrusive thoughts are not overpowering. They leave as quickly as they come, without occupying much space, and I easily return my focus to my breathing. As I ran along the boulevard, I attempted to apply the concentration techniques I had successfully practiced many times.

I failed miserably. No amount of mental effort, no gentle letting go of my thoughts, no repetition of a "holy word" could clear my consciousness enough to allow room for a spirit-filled run. Why was this? Certainly the sensory stimulation of Las Vegas Boulevard was overwhelming. The noise, the lights, the garish architecture all bom-barded my senses. Yet, as I said, I have gone for runs in many big cities. The sights in most cities are interesting, sometimes distracting, and sometimes awe inspiring. Running in New York, for example, allows access to the wonderful parade of humanity, a sea of faces with real lives, buildings that may be grand or squalid, but each reflecting a human spirit, a sense of history.

In Las Vegas, each casino is in competition with its neighbor to be more spectacular, more attention grabbing, more distracting. Each is designed to lure the potential customer off the street and into the hands of the money extractors. It's Disneyland. It's a shopping mall. It's a collection of carnival sideshows. Las Vegas is unique among the myriad ways man has devised to get the attention of those willing to part with money in pursuit of pleasure. The magnitude of the enterprise, and the means by which it has perfected this disingenuous art, set Las Vegas apart from less skillful money grabbers. The city's success is phenomenal, but I think it is at a tremendous price. The builders of Las Vegas have managed to create a soulless environment.

I am not sure that I would have sensed that "soullessness" had I seen the city in any other way. My visit was brief, and I am confident that, given enough time, one can find many—thousands—of very real individuals living and working there. There are undoubtedly people living fulfilled and happy lives behind the facade of reality that I experienced in Las Vegas. I also know that had I only driven through town, I would have received a very different impression of the city than I did while running. As I have said before, running provides a very unique perspective to the person experiencing a new environment. The runner is exposed directly to the sights, sounds, and smells of the place. No pane of glass separates the runner from all the sensory elements present. There is the possibility of a more in-depth experience of the physical environment than when the world is whizzing past at automobile speed. At the same time, the runner, because he covers more distance than the stroller, is confronted with a wider range of experiences to absorb.

Upon reflection, the reason that I was so incapable of shifting into the spirit-filled run is quite obvious. My journey through the city of Las Vegas left my head spinning. It was clearly a case of sensory overload, a deadening of the spirit that was the result of receiving too much without a chance to process it. The effect was so pronounced because running is usually such a different experience for me. It is usually a time of emptying the excess mental baggage I accumulate. On this run more sights and sounds were added to a brain that was already filled with an abundance of travel experiences. The run provided no opportunity to empty my head and allow room for God. The contrast of this desert experience with the desert run along Old Ore Road is blatant—the God-less and the God-filled— but the truth is that we don't consistently live our lives in either of these environments. We live somewhere in between, and our task is to learn how to structure our lives, and mold our souls, so that we can communicate with God even in "inaccessible" environments.

8

Happiness is an inexpressibly misleading and temporary thing, decides
nothing; the true stations of joy are on the road which lies through
simple endurance.

RAINER MARIA RILKE

Ten thousand flowers in spring, the moon in autumn,
a cool breeze in summer, snow in winter.
If your mind isn't clouded by unnecessary things,
this is the best season of your life.

WU-MEN

Purgation, Illumination, and Union

In her influential book *Walking a Sacred Path*, Lauren Artress uses the
classic stages of Christian spiritual growth—purgation, illumination,
and union—as a means of understanding the transformation that
occurs when one walks through a labyrinth. For Artress, the walk
from the entrance of the path to the center of the labyrinth is a time
of emptying, releasing, and letting go of control. Illumination occurs
at the center of the labyrinth where resting (in prayer and meditation), insight, and understanding may occur. The stage of union, a
retracing of your steps as you move from the center of the labyrinth

to its edge, is a time in which insights can be absorbed and energy is gathered to face the world outside the labyrinth.

These same categories of purgation, illumination, and union can also be a useful means of conceptualizing the spiritual process embedded in an individual run. Unless you are participating in an organized race or have prearranged shuttles or some other means of returning to your starting point, your run is likely to consist of a loop or a run to a certain point and back to where you began. Typically, then, most runs can be divided into three parts: an outward run, the midpoint, and the run home.

Think of the first part of the run, the run outward, as purgation. This is a time of releasing negative energy and letting go of yourself. If your day has been full, you are likely to be overwhelmed by a barrage of thoughts, a rehashing of earlier conversations and a rising to the surface of the most troubling and significant of the day's concerns.

This first period is a coping stage. Running becomes a tool to cope with the difficulties you face, a way to lessen the pain, or to hide it behind the endorphins your body is producing. Anger, depression, and heartache can be alleviated. If your spirits are low, running is likely to elevate them during this period of purgation. Running in this stage can be used as an escape, in the same way that alcohol and drugs can be used to numb the pain. Still, running has several advantages as a means of escaping the pain—no hangover, little cost, improved fitness and health. Running in this stage alleviates the symptoms and eases the pain. The immediate, pronounced effect is temporary—lasting only an hour or two, but a residual, barely perceptible elevation of mood may persist throughout the day.

I usually start a late-afternoon run with a burst of energy, with a feeling of immense release from the pressures of a workday or the trials of relationship. About twenty minutes into the run, probably due to the endorphin effects as much as anything, the concerns of the day typically diminish. Often the negative images I held in my mind will remain, but their effect on my mood is less pronounced.

Running at this level is as good as an antidepressant drug, with a short-term duration and only positive side effects. The danger from remaining in this stage is that it is merely an escape and may prolong the avoidance of engagement with a troublesome world. It is possible, indeed likely, that your entire run will remain in this stage if you do not adopt a conscious intention to move beyond it. The palliative effects of running are very gratifying and it is tempting to remain in a stage that merely enables them to feel better.

But the self-inventory that sometimes takes place in the stage of purgation may not always be pleasant. You can find yourself wallowing in self-pity, expressing regret, in fearful anticipation of the future, and recounting past failures. It may be that this kind of experience occupies most of your run. If so, it is work that needs to be done. Eventually, as you become more practiced at returning to your breath and to awareness, this stage can be moved through more quickly.

In the early 1990s, in the throes of separation and divorce, I was stuck in the first stage. Often running with tears in my eyes, I piled on the miles, finding that I needed increased dosages of pain-relieving physical effort to escape the sting of loss and rejection. Working in San Antonio for the second time, I spent most evenings traversing the affluent neighborhoods of Alamo Heights and Monte Vista. Surrounded by wealth, the poverty of my soul was laid bare. Later, back in Austin, I ran countless miles around Town Lake in anguish, waiting for the endorphins to kick in. Eventually, it was God's grace that allowed me a glimpse of illumination, permitting a release from the endless road of purgation.

Recognition of what you are doing, where you are—both physically and emotionally—occurs at the stage of illumination. It is here that a sense of being grounded comes into play. The runner can say, "Yes, I have made a mess of my life in all the following ways . . . but be that as it may, here I am moving along this trail, improving with every step, not languishing in self-pity on the couch, advancing through this difficult time." The indisputable fact that you are moving forward, even if only physically, adds momentum to your emotional healing. The link between mind and body is often ignored in conventional therapy. At this stage, the runner who can muster the energy to put himself in motion can use that physical momentum to propel himself through the purgation stage and toward illumination.

The stage of illumination usually occurs somewhere around the midpoint of the run. This is a time of intense awareness. Usually, the seemingly incessant noise in my brain that accompanied the first stage of the run has quieted. I often stop for a few moments, make sure that I am fully in the present, and perhaps walk for a few yards. In general I see it as a time of deep recollection, a reflection on where I have been and where I am going. It is a moment to take a reading of my spiritual condition before beginning the homeward journey. On a Saturday-morning hill run, the transition between the outward run and the run home is a long steep rise up Mountain Climb. My body is usually absorbed in the difficulty of the ascent. My rambling thoughts are rambling less there than on any part of the run. I am most open to divine inspiration.

The stage of Union usually begins somewhere along the run home. There is the sense of moving in union with the Divine—a feeling that God is with you. The thoughts that arise are usually less troublesome, more manageable. Artress describes this as a time to begin to integrate the labyrinth experience with the waiting-outside world. While I do sense an integration of the running experience with what awaits, I also tend to continue to move closer to the Divine as the run proceeds. The heightened sense of awareness that has developed over the course of the run is retained and spills over into the secular, making it sacred as well. The union that occurs is not merely a sense of closeness between my own soul and a separate deity, but a unity of spirit with all creation. More often than not, I end the run tired, but with faith renewed and a certainty that all is well.

The Benedictine Run

The Benedictine run is done in the spirit of the Benedictine life. This is a run of balanced activities, just as the Benedictine life is one of balance. For the Benedictine, each day must include some time spent in work, some in prayer, some in sacred reading, and some in community building. It is possible to achieve this kind of balance in a condensed form during the course of the run. Practicing the Benedictine lifestyle within the microcosm of the run makes it more likely that the practice will extend beyond the run's confines. The run is completed with a sense of balance, of order, of awareness.

The Benedictine run can be practiced as follows: The goal is to achieve balance and harmony over the course of the run. Devote the first third of the run to sacred reading. I prefer the Psalms for this purpose, but any sacred text or meaningful poetry will work just as well. Select a short passage and copy it onto a small piece of paper. Before beginning the run, read over the passage a few times. Carry the text with you, glancing at it occasionally, perhaps memorizing it as you run. As you recite the words, look beyond their literal meaning for a deeper understanding of what the passage has to say to you at this moment in your life. Hold the text in your hand and your heart throughout the first third of the run.

Devote the second third of the run to explicit prayer. If your prayer takes the form of verbal communication with God, that is fine. If opening your heart in silence and listening to God's voice is your customary way of praying, then do that. Simply be aware that this fifteen or twenty minutes is time for prayer alone.

The last third of the run is devoted to work or community participation. You may not find a lot of work to do along the way, or the tasks that you encounter may be too large to tackle in the midst of a short run. Still, keep your eyes open for work opportunities, and they are likely to appear. Pick up bits of trash along the way.

Remove a large stick or stone from the path. Be of assistance to anyone in need along the way. Show kindness in your eyes and smile at those you encounter. Be aware that you are part of a community of souls using the trail. Most likely they are people you have never met, but be aware of the shared responsibility you have for the maintenance of the trail and the well-being of those who use it.

When you finish the run, take a moment to reflect on the sense of balance that results from such a run. Carry that harmony and balance with you throughout the day.

Nature, Sin, and Grace

Another traditional way of looking at spiritual development within the historical Christian tradition is to consider the following:

1. Who we are by nature.
2. What we have become through sin.
3. What we might become through grace.

By nature we are perfect. We come into the world flawless, created in God's image. Our falling away from God (sin) happens when we make choices that separate us from God. Eventually, if we are receptive, God's grace brings us back into relationship with the Divine. These stages that take place over the course of a lifetime cannot, of course, be compressed into a single run. However, the changes that can occur during the course of a run can be used to symbolically represent much larger changes that take place as the spiritual life progresses from natural perfection, to sin, and into grace.

A run begins with a clear sense of presence in the natural world. You breathe deeply and easily, fully aware of the sun, the wind, and every sound—especially conscious of how your body feels in this new environment. As you run, your mind begins to wander. Think of this wandering of mind as sin. Not sin as the committing of an immoral act, but as action that takes you away from your divine purpose. The thoughts have taken you away from consciousness of the present moment—that moment where the Divine resides. In due course, if you continue in the practice of returning to your breath, you will find yourself returned, through grace, to the presence of God. The pattern may be repeated many times over the course of a run: running in Divine Perfection, lost in the sin of mindlessness, and arrival back into the arms of God's grace.

July 20, 1999—The Inward and Outward Runs

I began yesterday's hill run with the heavy burden of my unhappiness. As I ran, I chanted, watched my breathing, and maintained, as best I could, a sense of presence in my surroundings. As is usually the case when I run with awareness, the unhappiness began to dissolve. The despair that I had earlier felt was replaced by love. I longed to connect with the larger environment around me, but especially with the people I encountered. I felt a strong desire to reach out, to express to others the peace and love I felt.

I tasted, on the run, a bite of the process that I have truly only read about. It is clear that the journey to God begins with an inward passage. For many years now I have explored the nature of my relationship with the Divine—seeking to know God. Intellectually, I am aware that ultimately this journey must change directions. I know that the God I seek will be found, eventually, in the faces of those God loves, his creations. In the daily pattern of my life, I make the inward journey, and as the concerns of making a living press in on me, I forget to love. I have even structured my life so that the opportunity to show God's love to others is limited. It is no wonder that my son can't see God within me. I feel His presence, but nothing about me shows others that it is there. I no longer show joy. The life I lead is nothing to emulate.

Yet on my run, I was given a glimpse of what it is like to make the journey complete. I was loved and then I loved. I felt God's presence and I radiated it. Returning from the run, my daughter and her friend could tell I was being "weird." Indeed, it was unusual behavior for me. I pray to God that it will not remain unusual.

A run could be structured to replicate this pattern. On the outward journey, practice breathing, chanting, and awareness. On the return home, practice showing God's love to all you encounter. Offer a kind word, a smile, or a blessing to everyone you meet. (Judging by the kinds of smiles I received on the run home yesterday, I must have been grinning quite largely.) Thank God for the blessings you see and hear and feel along the route home. Intentionally, reach outward to share the blessing of having spent time in close communion with God. My own experience has been that this time of reaching outward extends well beyond the duration of the run. Yesterday, my awareness of the desire to reach out stretched for several hours into the day. It is my prayer that this willingness to share God's love can become the norm, the way I live my life.

The Path of Gratefulness

The spiritual path practiced by Brother David Steindl-Rast, the highly influential Benedictine monk, can best be described as one of gratefulness. Brother David taught us to cultivate a sense of surprise, not only in the extraordinary, but in the ordinary, as well. He said that our eyes are opened to the surprising character of the world once we wake up from taking things for granted. Almost inevitably we experience both surprise and gratitude at the sight of a rainbow. However, as e. e. cummings once noted, "the eyes of my eyes are opened." This same sense of wonder can occur when we encounter the ordinary as well. This fullness of gratefulness, for Brother David, is recognized in "Gerard Manley Hopkins' 'dapple-dawn-drawn Falcon, in his riding,' or simply it may be this morning's inch of toothpaste on my brush."

Run in this spirit of gratefulness. Before beginning the run, declare your intention to look upon all you encounter with the freshness of the unexpected. Brother David taught that, "surprise leads us on the path of gratefulness." Run with a sense of miraculous expectation and allow a feeling of gratitude for the extraordinary and the ordinary to flow through your being.

Running with Money

I had long been aware of the homeless I would encounter on my run along the Shoal Creek Trail. I make a point of greeting them, smiling, and silently offering a blessing. They are usually surprised at my greeting and sometimes ask for money. Thursday afternoon, before stepping out of my car, I slipped a dollar bill into my key pocket, anticipating such an encounter. I ran, watching for someone in need. Eventually, just past the halfway mark, I came across a fellow sitting at a picnic table drinking cheap beer. I had noticed him before reaching the turnaround point, and could tell by his worn and dirty clothes, his leathery skin, and his tired vacant eyes that he lived without life's comforts. As I drew closer, I slowed down and walked up to his table. "What's up, man?" he asked. In response I held out the dollar and said, "Here, my friend." Surprised to receive something without even asking, he said, "What's this for?" I shrugged and replied, "God bless you," then turned and continued on my run.

He might have said thanks, but I didn't listen for it. A single dollar was not likely to have any impact on his life, but it might on mine. The exchange was not particularly gratifying, but I didn't have any such expectations. The impact came in the way that I moved on my run with a sense of hope that I might offer some relief, some help to those I met. Most significantly, I was eager to reach out to them during the time that I spend most fully in communion with God. I wish to try this more. I wish to share more than dollars.

The Laundry Run

For several years after the separation from my wife, I washed my clothes at the neighborhood laundry. Initially, I resented that I was now in my forties and was spending time at a place that I thought I had left behind in my college days. I was angry when I was there, typically angry with my ex-wife, but also angry with myself. I tried many approaches over the years. I would be overtly friendly to my fellow patrons or especially kind to the children there. I railed against the inherent unpleasantness of the heat, the noise, the detergent smell, and the forced close involvement with strangers who felt an equal distaste for their circumstances. I resisted buying a washer and dryer, partially because of the cost, but also because of the permanency of buying a major appliance. Such a purchase would be a clear indication that I accepted being single. No reconciliation with my ex was going to happen. I wasn't going to marry any of the women I had dated. Buying a washer and dryer made the reality of my single life too real.

I settled into a pattern of drinking when I had to wash clothes. I wanted to anesthetize myself against the laundromat. The routine became clearly established over the years. I would stuff my clothes in the five or six washing machines required to clean two weeks' worth of dirty clothes. I would then sheepishly walk across the street to the convenience store, buy a bag of popcorn and whatever beer was being offered at two cans for a buck, and retreat to the confines of my car. I always hoped that no one would see me. I was ashamed of being at the laundromat, ashamed of drinking two cheap beers by myself, and embarrassed to be seen wearing my ragged laundromat attire. (I always put off the trip to the laundry so long that I had only my shabbiest clothes left.) Drinking the beer, munching, I would immerse myself in a book or magazine. I always brought something I was interested in reading, something that, with the aid of the beer, would transport me to a place other than the laundry.

Once I settled in, I thoroughly enjoyed the time. When the spin cycle was complete, I would reluctantly leave my book and beer behind, load the sodden clothes into a wire-mesh cart, vie with the other patrons for a few working dryers, return to the car, and nestle in with my comforting companions. But timing was important and my return visit to book and beer would be brief if I intended to snatch my warm shirts from the still-spinning dryers before they could languish in a wrinkling pile.

It was at this point that the problem with this routine appeared. I was folding clothes in my sleep. I wanted to be someplace else: back with my buddies in the car, at home, away from where I was. The desensitizing effect of the beer faded quickly and I was stuck in a place I didn't want to be. The effect would last the evening, even after I returned home. Typically, I spent the rest of the evening in a funk and would go to bed dissatisfied with my life.

Eventually I adopted a different approach to laundry day. Instead of driving directly from work to the running trail, I stopped by my house, gathered my dirty clothes, changed into my running clothes, and headed to the laundry. I loaded the big machines with separated whites and darks, noted the time, climbed back in the car, and drove the short distance to the trailhead. I didn't run quite as long as I might have had I not been occupying washers that other laundry patrons might need. I finished the run refreshed and renewed.

Returning, I would make the transfer from washer to dryer, then attend to a quick errand or two before returning, yet again to pluck shirts from the still-spinning dryers. Carefully, I folded each item. Instead of being depressed, my awareness of the surroundings was heightened. I smiled more readily to the strangers willing to return my gaze. The entire washing experience was pleasurable. What I had earlier found to be an oppressive physical atmosphere proved to be an opportunity to practice mindfulness. I realized how hard I had been working to detach myself from what I had regarded as a distasteful environment.

I learned to fold clothes mindfully and happily. The former resentment that resided in the shadows of a two-beer fog was not there. Now, fully aware of my presence in a laundromat, I did not find it objectionable. This was no revelation for me. I have known that a cultivation of awareness is the key to happiness for some time. The difference is that, aided by the consciousness-enhancing effect of a run, I was able to act on that knowledge.

The wash/run became an established part of my routine. I learned that a run could be coupled with any task that I find unpleasant. I often sandwich a run in between housecleaning tasks, shopping, or paying bills—any job that I find disagreeable. The anticipation of the run makes the burden of the first part of the task less burdensome and the heightened awareness, sense of self, the effect of beta-endorphins, make the second half of the task less of a chore.

The Smiling Run

Maintain a Buddha half smile while running. You might also think of it as a Mona Lisa smile. I have found that it helps maintain focus. I've also noticed that people smile back, and the returned smile uplifts me and lightens my step. When you find that the smile on your lips has dissipated, re-create it, just as you return to your breath after a moment of forgetfulness. In the Anglican *Book of Common Prayer* the sacraments of Baptism and Holy Communion are described as "outward and visible signs of inward and spiritual grace." I think of this "running smile" as a similar outward manifestation of a sense of having been graced with God's presence. Maintaining a smile while running is not always easy, but I don't know of a clearer signal to indicate where your consciousness lies. It may be natural and spontaneous to smile during the course of your day. While running, smiling usually requires purposeful consideration. The attention to the smile, like the focus on the breath, helps empty the mind of random thoughts. Simultaneously concentrating on breathing and smiling brings you home. While smiling and breathing may both be executed either consciously or unconsciously, maintaining a purposeful regulation of breathing while keeping a smile on your lips leaves little room for extraneous thought. Holding an awareness of both the smile and the breath helps move you toward a keener sense of presence.

Decision-Making Run

There are times when important decisions must be made about the direction one's life is to take. Much of this book has been devoted to instruction regarding ways of clearing the head while running. Running, however, can also be a very useful time for engagement in serious thinking. The same kind of discipline required to empty the mind of thought to allow for spiritual processes to take place can be utilized to focus the mind on a single important topic. As one becomes more proficient at running meditation, the state of mind reached when you are in touch with the spiritual self becomes "holy ground." As the practice develops, it becomes a place that you can gain access to more frequently and more easily. You develop an understanding of the path that leads you there. This holy ground is where spiritual formation takes place.

This sacred space can be used as a place for decision-making. The facts needed for making choices can be gathered elsewhere. This is the place where, if divine guidance is sought, it can be found. Running in the ways we have discussed can produce a change in mind and heart that makes one receptive to divine intervention. Bringing to this sacred domain the problems faced in the secular world is a way to find answers that are beyond the purely rational.

It is not that the rational is left behind. In fact, tremendous clarity of thought can develop while running. Thoughts can be most clearly held when the run has moved beyond the initial stages and before excessive fatigue has developed.

Plan the decision-making run carefully. Determine the topic you wish to consider on the run. Be clear about what it is that you really are deciding. Develop a list of the pros and cons. Consider the question rationally. Then leave this approach behind. When it comes time to hit the trail, prepare for the run as you normally do. Meditate, pray for guidance, clear your head, and then simply run and breathe.

Run until your mind and body have arrived at the place where you recognize peaceful presence. Introduce the topic to the emptiness and let it rest there. This is not a time to engage in an internal debate over the merits of one choice over another. It is a time to turn the discernment process over to a nonrational mode of being. Relinquish control over the process; allow your anxiety over the outcome to slip away. Simply breathe, run, and permit the spirit within to hold your problem.

What can you expect? Anything from the answer to your questions written in lightning bolts across the sky, to a temporary and subtle sense of serenity regarding the issues at hand. Finding direction in your life is a difficult task. Those who run the spiritual path have at their disposal an alternative to the typical decision-making process—a way of taking the question to a higher source of wisdom.

Zen Run

The Zen walk is a normal practice for many practitioners of meditation. This slow, thoughtful walking interlude is used as a way of breaking up the physical strain of remaining in one position for long periods, while still maintaining a meditative state. Known as *kinhin*, the walking form of Zen may be thought of as Zen in motion. Various Zen disciplines practice *kinhin* in different ways. In the Rinzai sect the pace is brisk and energetic. In the traditional Soto practice, the pace is slow and leisurely. Counting of breaths or recitation of a koan is continued through the walk. The *kinhin* is seen as an extension of the sitting meditation. A practical way for us to use the *kinhin* is at the end of a run to extend the meditation.

> *September 29, 1998—Retaining the Spirit of the Run*
> *Leaving a run behind over the weekend, I Zen walked to my car.*
> *The walk was not planned, I had made no unusual effort to retain*

the spirit of the run, but the sense of still being in God's presence remained with me. Wanting to savor that moment, I walked slowly— not as slowly as with a traditional Zen walk—but slowly, deliberately, conscious of my breathing and reciting the Trisagian. I felt that I wanted to always walk with the same sense of well-being, of confidence, of happiness. The distance to my waiting van was far too short. Even now, as I write, I want to get up and go for a very long walk, remaining conscious the whole way.

November 16, 1998—Zen Walk with Robert
I visited with my good friend Robert, who is dying of liver cancer and is in a great deal of discomfort. He has difficulty staying in one position for long. Eventually, he said, "I need to walk." He got up from his bed and began to pace fitfully around the house. I watched him for a moment and could feel his distress. Knowing how receptive Robert is to prayer in its many forms, I suggested that we turn his disturbed pacing into a prayer. I told him how to Zen walk: taking careful, deliberate steps; focusing on the way the walking surface feels on the soles of the feet; noticing how the heels, the instep, the balls, and the toes of each foot, slowly, in turn, caress the earth. I suggested that he breathe deeply and slowly, synchronizing each footstep with a respiration—drawing God's spirit in with each breath.

Robert was too weak to walk unaided for more than a few steps. I asked him to place his hands on my shoulders and follow me as we walked throughout the house. As we walked together, we chanted the Trisagian: "Holy God, Holy and Mighty, Holy Immortal One, Have Mercy Upon Us." We began the chant loudly, then more quietly, until it, after some time, was barely a whisper. Approaching death, children of God carry with them an almost palatable sense of the Divine. With Robert's hands on my shoulders, his pace in step with mine, and his trembling voice at my ear, I was drawn into God's presence in a way I have seldom known.

Cruising

I sometimes choose to do a lighter sort of run; not every run needs to be a search for life's deeper meanings. Yet even a run without specific spiritual intentions can be run with a purposeful openness. The young man named Speed in the 1998 film *Cruising* beautifully depicts this kind of receptivity to whatever he encounters. In the film, Speed spends most of his time working as a tour bus guide in Manhattan. Speed moves through life looking for bliss, open to whatever joy is presented. Speed is not in an active search for the spiritual, but is on a journey that takes him wherever it might, and along the way he pays attention and finds joy in all he encounters. Try running in this same way. Anticipate joy as you run. Approach the run unencumbered by whatever mindset you usually adopt. Look for the unexpected and look at the expected in a different way. Just cruise.

Organized Marathons

Racing can be great fun. The enthusiasm of the crowd, the anticipatory excitement, conversation with friends along the way, and the thrill of crossing the finish line make racing an experience all runners should try. Organized races are not, however, good opportunities to practice running meditation. The distractions are simply too numerous and powerful to overcome with any constancy. Paying attention to breath, praying, saying mantras, and visualizing are made more difficult when running in the midst of sensory excess. The crowd, the noise, the challenge of other competing runners may help the runner achieve victory or attain her personal best. For me, they are unnecessary diversions from the object of my run. I would attempt to focus my attention on breathing and would lose concentration almost immediately. Water stations, energy boosters, Powerade stands, medics, helicopters, loudspeakers, music, cheering crowds, friendly runners, frequent mileage markers . . . all of these things are very useful for the runner intent on marking his pace, finding distraction, or filling his mind. But the carnival atmosphere of such a run is in stark contrast to the solitary run I usually choose.

When I compare these two types of runs, I find few of the spiritual qualities in the marathon that I find in many of my solitary runs. It was useful for me to compare my time and pace with other runners. I am probably a smarter runner now and I know more about how to prepare for another race. It is certainly possible to run a race like this and evolve spiritually, but in my experience, the odds are against it. This kind of run is as filled with distractions as any other aspect of my life. The distracting influence of life's externalities can certainly be overcome, embraced, and incorporated into a spiritual life. However, if you haven't achieved saintly status, it takes practice in a setting that lends itself to spiritual encounters. Running in the setting of a major race is simply more of life as usual, filled with people, events, and goals that can so fill your mind that there is little opportunity to encounter Divine Presence.

I ran my first marathon without exploring the possible silence and without a clear sense of the present. It would be foolish of me to blame the organizers, the other participants, or even myself. The race was the place where I was called to find God; instead I learned, yet again, that the world's distractions can be a formidable challenge to an effort to rest in God's presence. Yet this is the world in which we are called to live. I was distracted because I was accustomed to running in a quieter atmosphere—one more conducive to contemplation. In retrospect, I failed to embrace the sights, sounds, and energy of the race. Instead of viewing these elements as distractions, I would have been better served if I had recognized the divinity behind every cheer, siren, and blaring loudspeaker.

February 21, 1999—Recovery Run
I ran yesterday for the first time since the marathon. Halfway around a short three-mile loop, my legs felt very, very heavy. All the

pain and heaviness I felt in my thighs during the last third of the race came rushing back to me. It reminded me of how I had ceased to breathe properly during the run, so I focused on moving into a steadier and deeper breathing pattern. My speed diminished greatly and it took great will to keep moving at anything faster than a snail's pace. I had begun the run quickly, having been eager to run fast, to shake off the sluggishness I had felt since the race. The last quarter mile I managed to push myself into—what is a stretch to call—a sprint. As a training run the workout was close to being a failure. As an awareness exercise, it was just what I needed. I was aware of my breathing (even though it was extremely labored) and I was conscious of the gnawing pain in my thighs without allowing either to overwhelm me. It was a short run, and certainly did not provide me with the test of my awareness skills that a marathon provides, but it indicated that all was not lost. The skills that I had acquired over the past few years were clearly working. The marathon had taught me, however, that those skills were far from finely honed. I learned that, under duress, I could fall back into the mindless struggle for existence that consumes most of us, most of the time. Even in the territory in which my mindfulness is most practiced, when put to a severe test, I lapsed into a pattern of avoiding the present. I have much to learn.

the joy of the ill-fitting shoe

I appeal to you therefore, brethren, by the mercies of God, to present your bodies as a living sacrifice, holy and acceptable to God, which is your spiritual worship.

ROM 12:1–8 (NEW INTERNATIONAL VERSION)

When the shoe fits, we forget the foot.

ZEN SAYING FROM *WATER BEARS NO SCARS*

Suffering is the sole origin of consciousness.

DOSTOYEVSKY

As runners, we repeatedly experience the duality of pleasure and pain. We seldom experience one without also facing the other. Even the joy of a run on a windless day, with cool air and sunshine and no troublesome injuries, is tempered by the measure of toil required to move swiftly down a trail. It is no secret that the runner's delight is often accompanied by difficulty, discomfort, and pain. The hardship is far from pointless.

The most obvious benefit of experiencing pain is the direct encounter with the cessation of that pain. The concentrated effort required of the runner stops at the end of the run. Breathing returns to a normal state. Soreness and aches may persist, but the intense physical demands of a hard run subside when the run is over. Relief, a feeling of accomplishment, and joy that a part of the journey is done replace the difficulty of the run. Wearing the ill-fitting shoe, pushing your body beyond the comfort zone, enduring the agony of running on a hot summer day, all enhance the pleasure of a post-run stretch, a cooling drink, a nap in the shade, or a well-deserved rest. Put simply, the flip side of pain is the simple pleasure of nonpain.

As a college student, my holidays were often spent hiking in the lower Rockies, canoeing down isolated stretches of white water, or cycling endless country roads. I returned to my studies exhausted, sore, bruised, and renewed in my appreciation for the student's life. The discipline of study in the comfort of the academic center library was no longer drudgery, but relief. Long hours spent preparing for exams were nothing in comparison to the rigors of wilderness adventure. The juxtaposition of the relatively soft academic life with the physical challenges of mountain trails and raging rivers kept me balanced and appreciative of whichever state I found myself. The experience of pain allowed me to recognize and enjoy the pleasure.

Now that I am older, and have fewer opportunities for extended adventures, running provides a similar outlet. Running allows me to engage in a vigorous physical activity that contrasts with my sedentary work-a-day world, allowing me to maintain that balance.

Yet it is not just that "runner's high" that I'm seeking. Nor is it simply the feeling of satisfaction that comes from having completed a challenging run. The primary benefit comes during the run itself, in the midst of the pain and difficulty. The chance to grow in the spirit occurs during the time we feel most challenged, not once the challenge has been met. As runners, we can learn to take advantage of an opportunity to enter a spiritual realm through a portal that is less available to the nonrunner.

Running meditation is not about the peak experience, that rare moment of personal triumph occasionally achieved by athletes. The performance of a competitive athlete is motivated by this goal of winning, setting records, achieving a measurable victory of some sort. In contrast, the meditative runner is simply moving, swiftly or ploddingly, toward union with the One. While the athlete's competitive experience may contain some of the same elements of the meditative runner's—focused awareness and a higher sense of self—it is the degree of occurrence, along with the intentions behind the run, that separates the two. The meditative runner achieves his goal every day. There are no good runs. There are no bad runs. There is always victory—a steady movement toward spiritual release.

It is not necessary to be a superb athlete to engage in running meditation. The practice is available to anyone who likes to run. Still, there is a certain level of physical conditioning that is useful to attain before a substantial benefit can come from running meditation. The ability to run a minimum of twenty to thirty minutes, at whatever pace suits you, is a prerequisite. Even if you are not running now, it shouldn't take too long to work up to that level. There is no hurry. God is waiting for you. If the struggle is too great, and too constant, it is easy to lose sight of the intention to connect with the Divine. Ideally, the run is challenging enough to keep the runner focused on the present, but not so difficult that awareness of the intention behind the run is lost.

The presence of pain can serve as a reminder of these three things:

1. That you intend to focus on breathing. When your attention drifts away from the breath, feeling the pain reminds you to bring your focus back to breathing.
2. That with each breath, you are taking in God—*spiritos*—and that as you run, God's spirit is moving through your body.
3. That the pain can bring you repeatedly back to the recognition that you contain a divine spark, that to be fully human is also to be divine, that we were created in God's image.

Please do not take this emphasis on the positive aspects of pain to mean that one should purposely bring pain into the run. It would be absurd to put a pebble in your shoe, run with an injury, run in excessive heat, or do anything that is likely to bring damage to your body. And it is hardly necessary. Without intentionally bringing about pain and discomfort, running, itself, will supply the hurt. St. Benedict taught that no self-inflicted pain was necessary—the world will provide enough.

When running gets harder, when you get tired, when you are climbing a steep hill, these are reminders to come home to your breath, to your awareness of God. Runners are constantly developing injuries. The aches and pains that develop when training are the most consistent topic of conversation among runners. Honor these discomforts as blessings. They are signals that God uses to call you back home, back to an attentiveness to breathing, even to smiling. The pain can be a very effective focal point for meditation.

July 10, 1999—A Christ-Centered Run

Several conversations of late have led me to consider the nature of the Trinity. It may be that I have not grasped the importance of the image of Christ on my journey. As I made the long, hard run up Mountain Climb I was reminded of the words from the invitational hymn we sang when I was a child in the Baptist church. The reference was to Christ on the cross, "the emblem of suffering and pain." When pain is so much a part of the distance run, how can I ignore the connection with a Christ for whom suffering and pain are emblematic? Certainly love, redemption, and forgiveness occur at the end of the suffering, but the most widely held image of Christ is his Passion—his suffering and death on the cross. Can each run be an expression of the Passion? Within each run, is there the opportunity to experience suffering, death, burial, and resurrection?

Evaluating the Quality of a Run

> Judge a moth by the beauty of its candle.
> RUMI

If the intent of your run is to move closer toward a knowledge of God, if in your run you are seeking an audience with "the Friend," it really doesn't matter if your stride is uneven, if your breathing is shallow, or if your pace is erratic. Judge the quality of your run by the steadfastness of your movement toward His flame.

After finishing a run, the first question I am usually asked is, "Did you have a good run?" My reply, if it is in the affirmative, usually involves a description of favorable weather conditions; the absence of small, nagging injuries; my speed; or perhaps a feeling of lightness in my legs. If the run didn't seem like a good one, I usually offer complaints about the heat or cold, fatigue, soreness, or my inability to achieve a steady momentum. But a good run isn't really dependent on the environmental conditions, and its success can't be measured by swiftness of pace or lack of physical ailments. In fact, the success of the run is not even measured by how attentive we are to it or whether or not we are able to maintain a sense of presence. The successful run is one in which we engage in the practice of returning to consciousness. We may or may not run easily. The weather may be perfect or wretched. We may have aches and pains and we may not. It doesn't matter. Perhaps we say that we have had a good run because our level of consciousness was high. That's a fine thing. Enjoy it. However, the really successful run is one in which the work of returning repeatedly to the present is practiced over and over again. A run may contain long periods of time during which we are completely awake, or we may begin the run with the firm intention of focusing on the breath and find that thirty minutes later we have focused entirely on an argument with a spouse, for example. We have not failed. This is practice as well.

This work may be better accomplished when running in the midst of difficulties than when running in the midst of unadulterated happiness. It is very easy to forget about running in the presence of God when we are surrounded by abundance. When all is well, our thoughts wander easily. When difficulties arise, we are brought back into the immediacy of our suffering. In the end, it doesn't matter whether the run was filled with pleasure or with pain. The important question is whether or not these sensations were used as vehicles to carry us to the Divine. Learning to repeatedly return to the bodily experience of the run itself, whether our sensory receptors register pleasure or pain, is the essence of a good run.

In running meditation, as in sitting meditation, it is important not to allow the glimpses of God, the rewards of earnest prayer, the sometimes-ecstatic feelings of joy to become the center of your attention. Remember that the focus is on the breath. Shifting your attention away from the breath and onto either the pain or the pleasure accompanying the run results in a loss of consciousness. Breathing has taken you where you are. Stay with it. All else, the discomforts as well as the delights, are distractions.

Running with Pain and Sacrifice

Running the spiritual path is not an easy task. Difficulties are encountered along the way. One grows tired, muscles ache, joints creak, blisters form, the heat can become unbearable, the cold can bite, boredom can set in, and the surfacing of remembered heartache can bring tears to your eyes. Yet, as with any pilgrimage, it is the difficulties that deepen the mystery. The running pilgrim doesn't undertake a run looking for adversity, but it inevitably arises. The idea is not to regard these hardships as obstacles, but as avenues leading to an enlightened sense of the self. They are opportunities to see oneself in a different way, to experience God's help in a moment of trial, or to acknowledge the feeling that God, in the narrow way we tend to conceive of him, has abandoned us. The mystery of how God intercedes in our lives, amid both pain and joy, is deepened. It is in the midst of pain that we may be compelled to acknowledge that God, in the old way we may have thought of him, has disappeared. Don't expect a God that will take away your pain, only a God that will experience your pain with you.

As my own running has become a sacred act, I've found it useful to remember that the origin of the word *sacred* is the Latin word *sacraficium*, meaning to cut up, or sacrifice. The element of sacrifice is a part of running that cannot be ignored. The spiritual run involves the sacrifice of time, energy, and comfort. The most significant sacrifice involves the giving up of an old way of being. Running in this way requires that life is faced head on, lived wholly in the present, and enjoyed or suffered through fully. Every pain and every sense of pleasure we experience while running can be an offering to God—a sacrifice. Savor each emotion, each sensation that arises, and then give it up. In letting go you will be rewarded by new experiences, deeper understanding, and more profound mystery.

In order to learn from the pain, it is necessary not to be overwhelmed by it. Detachment is the key. Carefully examine the pain— its source, its intensity, its rhythm and duration. View the pain as something to be experienced—just as you experience the breeze, the texture of the trail's surface, or the sunlight. If a pebble in your shoe causes the pain, stop and take it out. If the pain is the result of the unnoticed pebble in your shoe the day before, then accept it as a gift, an opportunity to learn about dealing with discomfort.

Stay unattached to the outcome of the run. As with everything, remain in the moment. Don't worry about whether a run was good or not, fast or not, conscious or not. The run is exactly what it should be, fulfilling whatever need exists. If your mind wanders, it probably needed to wander. If you find yourself stumbling along, filled with self-pity, remorse, and anger, don't give yourself a hard time for having such feelings—acknowledge and accept those feelings, then simply run through the pain.

I had lunch with an old friend, Dave Malone. Dave and I had

played football together as freshmen in college. I was talking with him about distance running and this subject of pain. Dave asked, "Didn't you get enough pain playing football at Baylor?" It was a curious question, but I dismissed it with a casual, "Apparently not." I don't seek the pain, but I don't avoid it either. Pain is an undeniable part of long-distance running. I have learned to regard it as a companion—a companion that requires patience and attention, but from whom much can be learned. The pain can keep me present. A sensation, like a flash of pain in my calf, startles me back into a fully conscious state. A nagging pain, like a pulled Achilles tendon, or a stone bruise, is a constant reminder to stay present. I have had many headaches disappear over the course of a run. They seldom can persist throughout a run, though sometimes they return afterward. Muscle soreness usually dissipates after a couple of miles. Many times I have experienced the soothing of heartache while running. Sometimes petty concerns simply evaporate. Other times the run provides a welcome respite from a battle with more deeply seated problems and even more elusive solutions.

January 20, 1998

A very interesting run today. The weather was perfect. I ran later than usual, beginning at six P.M. The last half of the run was in the dark. I don't usually like that, but today it was fine. I'll begin at the end of the run. My toes are in severe pain. I have blood-filled blisters covering the bottoms and sides of my little toes. When I put my orthotic inserts inside my running shoes, I rather stupidly forgot to remove the insoles that were already inside. I should have noticed that the shoes felt more snug than usual. I felt discomfort in my toes early in the run, but I was quick to attribute it to several factors—the socks I was wearing, the speed I was going, a slightly different stride I was trying, and my recent erratic running schedule. Three quarters of the way through the run an excruciating pain shot up from each of my toes and jolted my awareness. It was as if they had decided to simultaneously send me a message in order to get my attention. In that moment I knew that blisters had not only formed, but had also burst. It hurt, but as all the conditions were there for a good run, I was determined not to allow it to slow me down. I have in the past used pain as a focal point for concentration. This evening I recognized the pain as nothing more than another element of my environment of which to be conscious. By the time I was aware that the blisters were really painful, I had returned to my breath. That is, I was at the stage of my running where I had refocused my attention solely on breathing. As such, the pain wasn't an obstacle; it was something apart from me. It was there, but exerting no control over me.

I'm rather exhilarated at that thought. I know that this is a breakthrough and an example of how I wish to live my life—aware of its joys and sorrows, feeling its pleasures and pains, but not being consumed by them. Knowing that the difficulties of my life do not define who I am and that I can rise above them.

The practical danger in this for the runner is real. I am, in fact, experiencing the effect of that danger while I write. I have very real blisters on my toes and will experience pain as a result of them for several days. The practical lesson here is that simple awareness of pain may be a signal that action should be taken. Not all pain should be ignored. In retrospect, I should have spent a few moments really searching for the source of the pain and, in this case, eliminating the source before it did any physical damage. Furthermore, if I had been fully present as I dressed for the run, if I had consciously laced my shoes as I geared up to run, I would have realized I was preparing to run with "ill-fitting shoes."

October 7, 1998

Yesterday evening I had the Wisdom class at St. David's Episcopal Church and had to shorten my run to about twenty-five minutes. I found that time to be too short to feel all the beneficial effects of running that I normally experience. Although the run had been brisk, I didn't feel the good tired sense that normally allows me to "rest in God." I often attempt to begin praying, chanting, or focusing on breath at the very beginning of a run. Usually, however, it is not until halfway through the run (at about the point where I stopped the run today) that I begin to feel the connection with God that I seek. It's often through suffering that we find God, and running involves a certain amount of suffering, but not every run is excruciatingly painful. In fact, some runs offer such a sense of release from the concerns of the day that I can hardly restrain myself from bursting out into a full joyous sprint at the beginning. Yet with each run a pattern is developed that points the way toward God. Whether in joy or pain, we are being led to the Divine. When experiencing pain we often find God readily, because we are exploring territory where God typically dwells—within the spirit that is tired, in pain, suffering. God waits for us within that broken spirit. As the Psalmist wrote, "The sacrifices of God are a broken spirit, a broken and a contrite heart" (Ps[s] 51:17). The broken spirit has fewer defenses, fewer concerns with the trivialities of life, and is more receptive to the relief that God offers to the troubled heart.

The act of running simulates that condition of suffering. We embark on a well-trodden path that leads to the Transcendent. Physiologically and psychologically, when we run, we experience many of the same sensations that we undergo when experiencing life's sorrows, crises and hopelessness. We are, therefore, open to God's intervention—seeking answers, assistance, relief, and companionship.

It is important to make the distinction between suffering and pain. Suffering is an overreaction to pain—the emotional or psychological reaction to pain. Pain cannot, and should not, always be avoided. It is possible, however, to avoid suffering as a necessary consequence of the pain. This can often be done by objectifying the pain, seeing it as something that touches you, impinges upon you, but does not become a part of your being. This applies to physical as well as psychological pain.

Tong Ling

The Buddhist practice of Tong Ling is a form of meditation designed to encourage compassion for others. It involves the visualization of actually taking on the suffering of other sentient beings. At its core it is an asking of God that one's suffering be a substitute for the suffering of others. This is one way in which the apparent meaninglessness of suffering can be overcome: The suffering takes on meaning when it is seen as being experienced so that another person does not have to suffer.

Yet the practice of Tong Ling carries this conception of pain beyond the point where it overwhelms you with discomfort and to the point where it can actually have a positive impact. The practitioner of Tong Ling might first imagine some group of people suffering, then selfishly imagine himself far removed from the suffering, then see if the natural self is drawn to the suffering group or to the selfish individual. When the feeling of empathy toward the suffering group is experienced, then the suffering of the group is taken on and you practice moving toward the sufferers and giving them your energy.

Although Tong Ling is a sitting practice, we can incorporate it into our running meditation; I find it best to keep these kinds of visualizations as close to the here and now as possible. To bring the practice to the present, it is not necessary to imagine the suffering among people far removed from you. On any urban running trail it is easy to find people whose experience of running has moved beyond objectified pain and into suffering in full bloom. I can suggest two practices:

1. When running in your own pain: Perhaps you have a small injury that you are running through, or you have experienced the pain of rejection from a friend or lover, or perhaps you are simply stepping up your training regimen and the increased speed is taking its toll on the leg muscles.

Imagine that the pain is experienced for the benefit of those you encounter. People you meet on the trail hurt less, because you are absorbing their pain. You are not asking for their thanks; just know that you are doing them good.

2. When you see suffering on the trail, take it as your own: With practice, it becomes easy to recognize suffering in the anguished faces of those you encounter. Suffering is everywhere. If you consciously look at those you meet, you will find it. For yourself, the suffering of those you encounter can be felt as objectified pain, not the crippling suffering they are experiencing. Empathize with the suffering you see. Then connect the experience with your breathing. When you inhale, be aware that you are taking in the nourishing breath of the Divine—divine inspiration. As you exhale, you are offering that divinely touched breath as energy to those who need it. You are nourished and, in turn, are providing nourishment for those around you. You are in the process of learning how it feels to offer compassion, and making it more likely to become a natural practice.

How Pain Brings Us to the Present

In Ernest Hemingway's *Old Man and the Sea,* the fisherman and baseball fan Santiago, in the midst of his struggle with the great sailfish, says, "I must have confidence and I must be worthy of the great DiMaggio who does all things perfectly even with the pain of the bone spur in his heel." Under the baking sun, Santiago later wonders if it isn't because of the bone spur in his heel that DiMaggio does all things perfectly. Santiago, suffering himself, made an important discovery about the nature of pain and how that kind of constant pain can serve as a focal point, a way of not being distracted by the noise of the crowd or the chatter in the brain.

While training for my first marathon, I was constantly fighting the discomfort of a strained Achilles tendon. I conscientiously stretched each tendon before and after my training runs. In retrospect, I realize I overstretched, especially before running, making it more likely that I would eventually be injured. On the Saturday morning before the Sunday race, I was merely walking to my car when a sharp and intense pain shot through the back of my left ankle. Oddly, most of the Achilles problems I had experienced earlier on had been in my right ankle. Gradually, as the day progressed, the pain subsided. Some discomfort lingered, but I chose to ignore it.

As I walked through the house on the morning of the race, I knew that the injured Achilles tendon was going to cause me some difficulty. However, the pain seemed minor and after having trained for many months, I didn't even consider not running. I can't say that was a wrong decision, but it was a fateful one. Less than a quarter of the way through the race, the pain in my ankle began building. It wasn't the kind of pain that caused me to limp, or that slowed my progress in any way. It did, however, continue to grow in intensity. At first I worried about the pain preventing me from continuing and I struggled to ignore it. Eventually, I realized that this pain was going to be my companion and was going to make its presence increasingly known. I chose to accept this pain as a reminder to stay present. My mind never wandered very far before the pain would bring me abruptly back to the moment.

I finished the race within the time I had hoped. The pain in the tendon persisted for some time, no doubt aggravated by the twenty-six-mile run on an injury, but it eventually healed. I still recall the race with clarity, and remember it as a difficult time, but a time in which adversity provided me with yet another opportunity to grow in spirit. With God's grace, I ran a conscious race.

August 8, 1998

We've had a bit of rain and it has cooled off slightly. It is amazing how much easier it is to run when the temperature drops only a little below the oppressive one-hundred-degree mark. Saturday morning I did my usual hill run—though at a somewhat earlier hour

than normal. I had gone to bed early, slept well, and awakened re-
freshed. I got out of bed early enough to enjoy the lower tempera-
tures of the morning.

I glided up the hills without giving them much of a thought.
Now, this might seem to be a blessing, and I truly did enjoy the
escape from the heat and the relative ease of the run, but the mind-
lessness with which I climbed the hills pointed out to me how impor-
tant the struggle of the heat and uphill climb can be. When sweat is
pouring off of me, when the muscles in my legs are begging for re-
lief, when my lungs are screaming for air, there is an acute awareness
of my present condition. The awareness is unavoidable. Accompany-
ing that awareness of the present is an inevitable awareness of God's
presence as well. When I am not challenged physically, my mind
tends to wander, both from an awareness of who I am and where
God is.

Learning from Pain While in the Midst of It

During a recent weekend, discussion revolved around the often-
asked question, "Why do bad things happen to good people?" Part
of the explanation commonly offered includes an observation that
after the "bad" event, it is often possible to see the good that has
arisen as a result of the experience. Generally the incident involves
deep emotional pain and brings with it the opportunity for accompanying spiritual growth. But it is difficult to regard pain as an opportunity when one is in the throes of it.

Running provides an occasion to practice learning from the experience of pain in a controlled setting. Let me emphasize that the
runner must listen to the body's pain. If the pain is sharp or severe,
rest and treatment may be in order. However, you can run through,
and learn from, the kind of pain that comes with the process of
improving your physical condition, the sort of pain that is an unavoidable part of the building of stamina.

The Joslin Bowl

According to our usual holiday tradition, the Joslin family treks en masse to the local high school football stadium after each Thanksgiving and Christmas Day dinner. Players from generations spanning almost sixty years—athletes, former athletes, and future athletes—loosely split up into two sides and attempt to prove to themselves and to their brothers, cousins, uncles, nephews, and in-laws, that the passing year has aged them not a wit. After two to three hours of running deep patterns, sprinting, cutting, colliding, and crashing to the ground, we limp back to the house and regale the awaiting sedentary members of the family with tales of our glory on the gridiron while feasting on leftovers.

As much as I love this ritual, I know that I will pay a dear price for it the following few days. The frenetic pace required in our annual family football game bears little similarity to my usual steady long-distance running routine. For several days afterward I emerge from bed struggling to walk. This year, unlike the year before, I had no broken bones, but I ached to the core of my body. I knew that the only cure was "the hair of the dog that bit me." So the following day I got up, limped around the house a bit, stretched, grimaced, and stretched some more. Even sitting and bending over to put on my running shoes were painful.

I began the run with a pace as slow and deliberate as I can ever recall running. It was less than a jog, barely more than a nursing-home shuffle. Slowly, carefully, I extended my stride and began to raise my knees a little higher. Each extension found a new pocket of soreness, but eventually I was able to regain my usual pace and the pain lessened. Running downhill brought on a new wave of soreness and I made the mistake of resisting it. The way to face pain of this sort is to run through it—not ignore it, not avoid it, but to recognize it, focus on the breath, and let the pain move through you and go away. That is not what I did. Instead of surrendering to the liberating abandon that downhill running usually offers, I held up my momentum. Instead of allowing gravity to pull me down the hill, I allowed the pain in my thighs to dictate the pace of my downhill stride. The tension I maintained to protect myself from the pain suddenly transferred to my lower back and a jolt of pain shot through my back muscles. Luckily, that pain left me as quickly as it had arrived, but what remained was an awareness of the mistake I had made. Pain cannot be resisted. It has to be felt. There is no need to dwell on it, but to try to avoid it is simply to send the pain to another part of the body where it may show itself more acutely. Recognizing this, I relaxed into it, remembering to breathe and allowing my body to take advantage of the break from exertion that running downhill provides. I was determined not to resist the gift because the acceptance of it seemed too frightening. As I continued the run, memories of painful experiences and my reluctance to allow them to be felt and then released flooded my consciousness. It is a similar but harder lesson to learn that the pain and soreness remaining in a wounded heart can be eased by allowing the pain to be experienced fearlessly and then moving on.

August 18, 1999

Despite the sorry state of my finances, or perhaps because of it, running has been richly rewarding of late. On those days when my spirits were low (and many days I have felt a deep melancholy), running has lifted me to a peaceful state. I have worked constantly to remain present during this trial. When I begin to dwell on the past, on failure, I struggle to return to the present. Usually I succeed. I wonder how running will be when times get better. When I have fewer negative thoughts to battle, will I be able to take running to a higher level, or is the struggle to remain present in the midst of pain and adversity the essential nature of my quest?

October 21, 1999

I am in the midst of the longest period I have gone without running in a very long time. The balls of my feet are bruised. My
shoes have grown thin and I really don't have enough money to buy
a new pair. Perhaps I will get paid tomorrow. I leave shortly for
Waco and Cameron to talk with two firms about selling church fur-
niture. God help me.

October 25, 1999

Amazing. I have been having continual back pain for over a
week. Today I finally bought new shoes and went for a very short
run. Upon my return I realized that I no longer hurt in my back,
neck, and shoulders. Perhaps the tension had finally been released,
the joints loosened, whatever. . . . I need to run. Unfortunately, the
shoes felt terrible and seemed to cause knee pain. I'll return them
tomorrow. But it is so good to be running again.

November 4, 1999

Yesterday's run around Town Lake was glorious. The sun was
bright, the air was cool, and I felt present. There were no baseballs
from the sky, only a deep abiding sense that where I was, was exactly where I should be.

Traveler, there is no path, paths are made by walking.
ANTONIO MACHADO

For though by this time you ought to be teachers, you need someone to teach you again the basic elements of the oracles of God. You need milk, not solid food; for everyone who lives on milk, being still an infant, is unskilled in the word of righteousness. But solid food is for the mature, for those whose faculties have been trained to distinguish good from evil.

HEB 5:12

When running becomes a part of your life, you run in all kinds of conditions. Some days are hot and dry; others are cold and rainy. Some days the trail is in excellent shape, while on others the terrain is barely passable. Some days you are infused with the joy of running; other days are filled with fear, dread, or sorrow. This chapter is about continuing to run despite whatever circumstances you encounter. There is a lesson to be learned from running in various emotional states, just as there are lessons to learn from running in a wide range of environmental settings. Don't shy away from running in an unaccustomed state of mind or an unusual situation. Opportunity for enlightenment often waits in the unfamiliar.

July 6, 1998—Fire and Rain

It has been one of the driest summers on record. The heat has been oppressive and El Niño is to blame for drought here and monsoon elsewhere. The lack of rain has left both Texas and Mexico parched. Thousands of acres of Mexican forests, in dozens of locations, have been burning since early spring. The smoke from a smoldering blaze south of the border has blanketed Austin in a thin cloudlike haze. The sky, usually blue on these long, rainless days of summer, is now gray and apocalyptic. It is both reminiscent of ancient plagues and laden with a frightening sense of what the future might hold. Meteorologists urged those with respiratory problems, young children, and the elderly to stay indoors and avoid prolonged breathing of the tainted air. Propelled by my need for movement and prayer I continued to run, though perhaps not as much as usual. Because I was so aware of the particulates in the air, I didn't breathe as deeply while I ran beneath the dark but cloudless sky.

We greeted the summer rain that evening with the joy of reunited friends. The drizzle continued through much of the night, leaving the morning air cooler and cleansed. As always, I was eager to run on such a morning. It was Saturday, my hill-run day. As I ran, my focus was on the long-absent rain. During the first leg of the run, the rain poured from the sky. Later it stopped altogether, then it sprinkled steadily. I responded to each change in the weather in a different way, but with each variant I focused on the atmosphere, on the way the drops felt as they fell on my body. I was aware of the sound of the rain landing on the rooftops, the street, and the cars. I heard the water rushing down the gutters, flowing toward the neighborhood creeks. I noticed the single splash that each foot made as it landed on the puddle-filled pavement. Cars passed, every tire creating a waterfall.

I ran, on that Saturday morning, in the way that Natalie Goldberg talks about writing in Writing Down the Bones, or the way that Betty Edwards instructs students to draw in her Drawing on the Right Side of the Brain. Write what you see, hear, and feel.

Draw what you see. Don't draw or write about what you think the thing you are experiencing might be like. Put yourself in the place, see its every detail, and be there. Run the same way. Be in the run. Fully experience it. Don't do your shopping list (or if you must do it, be done with it and get on with the run). On that rainy Saturday, I concentrated my focus on all things connected to the rain. The renewed freshness of the air, the drops of rain landing on my forehead and nose and running down my face—these were reality.

December 22, 1998—A Winter's Run

The weather turned very cold overnight and it was with some reluctance that I donned multiple layers of clothing and embarked on a late-afternoon run on the Shoal Creek Trail. The reality of the cold was not nearly as unpleasant as the dread had been. Only my face and ears remained cold after the first five minutes into the run. Even my hands, usually chilled during the cold weather, stayed fairly warm in my cotton running gloves. I began the run by almost immediately chanting "To-ward-the-One." I tried accompanying the chant with the successive touching of my thumb to each finger, but I found that moving my fingers allowed the cold air to surround and chill them. I modified the action by simply pushing the fingers of my closed hands against the palm of each hand. In that way the fingers could share their warmth with one another and I still had an additional motion to keep my breathing company.

The returning half of the run was almost in darkness. Yesterday was the winter solstice, the shortest day of the year. Precious little daylight remained for me to see my way home. If possible, the Shoal Creek Trail was in worse shape than ever. Now park personnel, prior to construction beginning, have fenced off several sections. Impatient runners and walkers knock down the succession of fences as quickly as city crews put them up. Now, in addition to the hazards of ruts and washed-out trails are the dangers of fallen fences and other artificial barriers. I made my way gingerly through the *darkness, aware that a false step could lead to a twisted ankle, but attentive to my breath, exhilarated by the cold, and enjoying each forward stride.*

May 12, 1999—Running Meditation Tape

Some time ago, out of curiosity, I had purchased a tape designed to facilitate meditation while running. I listened to parts of it when I received it in the mail, didn't find it particularly useful, and shelved it. Finally, yesterday, I decided to try to use the tape while running. The tape consisted of running music on one side and the same music on the reverse side with a female voice popping up in the background saying things like, "She can run!" and offering rhythmic advice on creating a new self from the earth. The beat of the music was good to run with. Experiencing the images created in my mind by the encouragement to run with the earth was fun. I may have run a little faster. However, the tape lost me when the background voice mentioned how the imagined runner was "oblivious to all noises." Some of the suggestions about developing a kinship with the earth made sense, but the approach to that goal was completely misguiding. Ignoring the noises, or any of the sensory elements, takes the runner away from the aimed link with the universe. The music itself, and the effect of wearing headphones or hearing anything but the sound coming through the headphones, transports the listener away from the present. The universe is not "out there," but in the here and now.

The sound that I found most compelling was not the music, or the soothing voice of exhortation to run, but the muffled sound the wind made as it rhythmically blew past the narrow space between the headphones and my ears. That unintended sound connected me with something deeper, something more primordial than the pronounced syncopation of the recorded music or the urgings of an audiotaped Siren's cry. The sound was reminiscent of a lonesome wind moving through narrow canyons. It was the kind of sound that the runner who listens hears without tapes on every run.

January 3, 1999—Wearing a Radio Headset

This Sunday evening I ran a short five- to six-mile run on the Shoal Creek Trail. I was dealing with an afternoon of depression— perhaps from the allergy medicine I took the night before, or perhaps a result of the continued difficulties I am experiencing in my relationship with Donna. I could see that I needed to run and had enough presence of mind, despite my mood and the bitter cold of the afternoon, to put on layered running clothes and head to the trail. However, I did not have the presence of mind to run, as I always do, without headphones. While sweeping the house I had begun listening to a Buddhist Lama discuss Western Buddhism on a radio talk show I often enjoy. I decided to listen to the conversation while I ran. I had been running, and listening to the radio less than five minutes, when the station experienced transmission difficulties and the program went off the air. The fill music that replaced the program did not interest me, so I clicked off the radio. Immediately, I became acutely conscious of the sound of the winter wind blowing through the radio receiver set still in my ears. In addition, having the earpiece still in place shut out some external noise, but amplified the sound of my breathing and the sound of my feet striking the pavement. I was, as a result, immediately and suddenly brought back to the present. It was as if I had returned home.

I am sure that there was wisdom to be had from listening to the radio program. I might have missed some insight; some thought that would have been useful on my spiritual journey. However, I think it far more likely that the act of coming home to my breath, recognizing the sound of my own steps on the trail, moved me farther along the spiritual path that I have chosen. Vividly, I was reminded just how personal, how experiential this journey is. Learning of a variety of spiritual practices, learning of the wisdom of the ages, understanding theology, all have their place. In the end, each of us has a journey to make alone. It is not enough to read about it, listen to the stories of other journeys, or speculate about the relative merits of one path over another. We have to begin our own journey, listening to the sounds of our own heart, breath, and feet—there God lies.

April 4, 1999—Running While Fasting

I observed Good Friday, as is my custom, by fasting. Saturday morning, Holy Saturday, I decided to run without breaking my fast. It was difficult. Since giving up beer and wine entirely during Lent, I have lost a few pounds and I am at the running weight I should have been at for this year's marathon. Consequently, I felt light enough. However, not eating the day before left me with little energy. Aware that I didn't have my normal strength level, I deliberately paced myself, focusing my attention on form rather than speed. Despite my efforts to retain energy, after making it up the steep incline on Mountain Climb, I was exhausted. I was having such difficulty catching my breath that I slowed to a walk for two or three minutes to regain normal breathing. I took advantage of the walk to concentrate my focus on my physical self and the immediate environment. My breath returned and I regained my pace. Nonetheless, after completing two more sharp inclines, I again walked for a few minutes to catch my breath. Again, I used the walking interludes to regain focus. I completed the run exhausted and it took me several hours and two small meals to feel at my normal energy level. I'm not sure that I would recommend this practice, but it was insightful. I never felt tired in the way I sometimes feel when my blood-sugar level plummets. It was much more a need to stop and catch my breath after the more strenuous parts of the run. At one point I felt the kind of depletion of energy that I remember from the marathon. At that level of depletion, I stopped and walked. I had no reason to further diminish my bodily strength that morning. I finished the run tired but happy.

December 22, 1998—Running with a Friend

Saturday morning my friend Kinley joined me on my hill run. In fact, it was Kinley who had introduced me to hill running a few *years ago. I liked it so much that it immediately became a permanent part of my running routine. Although I owe my love for hill running to Kinley, my hill run is usually made alone, in the quiet early hours of the morning. This Saturday, with the promise of posttrun migas at a downtown Mexican eatery, we agreed to run together. Kinley is one of my closest friends and of a strong spiritual bent. I suggested that we experiment with a hill-running mantra and he agreed. As we started out at a warm-up pace on the flat terrain leaving his house, I taught him the "To-ward-the-One" chant and showed him how to couple it with exhalations. We practiced that a bit until it felt comfortable. I then demonstrated how to use the hand motions called mudras to further focus the attention on the purely physical aspect of the breath.*

The surprise for me was that our breathing synchronized. We are different body types and at different levels of conditioning. I had never before noticed that we breathed together as we ran. Now climbing these hills, both of us breathing heavily, occupying our minds with the mantra, we were linked in spiritos, in spirit and in expiration. I have always felt a kinship with Kinley, but now within sharing what I had learned about spirit running and recognizing that in that communion we were sharing breath, lay a significant revelation.

Running with My Daughter

Sunday afternoon I ran the Shoal Creek Trail while Lillian cycled along with me. In the beginning, there were no elaborate chants, no Sufi practices, just close attention to my breathing and the joy of being in the presence of my daughter. I watched Lillian gain speed and cycle ahead of me. Finding a smooth part of the trail, she raised her hands from the handlebars and carefully spread her wings. I held her in my gaze as the distance between us grew. I felt proud and thankful and involuntarily began to chant the Jesus Prayer and focus on my breath. I felt an immediate outpouring of love for my child. She was wrapped securely in my prayer, encapsulated in my love. I continued the prayer in my usual manner until we reconnected. As she talked, I listened and prayed. The prayer became a vague awareness of my breathing while I focused attention on my daughter's voice. My prayer had not ceased while I spoke with Lillian. I was able to remain mindful of my intention to pray while talking and listening. I have always found it difficult to remain mindful when talking, but here with my daughter, it was perfectly natural. This was, admittedly, a completely nonthreatening situation. I was in the most comfortable of settings. However, it was a step forward. Remaining present to God, while in the presence of others, presents a challenge. This is a way to learn how to meet the challenge. Start small. Practice the presence of God in ways and situations where the chance of success is good. Practice remaining in God's presence among those you love. I am probably more comfortable with my children than with any other human beings. I am also very secure and practiced in my running. I am comfortable in the situation. When I run with those I love, I am automatically closer to God and happy.

In his book *Living Buddha, Living Christ*, Thich Nhat Hanh speaks of the Buddhist concept of "Pure Land." Pure Land is a place, or a state of mind, where the practice of mindfulness is easily shared with others. There exists a common spirit of love, compassion, and understanding. It represents a safe place, a refuge where one's spiritual journey is nurtured. Running in the company of those you love, or running with those whose purpose in running is to move with the Transcendent, is a natural, easy step beyond the comfortable solitude of running alone.

The next step is to take God with you as you move away from a comfortable setting; practice breathing and praying while in the presence of people with whom you feel less of a kinship. Practice in situations that are less womblike. Take the knowledge of God to the streets. In order to bring the presence of the Divine to others, you must keep the source of divine love flowing within yourself. You must continually tap into that source of love, constantly available to you through your breath.

July 20, 1998—Running as Catharsis

Saturday's morning hill run was grueling. I got out the door later than usual and it was oppressively hot. The heat would have been enough to put me out of sorts, but during the past week I had failed to practice my usual early-morning prayer routine. I had also failed to write. When I do not pray and I do not write, I am not at peace. The run was not a prayer, but it was helpful. Many of the thoughts I held and emotions I felt churned to the surface as I ran. I could do nothing to stop them. They demanded to be heard. The usual listening kind of prayer comes later—when I am back into a more consistent pattern of communication with God. Until then, the run is cathartic and helps keep me in balance, but doesn't serve as the wellspring of a contemplative relationship with God. Unless my spiritual practice is consistent, I am not moving forward in a satisfying way. A single run only allows me to maintain the status quo, to keep from slipping into the mire. Sometimes that has to be enough. Today I feel that my values are out of kilter. The things that I value are not getting proper attention. Tomorrow morning I will begin anew. Even writing now, I can feel the spirit stirring again.

November 30, 1998—A Following Wind

I began Sunday's run heading directly into a strong southeasterly wind. Running against the wind, my pace seemed unbearably slow. Facing the wind, I was acutely aware of its constancy and I heard the sound of each gust building and making its way toward me. I had been sailing on Lake Travis the day before and with my mind still attached to the sailing experience my inclination was to trim my sails to a close-hauled position. Unfortunately that is not an option when running. I was, however, able to recognize that I was running directly into the wind only one fourth of the time as I made my way on the loop around Town Lake. It is easy to imagine that any wind that is not directly behind you is against you. Yet if I became aware of it, I could feel that the breeze was propelling me forward as *it blew first across my port side, and then from my starboard side. I imagined that I tacked as I ran with the wind at my side and, when truly running against the wind, I allowed my body to be slighter and slip between the breeze.*

The wind and I were moving at about the same speed. As I rounded the first loop and began to run with the wind, quiet prevailed and the wind ceased. The sound of the wind that had been howling in my ears stopped and silence took its place. A following breeze was pushing me onward, yet if I had not—only moments before—faced the wind's force, I would have been unaware of the aid that it was now providing. Silently, I was being propelled by this unseen and unfelt power. Without the drying and cooling effect of the now-vanished head wind, sweat dripped from my brow. I wondered how often I had received the help of a following wind and remained unaware of its presence. More often than not, it is only when the wind has seemed to turn against me that I know it is there. Learn to be mindful of shifts in the wind's direction, the boost that a following wind can provide, the cooling effect of a cross breeze, and the challenge of a head wind.

March 16, 1999—Running in Sadness

I began yesterday's run feeling distraught. I would like to say that I ended the run uplifted, but that would not be true. I did end the run feeling better, having learned something more about my relationship with God. Still, the unhappiness I carried into the run remained. Sunday afternoon and evening I had had an awful row with my son, Nate. I love the boy more than life itself and it grieves me deeply when we are at odds. I was much harsher in my criticism of him than a fifteen-year-old boy, or anyone perhaps, can usefully accept. I knew that, in my efforts to be a father who expects a high standard of his children, I had failed to be the compassionate, understanding father who my Father above exemplifies. This felt like sin to me and I was remorseful and full of pain.

As I ran, the incident of the day before kept rolling through my mind. I am now aware, looking back at the run, that I paid no attention to my breath. My immediate physical environment was of little consequence to me. I had not been elevated to any higher form of consciousness. Eventually, through habit, I fell into a familiar chant. I moved in and out of the chant, but even in the midst of chanting, I failed to link the phrasing with my breath. Finally, toward the end of the run, I found myself verbally asking God for forgiveness, for compassion for my son and me, and for wisdom. It was as if, in the development of a life of prayer, I had been climbing a ladder that leads closer to an understanding of God. While climbing the higher rungs of the ladder, I slipped and fell to the ground. My first impulses were to begin climbing the higher rungs from which I had fallen. I found that I had no choice but to begin at the bottom step where I first began to pray. At this level all that can be expected is a cry to God for mercy. As I ran, I talked to God as my confessor and asked for forgiveness. I prayed in the manner that I remember praying as a young man of Nate's age, when, full of myself, I had suffered through crushing disappointment. Sometimes in prayer we have to begin anew. When we suffer a fall from a great height, it is not possible to start anew from where we left off. It is likely to be a slow, deliberate climb back to the point of the fall, with some soul-searching time spent at the bottom rungs.

June 16, 1999—Running in Joy

Yesterday's run on the Shoal Creek Trail was delightful. On the return trip the heavy humidity turned into a cooling rain. When I crossed the creek, slowing down to avoid slipping on the rain-soaked stones, I noticed the pattern of the raindrops as they collided with the creek's silent surface. The sight brought my run to a halt. I imagined this scene of water colliding with water, as an artist's mad brushstrokes wildly moving across an empty canvass. Stopping only for a few moments, I carried the image with me while I ran. The rain, now very heavy, both cooling and disturbing, kept me present, each drop reminding me of where I was.

The outward run had been memorable as well. As I chanted "Toward the One," a tremendous joy came over me. I felt that with each step I was making progress. I wasn't merely maintaining my physical health, I was moving toward union with God. Each step moved me closer and closer toward Oneness. I was aware that each individual step counted; whether that step was faltering or with perfect form, I was simultaneously moving within and toward the Divine. I had the clear sense that I was where I needed to be and doing what I was meant to be doing. An awareness of that condition propelled me forward effortlessly.

It is a significant challenge to stay close to God during the good times. Right now, I have few troubles. I have a good job, loving kids, and a comfortable home. Yet I usually feel that I am neglecting my spiritual journey. The path is laid out before me, but I am only toying with the idea of a serious embarkation. I am not sure why. Little else intrigues me. Still, I hesitate and let other things fill my life. I can only ask that God fill me with the desire to know Him. Inside I fear this, because at the times I have longed for God the most, my life's circumstances have been the most difficult. I am not asking for more pain in my life. I am asking for God's continual presence in times of joy and pain and, especially, through the mundane. I am asking for the presence of God in the ordinary world— not just in the spectacular, the breathtaking, or in the midst of despair, but always.

July 22, 1999—Running When Depressed

Yesterday's run was in the rain. Since I knew the trails would be slippery, I chose to run on the neighborhood streets. This neighborhood is so boring, that I face few distractions. The houses are devoid of interest—uniformly brick, three bedrooms, a patch of lawn with shrubs bordering the front of each house. I am so depressed these days that it was difficult to get out the door. As usual, the run was therapeutic. I can't say that my spirits were lifted to new heights, but I clearly felt better. I focused on the rain, my breathing, the splash of each foot on the rain-covered pavement. I had difficulty staying with the "Toward the One" chant, so I switched to the Trisagion: "Holy God, Holy and Mighty, Holy Immortal One, Have Mercy on Us." This chant aligned more evenly with my mood. I was at a place where I needed mercy. The thought of being uplifted to the heavens seemed too far-fetched an idea.

August 6, 1998—Difficulties in Praying

I went for a Shoal Creek run yesterday. A brief but welcome rain had cooled things off a bit. Much of the run I spent in an attempt to pray verbally. I had a number of things on my mind, and I sought guidance. The attempt met with little success. Or so it seemed at the time. The attempt to pray, in whatever way, is rewarded. Reaching out to something greater than we are, in whatever fumbling manner, is an acknowledgment of our own frailty, a sign of an awareness of our connection with the Divine. I had difficulty maintaining that connection. My mind wandered. I wasn't running in a meandering way, I was following a well-defined path. Why can't my prayers be as direct? I kept losing track of my place on the list of things I wished to present to God. Each item of concern became a platform from which I began to dwell on the topic, mull it over aimlessly, and forget about my intention to offer it up to God. Was I in fact offering the problem to God by my intention to do so? I think that the intention takes me some way down the path, but truly offering the issue to God requires that I remain conscious of the process. When I forget my intention and simply mull over the problem, I'm leaving out God.

Running with Preoccupation

I began the day drinking tea and talking with a good friend who had contracted Lou Gehrig's disease. Later I took Communion to Kevin and Nancy—friends who were about to face the trials of beginning Kevin's leukemia treatments. I left their home to visit and pray with my friend Robert, suffering through the final stages of liver cancer. At the end of these three encounters with friends confronting either the possibility or the certainty of death, I was very grateful that I had enough daylight left to take a long run. It was a gloriously beautiful evening, with a few clouds gathering above the hills in the west, waiting to provide color and texture to the sunset. The air was cool and I was feeling strong. Quite naturally, my first running thoughts were of how fortunate I was to be able to run, when walking was a struggle for the good people I had just left behind. A prayer of thankfulness was ready on my lips.

My mind was consumed during most of the run with thoughts of my friends and how much they had given me. I knew that after I served Communion to Nancy and Kevin, I was preoccupied with thoughts of them and was not able to be as present to Robert as I wanted to be. Robert, with his unceasing kindliness and sound judgment, had already forgiven me for this sin. I was thankful that I had planned a long run. It took some time for my brain to process all that I needed to process. Eventually, the steady rhythms of the run had worked their magic and I could bring my heart and mind in conjunction with my body and finally engage the present. Eventually, the run was all there was. The demands and the mercies of the day were absorbed into my heart. My heart, meanwhile, was being gently massaged by God's breath. The cold beer I had later that evening to accompany leftover pizza also tasted of the Divine. God's blessings come in myriad shapes.

March 1, 2000—Marathon III

It has been one and a half weeks since my third marathon. It was a beautiful race. Thanks to my friend Kinley, I started out slowly and kept a slow, even pace throughout the race. We engaged in an easy conversation much of the time. Other times we simply ran along beside each other in silence. After milepost 18 the back pain that Kinley had been experiencing proved to be too much and he had to stop to stretch. Before the race we had agreed to run together as long as we wished, and that I might at some point pull ahead. I felt some regrets at leaving him behind, but the pull of the race compelled me to move on without him. Beyond twenty miles the run grew more difficult, but I was never exhausted and I was able to maintain an even pace to the end. In fact, I was actually able to accelerate somewhat in the last mile and had some energy left over for a slight sprint at the end.

I finished the race a few minutes ahead of my time the year before. I was pleased at that, but greater pleasure came primarily from the experience of maintaining a higher level of awareness throughout much of the marathon. I ran a conscious race. The conditions—that is, the crowds, the noise, the excitement—prevent me from running the contemplative kind of run that I experience when I run in solitude. Running a marathon in the company of thousands of other people doesn't allow for the same kind of spiritual encounter that running alone provides. Instead, I am compelled to run with joy, alive to the evidence of creation that surrounds me. Learning to joyfully experience the surrounding sights and sounds while my body steadily grows weary is an extremely valuable lesson. Only in the last few miles of the run did I turn inward and begin to focus on breathing. At that point I needed the much-practiced comfort of a familiar chant and an awareness of breath to bring me to the finish line. I had not been winded during the entire race until I picked up the pace at the final gentle rise leading to the finish line. Running uphill has always been my forte and knowing that the end was near, I accelerated through the rise, listened to my altered breathing pat-

tern, and pushed to the finish line. I had enough energy to run the last hundred yards with an awareness of form, running erect, bringing my knees up high, pumping my arms, and landing each foot quietly. Grace had brought me to this point and it was with grace that I wished to finish.

Enter through the narrow gate. For wide is the gate and broad is the road that leads to destruction, and many enter through it. But small is the gate and narrow the road that leads to life, and only a few find it.

MATT 7:13

Choosing to run the narrow road—the steep uphill climbs, the rock-strewn trail, the muddy path—these are choices made by few.

ritual, sacraments, ordinary and extraordinary

We ought not to think of building holiness upon action; we ought to
build it upon a way of being, for it is not what we do that makes us
holy, but we ought to make holy what we do.

MEISTER ECKHERT

People who manage to perceive and appreciate the sacraments of life are
very close to, or rather already immersed in, the life of the sacraments.

LEONARDO BOFF

Holiness isn't something we can build into a run. Neither will
running make us holy—anymore than baptism, communion, trek-
king to Mecca, or reciting a thousand names of God can make us
holy. Holiness is a way of being that transcends activities. However,
we can make the run holy by bringing to the run a sense of God's
presence in us. In this same way we can transform all of the ordinary
into the sacred.

The Importance of Ritual in Running

Athletes tend to be very ritualistic. I love to watch baseball players, from the little league to the majors, tap the bat to the toes of each shoe, spit, step out of the batter's box and take a practice cut, and cross themselves. Each action is a necessary part of a routine that the batter feels he must do before he is ready to take the pitch. Among ball players, Tampa Bay Devil Ray Wade Boggs stands out for the dozens of highly ritualized acts he was compelled to perform before, during, and after every ball game. Runners have their own patterns of behavior that they follow before competition—eating a specific food, stretching in a certain way, tying their shoelaces just right.

These rituals are a natural part of preparing for a challenge. When starting a spiritual run, use this tendency to develop ceremony to good effect. Turn every stretch into an act of humility, a bowing before the Almighty. Consider the last drink of water as a part of the sacrament of Communion. Make the preliminary splash of cool water on your face on a hot summer afternoon a kind of baptism. The parting comments to a friend you saw at the trailhead can become words of brotherly love. A walk around the water fountain can be done with the same reverence as the ceremonial clockwise circumambulation that pilgrims take around the Buddhist temple Borobudur in Java, Indonesia. Whatever actions precede the run, perform them with a sense of reverence. The run, and the preparation for the run, can become sacred acts. Regard them as such.

Response to Artress

The Rev. Lauren Artress, noted for bringing the ancient wisdom of the labyrinth to modern pilgrims, has said that the sacred path is a "pedestrian path." I think that by this she means that the way to God is open to all, available to those travelers without elaborate means of transport—to those who are journeying on foot. The footpath to the Transcendent that Artress specifically describes is available to all who are willing to go to a cathedral, church, or retreat center that offers a labyrinth. I strongly recommend the practice of labyrinth walking. Walking the spiraling path of the labyrinth enables you to follow in the footsteps of centuries of sojourners who have sought God along the same path. The experience of walking the labyrinth in solidarity with others can create a shared energy that is more powerful than any single person can generate. The relative absence of distractions and the singleness of purpose that surrounds labyrinth walking can be excellent mindfulness training. By all means walk a labyrinth. Visit labyrinths as often as you can. The run, however, is accessible to you every day. Approach each run as if it were a labyrinth, each trail a sacred path.

May 19, 1999—Running the Labyrinth

Late Sunday morning, Donna and I made the short drive to Cedar Park, where the parishioners of Christ's Episcopal Church have built a labyrinth amidst the oak trees behind their chapel. It is a lovely setting and the concentric rings and slashes of the labyrinth have been lovingly created from the creamy limestone rocks gathered from the grounds. Perhaps one of the nine-year-olds romping in the adjacent playscape had mischievously rearranged a few stones, resulting in a false start and a setting to order of the misplaced stones. The metaphoric qualities of the labyrinth were evident even before the walk began. Soon after setting foot inside the labyrinth, I knew that this was sacred ground. It came very naturally for me to walk slowly, deliberately, just as I walk when I get the morning paper after a morning meditation and just as I walk when I wish to catch my breath during a distance run. My emotional state changed as I moved inward and outward through the circles. My focus shifted between breathing, the pastoral setting of the hill country, the tiny wildflowers gracing the path, the quivering shadows of the small blooms lying on the faces of the path stones, and the chatter of the church members leaving the morning Eucharist. Eventually the children of the playscape found the labyrinth walkers irresistibly interesting and they joined us. An energetic young boy found our methodical pace to be painfully slow and he soon broke into a trot, calling to his sister, "I'm running the labyrinth!" Tears rushed to my eyes. I recognized that I, too, have been running the labyrinth. I am among those who are eager to find God at the center and must run to meet him.

The boy's sister called out, "You're supposed to walk the labyrinth!" Offering him the conventional wisdom, her advice had no effect on his pace. He knew that his method of making it through the labyrinth's path was right for him and he could do nothing else. The true seeker heeds rigid rules defining how God should be approached, as carefully as a boy listens to his younger sister. Which is to say, not at all.

Part of the appeal of the labyrinth is the circuitous characteristic. We tend to lead very linear lives. An opportunity to engage in a nonlinear activity can be a welcome respite. This is also the way we tend to run. My preferred run is a loop around Town Lake. Whenever I can make my run a loop, I do so. I begin the run, make the circuit, and return to where I started—a slightly changed man.

Shabbat

At first it might seem odd to think of a run, particularly a strenuous run involving miles of steadily paced exertion, as a kind of Sabbath. Traditionally, the Sabbath is thought of as a day of rest from the toils of life's labor. While this is true, it is the purpose of this rest that is of more importance. Man was ordered to observe the Sabbath in order to have an established time to commune with God. The Sabbath, according to Old Testament scholar Ellen Davis, is an invitation to intimacy with God.

During the time in which the Torah, the first five books of the

Old Testament, was written, work meant physical labor. The Israelites were an agrarian society, and observation of the Sabbath meant resting from the physical labor of the fields. Here, in the first days of the twenty-first century in Western society, most of us toil with our minds. A truer observation of the Sabbath, for us, would provide an opportunity to rest the mind. It is not coincidentally true that a mind at rest provides an opportunity for intimacy with God. The contemplative run is a time to experience the Sabbath in this way. You are using your body, but stilling the mind. Physical work, which can feel like recreation to the sedentary citizen of the second millennium, is accompanied by a practiced quieting of the mind, a listening for God's voice, a true Sabbath, available any day of the week. Next weekend, consider carefully who may be most properly observing the Sabbath, the well dressed filing into churches and synagogues or the T-shirted runners who may be in intimate communion with God.

Why Running Meditation Makes Sense for the New Millennium

One way to look at running is as a tool, a device or practice that aids the user in his quest to pray. Examined in this way, running can be compared to mantras, chants, labyrinths, rosary beads, prayer ropes, drums, the martial arts, or tea ceremonies. I bring up these last two practices because of the way each arose and flourished within the popular culture of the time. The Oriental warrior's study of combat techniques was, at its core, a spiritual training. The same could be said for the tea ceremony. People drank tea. It was part of their daily lives. To begin to use the serving and drinking of tea as a spiritual exercise seems perfectly logical when one adopts the aim of living a life in prayer. While the movements of the martial artist can easily be seen as meditative and it is easy to understand how the physical and the spiritual could be linked in a practice such as this, the important thing for us to grasp is that training in this kind of combat was a part of the culture of the time. Here, in the opening days of the twenty-first century, running is one aspect of our culture wherein spiritual insight can be gained. Running is something we commonly do and is a potential avenue for spiritual exploration. If one is intent about moving along a spiritual path, it only makes sense to utilize those aspects of our lives that already fill our days. One only need awaken to the spiritual undercurrents that flow through the most commonplace of our daily activities.

January 11, 1998—Run of the Mill

I've not been running much lately. The weather has been bad, I've worked late, and there have been other obligations. I ran this evening and it was glorious. No great insights. I wasn't particularly well focused on breathing or prayer. It was simply a good physical run that loosened the tight muscles in my body and elevated my spirits. This is good, too. Even an ordinary run can be a prayerful experience.

Running as Baptism

Baptism is thought of in fundamentalist Christian denominations as a rebirth. This rebirthing experience is usually expected to happen only once. Yet human beings are in constant need of renewal. Fortunately, opportunities to be born again abound. We are not limited to the ritual of Baptism to know the sense of regeneration of spirit that is symbolized by this holy rite. The renewing sense of baptism can be experienced in the nonformalized ritual of meditation. In each meditation session, the opportunity exists to be transformed, to experience a rejuvenation of the self. Just as the sacrament of Baptism is performed in a highly structured manner, it is important that the sense of ritual be made a part of the meditation. An appropriate setting, proper posture, the creation of a physical atmosphere conducive to making a connection to the Divine are all necessary ingredients. The exact nature of that ritual is less important than the cultivation of a sense of mindfulness surrounding the meditation practice. Meditation of this sort is worship of the highest order. Worship demands attentiveness, a conscious recognition that you are in the presence of the Divine.

Running can be experienced as a baptism as well. Running yesterday, with sweat dripping down my face, the cleansing effect of the run felt like a baptism. I was healed, cleansed with sweat, and made whole again—ready to face, in a present way, the remainder of the day.

Arising from a meditation session, I usually feel awakened and refreshed, but soon enough the activities of the day surround me, and remaining in the presence of God becomes more difficult. Engaging in activity like running enables me, more easily, to maintain an ongoing consciousness. It is as if I had been reborn in the time spent in prayer or meditation; yet being newly born, I still require careful nurturing. Running (or perhaps walking, gardening, yoga, folding clothes) provides an environment in which experiencing the presence of God can be practiced in a nurturing environment. Running shares many of the traits characteristic of prayer and meditation—principally the quality of bringing one into the present. Yet running also compels you to open your eyes and move about in the world. It is as if you are a child learning to walk, but in this case you are learning to move through the world mindfully. There comes a time when you must leave the comforting arms of your mother and walk on your own. We are learning to walk in the world and still remain present to our divine origins.

I will occasionally attend a stretching session that is held after a local running group's workouts. The stretching is useful. Like most runners, I find that my muscles have become too tight and badly need the stretch. The exercises are very similar to yoga postures, but without the spiritual element. The friendly coach chats with members of the class while she gives instruction to the class. We are encouraged to breathe, but only so that the stretch could be completed more easily. The exercises are good for the body but do little for the soul. The session pointed out to me how important intentions can be. The activity was much the same as yoga, but done without mindfulness. Running can be thought of in a comparable way. You can run in a way that is disconnected from your body and spirit, or you can run in a manner that engages your whole being. It is a question of intention.

Sacred Traditions

It is important that running meditation be part of a sacred tradition. There needs to be a context in which to apply the lessons learned while running. My own tradition is a Christian one, but a running meditation can exist as an authentic practice of prayer within the framework of any of the major world religions—Judaism, Islam, Buddhism, Taoism, or Hinduism. It is not a substitute for any of the practices of faith that have withstood the test of time. Trust in the wisdom of the ancient traditions, but don't be afraid to try a contemporary expression of an ancient practice.

Thinking of the importance of practicing running meditation in the context of a larger spiritual tradition reminds me of the oft-told Buddhist story of the newly initiated Buddhist disciple who wished to attain enlightenment without going through the rigorous disciplines of meditation and wholesome living required of those seeking higher consciousness. The teacher told the student that if he wished to give him an egg, he must hand it to him encased in the shell. If he attempted to give him only the yolk, what would be transferred would only be a sloppy mess. The yolk is enlightenment. The shell is the tradition that holds the yolk together. We need the practice, the discipline, the coherence of a unified body of religious thought in order to prevent the "truth" from becoming only a hodgepodge of ideas. Use running meditation to strengthen your own faith, not as a substitute for that faith. Do not be afraid to explore new avenues to God, but draw deeply from the ancient wisdom of spiritual teachers who have preceded you in this journey.

A Secular Activity Made Sacred

I attended a luncheon recently at All Saints' with Kenneth Leech, the author of *Soul Friend*. He quoted the Duke professor Alistair McIntire, who said, "The task of religion is to enable us to see the secular as sacred." When the sacred and the secular are divided, religion becomes compartmentalized, simply an aspect of a larger life. Running is a secular activity, but it can be a sacred one as well.

It is important to achieve balance in one's life. A balanced life is usually thought of as one containing a variety of activities. For centuries the Benedictines have practiced a life of balance that includes labor, prayer, holy leisure, and service to others. A contemporary expression of a balanced life would include work, play, spending time with family and friends, creativity, and perhaps, some place for the sacred. As Joan Chittister, a nun who has written extensively about the Rule of St. Benedict, has noted, "Daily life is the stuff of which high sanctity can be made." Whether one lives in a monastic community or a bedroom community, it is important that each day include an opportunity to practice the various dimensions that make up the human spirit. However, even more important than making sure that there is time for a variety of human endeavors is the realization that a sacred thread runs through each of the tasks we accomplish. Caring for the poor and handing a credit card to a gas station attendant are both opportunities to bring the sacred into the lives of those we touch. Purposeful recitation of a much-loved prayer and reviewing the box scores from the previous day's baseball games are both opportunities to mindfully conduct the business of divine awareness.

It is this divine awareness that enables us to lead an undivided life. Jesus provided the example in Logion 61 of the Gospel of Thomas: "I am he who exists from the undivided." Our lives are spent engaged in a variety of different activities, but we are able to bring unity to those disparate tasks by remaining conscious of the kingdom of God.

Certain activities can lead us more directly to an awareness of the Divine Presence. Depending on where one is on the spiritual path or the nature of one's spiritual practice, God is more apparent in some circumstances than others. It may be easier for us to sense God's presence in places and situations where we are already accustomed to finding God. That fact is an indication of our own limitations in perception, not a statement about where God resides. We may habitually find God only in the splendor of a "high church" setting or only in the solitude of a climb to a mountaintop in a national park. Yet God is just as available to us on the congested drive to the cathedral or in our conversation with the park ranger.

Learning to find God in the routine is a matter of practice. Running is one of a range of activities that can serve as a bridge that leads us from a place where we readily sense the Transcendent to a larger world where the Divine is omnipresent. It may be that you can readily sense God's spirit while kneeling at the Communion rail and that when stuck in snarling traffic you might as well be an atheist. Practicing the presence of God while running is one of the ways to bridge that gap. Learning to recognize God on the running trail is not a difficult task, but it is one that, when practiced, can make recognition of the Divine a part of ordinary time.

December 9, 1998—Running as a Sacrament
I am drawn to consider the mind-body connection, in particular, the spiritual nature of both. Increasingly, I find it difficult to separate the two. It is not simply that running leads me to a place in my head where I can sense the spiritual, though it does that. The truth

is that the running has become a spiritual act in itself. Does it lose
its spiritual sense if my mind has wandered? Do the sacraments lose
spiritual significance if the priest's mind has wandered? Running has
taken on the same sense of spiritual connection that is found in the
sacraments or in formal prayer. Not always do I run and consciously
feel a connection with God's spirit. Yet each time I run, the potential
for making that connection is there. Because I have engaged in an act
through which I have often made the connection, and in which my
intention to connect with God has been firmly established, it feels as
much like a "blessed and holy" sacrament as Communion at the al-
tar rail.

The Procession on Town Lake

Episcopalians love processions. The clergy, lay readers, the choir,
acolytes, chalice bearers, and assorted ministers, all proceed into
the church at the beginning of each service and recede out of the
church at the end. It is a grand parade—full of pageantry, pomp,
and a sense of the glorious. Running on the Town Lake Trail, I
often feel a part of such a procession. Sometimes the procession is
sparsely populated—on cold, dark, wintry evenings, for example. A
Saturday morning on Town Lake is another story. The procession is
constant and the runner need only find his place. The praying runner
can hold on to the idea that his role in the procession is unique and
blessed. He is bringing God's presence to the hundreds of runners
and walkers and cyclists whose sense of the sacred may be less developed. Whether you are ahead or behind of others on the trail,
you are leading them, showing them the way to tread on holy
ground.

When taking an active role in an Episcopal worship service, and
thereby, the procession, I have the sense of being part of much more
than a mass movement from the back of a church to the front.
Inherent in the procession is an act of transformation. Here is an
opportunity to deliberately leave behind the routine and, with each

step, move toward an awareness of God's presence in a sacred place. A run can be approached in the same way. Run with the realization that you are engaged in a process of transformation—each stride taking you closer to the Divine. With every step, you are being changed from a person mired in the concerns of a narrow world and moving toward higher consciousness.

William Segal, the noted magazine publisher who later in life devoted his energy to spiritual pursuits, refers to ritual as an awareness of what one is doing at the moment, even drinking a cup of coffee. He says that we can be fed, receive energy in a new way, if we pay attention. Segal believes that it is through ritual that we can learn to harmonize our whole being and learn to listen to a universal sound. The rituals can be as elaborate as those that make up the celebrations of Passover, Easter, or Ramadan. Or the rituals can be as simple as lacing up your shoes or stretching your muscles. In either case, it is the attention to the details of the practice, a mindfulness that transforms a routine task into an act that brings you into God's presence.

Lacing Up Your Running Shoes

I encourage you to turn the most everyday aspects of running into sacred ritual. Consider the manner in which you put on your running shoes. I try to dress for running in much the same way that a devout and mindful priest might put on his vestments before celebrating the Eucharist. I store my running shoes on an upper shelf in my closet—a "sacred" place. I wouldn't leave them tossed carelessly on the floor. I remove the orthotics from my everyday walking shoes and insert them into my running shoes. This simple action is a reminder that I am bringing an ordinary element of my life into the sacred. I pay little attention to the socks I normally wear, but I select my running socks with care. After all, they caress my feet as I move on holy ground. I pull the socks carefully around each foot, making sure they are not bunched in a way that would cause discomfort later. If I am properly mindful that day, each part of this process is punctuated with awareness of breath. I loosen the shoelaces on each shoe enough to allow me to easily insert each foot into the shoe. It seems thoughtless to only loosen the laces enough to allow me to force each foot into its shoe. I then take care in lacing up each shoe snuggly and evenly, so that there is balance in the snugness of each shoe's fit. Perhaps you follow a similar pattern each time you prepare for a run, but instead of moving through that pattern with a singularity of mind, you do so while ruminating over your day or determining your dinner menu. If so, recognize and be aware of the fact that you have established a ritual. Make the most of your dressing ritual. Or develop your own ritual. Simply remember to pay close attention to each step in the process. Do it mindfully.

The Ordinariness of the Run

The training run is often a very ordinary experience. Usually, nothing particularly interesting happens. The training run doesn't have the spark and energy of a race. The thrill of victory and the agony of defeat are not a part of the usual running experience. Yet it is this everyday run that has the potential to become a quest for life's meaning in the midst of the unexciting. The vast majority of my runs do not take place in the deserts of Big Bend, are not run on the sands of a Caribbean beach, nor are they made in New York's Central Park. Most of my runs, and probably most of yours, take place along one of a small number of very familiar routes. Epiphany is not a common occurrence. As in everyday life, usually nothing extraordinary happens. Yet it is in this ordinariness that God exists. He can be found in the empty space that exists among the triumphs, failures, ecstasy, and depression that typically command our attention. Running is an opportunity to search for God amid the commonplace, humdrum activities that occupy most of our time. That is, ultimately, the point—finding a way to mix the mundane with the mystical, to blend the sacred with the profane, to find heaven on earth.

In a similar vein, this kind of running is not just for extraordinary athletes. Running meditation is as accessible to the novice as to the professional. It requires a desire to run, however slowly or quickly your body permits, and a need to exist in the presence of God. Runs of only a mile or two may not allow sufficient time for your meditation practice to get beyond dealing only with the thoughts of the day. However, that alone can be encouraging enough to spur you on to greater distances. How quickly you make it through those additional lengths matters not at all. The devotion of additional time to running will allow you more opportunity to practice sensing God's presence while running.

The Cumulative Benefits of Running

In her book *Walking the Sacred Path,* Lauren Artress speaks of the cumulative benefits of walking the labyrinth, even in times when nothing significant happens. Running the spiritual path is a much more ordinary process. Never run with a sense of expectation that something significant will happen. Typically, I ask only that I run in the presence of God and that I run with a heightened awareness of that presence. Occasionally, insights arise or I feel an unusual closeness to God's spirit. Usually, however, I simply know that I am not running alone and I carry that sense of a shared journey with me long after the run is complete.

February 2, 1999—The Temple at the Run
   While sitting in meditation this morning, many thoughts crossed my mind—memories of the sail the day before, erotic thoughts of Donna sanding the tiller, Saturday's baseball game, and the work-week ahead. I fought none of these thoughts, nor did I dwell on them. Instead, I offered them up for blessings. I asked, though not in words, that each of the thoughts that crossed my mind be sancti-fied. It was as if I brought each of the secular facets of my life into a temple. Inside the temple they can remain as displaced objects

having no role to play in a holy place, or they can be blessed, and take their place among the sacred.

This is an important step toward achieving unity within one's life. I can no longer tolerate dividing my life between what is God's and what is man's. It all must be God's or I have no use for it. Is this to say that I do not relish earthly pleasures? No, it is simply that I am beginning to recognize God's hand in the world's most routine offerings. Finding God in the joys of an afternoon sail, in the subtleties of a pickoff play at second, in passionate sex with the woman I love—this is no longer something I strive for, but is unavoidable. This introduction of the sacred into the ordinary and the worldly into the heavenly has happened largely because of the practice of running and sitting meditation. In both spiritual exercises, thoughts intrude that can take you away from your breath, your mantra, or your focus on the present. These thoughts are not to be cursed, but embraced. The embrace, however, is only a quick hug before passing the thoughts on to God. In God's presence, in this temple of the run, the thoughts receive the blessing, the forgiveness, the purification, and the treatment that is needed.

The Spiritual Urge

Gail Godwin, author of a novel called *Evensong,* is an Episcopalian and married to a Jew. Both she and her husband possess what she calls the "religion urge" or "spiritual urge." It is this desire that moves me forward in my run. It is a longing for companionship that I don't seem to find on earth. It is a yearning to feel that I am part of a pattern, that my role makes sense, that I am fulfilling my destiny. When I run, I feel as if I am moving toward that goal.

The etymological root for religion is *religio,* meaning to link us back. Establishing a link, a connection, is the goal of spirituality and religion as well. Religion typically does this in a formal, established practice. If the formal practice fails to provide the linkage, then it is of little value. The practice doesn't satisfy the "religion urge." It is important, however, to point out that running is not a religion and it would be a serious mistake to try to make running one's religion. Nevertheless, running can become an important part of one's religious practice—providing another way to become closer to God— in whatever form God is conceived.

I was downtown when I finished a recent workday, only a few miles from the running trail around Town Lake. However, I didn't feel like running. In fact, I didn't feel like doing much of anything. It was only the knowledge, based on countless previous experiences, that my spirits would be elevated if I went for a run that kept me moving toward the trailhead. Without stopping to consider the matter, I proceeded to my usual starting point, changed into running clothes, and began the run. It wasn't one of my best runs, but it was spent in an effort to allow room for spirit in my world-filled head. While running, it seemed that I was having little success in achieving that modest goal. Even at the end of the run, my head was still swimming in the day's thoughts. Despite the absence of a singularity of vision that I am sometimes granted while running, the effort I had made to be open to God's presence was rewarded with a restoration of my sense of self. I recognized my place as a seeker after knowledge of God, not a person (especially on this day) who had achieved Divine Union, but a man with the clear sense that I was still on the journey.

At times it will feel as if you are merely "going through the motions" of running meditation. Don't despair. If all you can manage to do is go through the motions, then that is enough. Among the Sufis, the term *zhikr* refers to the repetition of Divine Names. Silently recited are names translated as "Lord of Peace," "God of My Vision," or "The Living God." It is said that the progression of learning the practice of repeating Divine Names goes like this: "First, you act as if you're doing the *zhikr*. Then you do the *zhikr*. Then finally the *zhikr* does you."

Initially, the motion, coupled with intention, is sufficient. The repeated use of the chant, the repetition of the Divine Name, simply running with an intention to move closer to an experience with God is, in fact, bringing you closer to the realization of that intention. Don't despair. Don't feel like a fraud. Stay with the practice and soon God will be running at your side.

godspeed

The race is nothing but a turning away from all created things and a uniting oneself with that which is uncreated.

THE PSEUDO-DIONYSIUS

Rapid motion through space elates one.

JAMES JOYCE

In an earlier age it was customary to bid "Godspeed" to someone as they embarked on a journey, as an expression of good wishes and safe travel. When beginning a meditation run, it is no less appropriate to bid yourself "Godspeed." However, more than an expression to invoke good fortune, in this, more literal, context, use of the term *Godspeed* can be thought of as offering up the hope that God will establish the nature and pace of the run—determining the optimal speed for running meditation. *Godspeed* used in this way denotes the pace set by God. Sometimes that tempo may be fast; other times, slow. Our challenge is to match the pace set by the Divine.

In a 1999 radio interview, William Segal spoke of the importance of pausing in the middle of mechanical processes to compose ourselves. He noted how being aware of each step in the process of living our lives gives us extra energy, "beneficent forms to help us." Running, too, can become mechanical. Even with the best intentions, the attributes of running that help move one along a spiritual path can also become obstacles on that path. The constancy of breathing and the steady rhythm of the stride can become automatic and stale. In order to avoid having the run become too routine, it is useful to vary the speed. In this chapter we will explore the effects of increased and decreased speed on the meditative qualities of the run, and how pausing to alter or simply recognize the pace can help enlist the aid of Segal's beneficent forms.

It is relatively easy to recognize how distance running can be a meditative experience. When I began, at the urging of a friend, to increase my speed, I feared that the meditative quality would be lost. Indeed, for a time, until my endurance increased, the extra push required to run faster seemed to interfere with my ability to meditate. Put in retrospect, I'm not so sure that it really did interfere. Clearly, until I got in better shape, I enjoyed running less. However, the focus on my breathing was a very natural consequence of struggling to catch my breath. Being rhythmic about breathing, however, was not so easy in those early, faster, runs. Overcoming the battle to fill my lungs with oxygen and to instead allow myself to be propelled by my breathing came easier as my physical conditioning improved.

For a long time, I balked at increasing my pace or doing any sort of "speed work." As a former football player, my attitude toward speed work was tainted by the memory of an endless series of "wind sprints" that inevitably followed a grueling football practice, or running sprints that were inflicted as punishment for missing a block or showing up late for practice. Only in the midst of marathon preparation years later did I begin to recognize the value of interval training. But even then I saw speed work only as a form of physical conditioning and failed to see that the running meditation I was practicing could be experienced while running rapidly.

Eventually I realized that the Sufi chant "Toward the One" was an excellent accompaniment to speed work. The breathing pattern I use while sprinting is as follows: "To (inhale), ward (exhale), the (inhale), One (exhale)." The syllables are short, corresponding with the rapid breathing required when sprinting. Moreover, the imagery of moving "toward the One," toward a finish line that is within reach, is an image that lends itself to short bursts of speed. This particular mantra also works well when chanted during the slower jogging intervals between sprints and is further discussed in Chapter 5, "Breath and Chant."

I have also found that chanting a short, fast-paced "Godspeed" mantra helps to recover momentum when I have grown tired. I chant "God-speed"—hearing "God" on the inhale and "speed" on the exhale. Awareness of the symbolism of taking in God with the breath and then letting the breath go with speed helps propel me along.

March 25, 1998—The Value of Changing Pace
   Yesterday's run was a short run down the Shoal Creek Trail. At the turnaround point I walked for a few minutes in order to capture a more complete sense of myself and of my surroundings. Later in the run I began to run intervals, alternately accelerating my rate of motion and then dropping into an easy pace. Both activities, speeding up and slowing down, heightened my consciousness. When I returned to the constancy of my normal pace, that heightened awareness remained. Changes like this, when done with intention, can provide a spark of recognition to the ordinary run—a realization of the purpose of the run—and can move you away from the mindless state into which you might have drifted.

June 6, 1999—The Effect of Slowing Down on Mindfulness
   On my long run yesterday, I carried the chant "Toward the One" with me. The Shoal Creek Trail is still in disarray and periodically I was forced to walk, gingerly skirting around the ruts and unearthed rocks. Each time I slowed down and made my way through the un-

certain terrain of the muddy trail, the chant resonated more clearly. I became acutely aware of breathing and finding my footing on the surface. As the trail improved and I accelerated, I continued to run with the same heightened mindfulness. The interval of obligatory cautious awareness added a dimension of clarity to the entire experience.

The state of awareness I felt as I carefully made my way through the uncertain terrain is the same sense of presence I wish to retain after the run is complete. If I can maintain consciousness while in the more difficult running state, then I can surely maintain a higher level of awareness when I slow down. Periodically, slowing to a walk and practicing mindfulness is excellent practice at retaining awareness for longer and longer periods after the run.

Upon reflection and with added experience, it has become apparent that awareness levels increase with both slowing down and speeding up. It is the change in pace that seems to be important. When moving at the same pace for an extended period of time, it is easy to fall into a pattern that allows your mind to drift off into random thoughts, losing your sense of presence. Changing pace, slowing down or speeding up, brings you back to the present.

The James Joyce Ramble

In Maine each spring, a race called the James Joyce Ramble is held. Each leg of the 5K race is named for one of Joyce's books—the *Ulysses* Leg, the *Portrait of the Artist* leg, etc. At every water stand, actors read selections from Joyce. The idea behind the race/performance is to reverse roles so that the actors remain still and the audience is moving—just the opposite of what we generally experience with concerts, plays, ballet performances, and other forms of entertainment. We typically enter churches, synagogues, and mosques in the same way, expecting to be passive participants in a worship experience. When moving, especially when running, we can use our bodies to actively seek communion with the Transcendent. The idea is to move our bodies in pursuit of God, while stilling our minds to receive him.

December 2, 1998—Speed Work

Yesterday I ran with the local track club, Run Tex. For many of the members it is quite a social occasion. I know a few of the regular members, but being a solitary runner, I interact sparingly, responding in a friendly manner to greetings, but seldom initiating conversation. The run set was fairly challenging, a series of 800-, 400-, 200-, 300-, and 1600-meter runs punctuated with resting jogs around the track. The run set was preceded with a few warmup laps and warming exercises and followed with backward and forward hill runs. I welcomed the speed work as part of my marathon training routine.

I was curious about how well running meditation would work in this kind of setting. I had run regularly with this group a few years ago and my memory of what the workouts were like led me to believe that the setting would be all wrong for a prayerful run. I was mistaken. I am increasingly led to the conclusion that the prayerful nature of the run depends far less on the circumstances of the run than on the intention and preparation that the runner carries with him on the run. It is what you take to the mountaintop that matters.

It was dusk when the run began, and before we finished, the track would be lit only by the nearly full moon and the ambient light from the neighborhood street lamps. I allowed my mind to wander through the initial laps and high kicks, cross-overs, and exaggerated skipping that constituted the warmup routine. However, once we settled into a series of short-distance runs (these were not fast sprints, but mostly meant to be run at a 5K pace), I determined to try to focus on my breath. Once again, I chose the "Toward the One" mantra. On my distance-training run, my breathing was slower and, therefore, the chant was slow as well. But in this case, particularly in the 400-meter and shorter runs, I was running fairly quickly, my breathing was accelerated, and the chant was said much faster. It worked beautifully. I was able to relax into the run in a way I had not experienced when sprinting. Generally, when I run fast, I feel my body tensing and can feel the grimace in my face. Focusing on my breath and the mantra, the tension was released, my stride automatically extended, and I fell into a more natural, and naturally rapid, pace.

For practical reasons, the swinging of my arms became a kind of mudra. The running coach pointed out that I wasn't swinging my arms high enough, particularly in the laps where we were concentrating on form. I responded by swinging my arms in a slightly exaggerated manner and incorporating the swing into the "Toward the One" chant. Breathing heavily, while running at just below sprint pace, I was brought beautifully into the present.

April 16, 1999—Intervals

On Monday evening the traffic to and from the Shoal Creek trailhead was so difficult that I decided to run in my neighborhood on Wednesday. I ran to the Pony League ballpark and scaled a few hillsides. Then I ran to the neighborhood soccer field for interval training. Practicing God's presence while interval training is relatively new to me. I have done it with some success during the Run Tex track sessions in preparation for the marathon. Now I was alone and I hadn't seriously done this kind of training since I was a teenager getting in shape for the demanding football two-a-day training.

Having completed a mile or so warmup run in the neighborhood, I began by doing a series of loosening drills: high kicks, cross-overs, butt kicks, skipping and running backward. Each of these drills was done mindfully, focusing on my breathing and coupling awareness with intention. Here, unlike my teenage routine, my intention was to solidify my connection with the spiritual, not merely achieve superior physical conditioning.

The loosening drills were followed with a series of almost race-paced 100-, 200-, and 400-yard runs. In between each near sprint,

I would slow down to a trot or a walk in order to regain my breath for the next burst of speed. Runners use the term intervals to refer to this kind of speed work—fast-paced runs broken up by a brief recovery period. For me it was the intervals themselves that captured my interest. During the fast run, I focused on my rapid breathing, on form, on running with grace and power. During the space between the sprints, my intention was brought to mind. I still watched my breath, aware of the time it took to regain my wind after each sprint. With clarity, I experienced the wind, the sun, the turf under my feet. Yet in this rest between the speed work, a recognition, of sorts, took place. This kind of training was so obviously a metaphor for how I strive to live my life: periods of activity, during which awareness is heightened, punctuated with moments of quiet reflection, moments during which it is possible to clarify my intention to find God's presence within the periods of action. For the remainder of the hour, I moved deliberately, back and forth, between the realms of awareness and intention, knowing that I was solidifying the practice for use in the nonrunning world. Use the intervals, the spaces in life that can be so quickly filled with meaningless chatter, as moments of reflection, times to find the center of your being.

January 28, 2000—Further Use of Intervals

I'm continuing to run intervals on the return leg of my Shoal Creek runs. The change in pace, in breathing patterns and the effort required, all combine to produce a change in the way I am present to God. Alternating back and forth between a hard charge up a hill and a slow moving recovery period awakens my consciousness. If I have allowed my thoughts to wander, the change from one mode of running to another brings my mind back into a focus on breathing. At the end of a fast-paced uphill climb, I am breathing very hard and am automatically focusing my attention on my breath. I can then watch my breathing steadily slow down, become less labored, and return to a more measured pace. As I later accelerate through the *next straight stretch of trail, or gather speed to make an assault on the next hill, my attention again inevitably turns to my breath. Running in this way ensures that my mind never strays for too long away from the purpose of divine connection. The breath not only serves as an avenue to the Transcendent, but also as the alarm clock that awakens the runner to a divine purpose.*

March 24, 1999—Walking

All conditions seemed perfect for a run on Town Lake yesterday. I had finished a meeting downtown at five, the temperature was seventy degrees, a little wind, sunny—a delightful day. Yet for some reason, at about two and a half miles I grew very tired. I slowed to a walk and turned around to head back to my starting point. As I walked I became acutely aware of the lack of consciousness I had maintained during the run. I now walked with deliberation . . . slowly, noticing every sight, sound, and smell. I walked until I felt at home on the trail and until I had regained the sense of my journey—the quest for kinship with God. After walking about ten minutes, I felt my strength return and I ran with renewed vigor. I began chanting in time with my steps, unusual for me since I usually time the chant with my breathing. While running I was able to maintain the same heightened level of awareness I had attained while walking. It was Tuesday and I often like to run intervals on those days. I now ran the intervals with good speed and enthusiasm. A smile returned to my face and I saw that smile reflected in the expressions of runners I met. My attention shifted to my accelerated breathing. When running quickly, breathing so dominates the competing forces for my attention that the focus on the breath becomes a completely natural act. This is part of the joy and ease of running meditation. At times, attention to the breath becomes all there is.

Running Laps

A secret turning in us
Makes the universe turn.
Head unaware of feet,
and feet head. Neither cares.
They keep turning.
RUMI

Most of my running is done on trails or city streets. Only rarely do I run on circular tracks. However, track running may be your preference, or perhaps the only choice available to you. The smooth, consistent running surface can be a delight and can certainly be much easier on your knees than unyielding pavement. Coleman Barks, in an introduction to a selection of Rumi poems about the dance of the "turn," the whirling meditation practiced by dervishes, writes of an added benefit from moving in circles. As the dervish turns round and round, ego involvement dissipates and "a resonance with universal soul" takes its place. A doorway to the spiritual center of the soul opens as the dervish looses himself in the dance.

As you run in circles around a track, I urge you to explore the idea of rotating around the center, running as the moon or the earth in orbit—loving the path, drawn in love to the center, feeling the gravitational pull of love from the center, running in perfect balance between the pull of the world and the pull of God's centering love. Technically, most running tracks are elliptical, not truly circular. In practice, this doesn't matter. In fact, the elliptical shape is a more accurate representation of the orbits of planets and moons and of the spiritual path. We sometimes move closer to the center, toward God, and then at the outer reaches of the ellipse, we move away from God. Staying with our path, we are repeatedly drawn back closer to the center, again and again.

Present to the Rhythm of the Moment

Ted Williams said that when he was in a zone, a fastball coming at him at ninety to one hundred miles per hour looked as big as a grapefruit. He claimed to be able to see the laces on the ball as it raced toward him. Ted was in sync, present to the rhythm of the moment. The meditative runner is not necessarily moving slower than any other runner. In a race setting, he is in tune with the racing challenge. Speed is the rhythm of the moment on race day. Still, it is about being present—fully present to the rhythm that presents itself. Remaining conscious of the intensity, of the excitement, of the expectations. Moving at a pace that is in keeping with the task at hand. Just as we are called on to move quickly through the work-day, to be busy, to accomplish a great deal, the task of the meditative runner is not to move slowly, but to move consciously.

February 8, 2000—More Speedwork
   Yesterday's run, on Shoal Creek, was beautiful and a little faster than usual. My legs are fully rested from the long training run nine days ago. I ran intervals two thirds of the way. My spirits were high and my focus on breathing was complete. Each time I picked up the pace, a smile came to my face. I wouldn't quite describe it as a feeling of ecstasy, but there was a tremendous sense of well-being, both in the midst of each burst of speed and afterward. I was breathing hard and I was happy.

The Beginning Runner

Running the spiritual path is not a method of awakening available to only the elite runner. It is a passageway that welcomes joggers, walkers, and even those who can barely manage to place one foot in front of the other. In fact, it is the beginning runner who can be most attuned to the breath and most aware of the immediate physical response to the running experience. Quickly, the new runner will unavoidably develop an awareness of the breath. Don't be discouraged because you are breathing hard. Regard the demand of your lungs for air as a call to consciousness, not as an obstacle blocking your way to physical and spiritual fitness. The soreness in your legs from the previous day's run is simply a reminder that you are experiencing a new approach to running and living—that you are using your muscles in new ways.

There is no need to worry if your pace seems dreadfully slow. Speed is not the goal. Instead, pay attention to your running form. Elevate your knees a little higher, extend your stride slightly, step a little lighter, and you will find that your pace is automatically boosted. Each run you take—fast or slow—is perfect, and accomplished at just the right speed.

As a beginning runner, you are capable of experiencing progress very rapidly. One day you may run fifty yards and the next day one hundred—doubling your running distance. Rarely does the veteran runner see such dramatic improvement. There is also a freshness and enthusiasm that the novice runner brings to the sport. People who have attempted to run in the past and have found it boring, difficult, or pointless may discover that running meditation can give fresh life to a practice considered tedious. It may be that going out for that first run is the biggest obstacle you will face. Buy new shoes from a store frequented by runners. Their enthusiasm is contagious. New shorts and a new top might also give you just enough incentive to begin what may prove to be a lifetime commitment to move with awareness.

physical, spiritual, mind and body

Don't feed both sides of yourself equally.
The spirit and the body carry different loads
and require different attentions.
Too often we put saddlebags on Jesus
and let the donkey run loose in the pasture.
Don't make the body do
what the spirit does best, and don't put a big load
on the spirit that the body could carry easily.

RUMI

The soul should take care of the body, just as the pilgrim on his way to
Mecca takes care of his camel; but if the pilgrim spends his whole time
in feeding and adorning his camel, the caravan will leave him behind,
and he will perish in the desert.

AL-GHAZZALI

The fully actualized human being can neglect neither body nor soul
in his striving to become conscious and whole. Some people rely on
the intellect to determine the course of their lives. Others look to
the heart to direct their choices. It is perilous to neglect any of the
resources available to us. It is important to remember that the body
can be a source of wisdom as well. The simultaneous development
of mind, body, and spirit is required to become absolutely human.

We often use our intellect in a vain attempt to solve problems that
might better be addressed via other means. Sometimes letting go of
a problem and bringing attention to the body allows the perplexity
to stew in a cauldron that transforms the physical into the meta-

physical. When running, allow the donkey, the body, to carry the load. Let go of the troubling thoughts arising and let them be processed by the breath of the Divine. The soul takes care of the body, but the body can be used to transport the soul. We have been given resources to aid us in our journey to God. Relying on a single resource and neglecting the other graces we have received—failing to achieve a measure of balance in our lives—makes for a much more arduous journey. Remember that we are not merely human beings on a spiritual path, but we are spiritual beings on a human path.

The seeker of Truth may take a variety of paths—the path of devotion, the path of love, the path of wisdom, or the path of contemplation. The runner's choice of silence, repetition, and solitude place him squarely within the path of contemplation.

Contemplative practices can take many forms, but the uniqueness of running stems from the extreme physicality of the act. Some types of yoga, the martial arts, and many of the Sufi customs are contemplative practices with a physical dimension. Running meditation can take a place firmly within those traditions. In the West, the number of runners far exceeds the number of people engaged in more traditional active meditation practices. It is possible to take this already well-established practice of running and look within it to find the elements that will serve to connect us with our higher selves. God does not exist solely within our minds. The presence of God permeates our being—mental and physical. The physical channel to God is just as open and receptive as the channel through the mind. In fact, for many people the Divine can be revealed much more readily through the body than through the head. Running can be pursued not just as a means of achieving physical development, but as an avenue of metaphysical development as well. The metaphysical runner seeks physical fitness and is also engaged in a search for truth and knowledge of the Divine.

Anyone who runs knows that running contains elements of challenge, difficulty, and pain. Rewards are plentiful, but only when accompanied by sacrifice and trial. The opening of the heart, the main objective of the contemplative runner, is possible because of this heightened state of receptivity. If running were easy, it would not so readily open our hearts. Running hurts, it wounds, it calls on you to rise above conditions that seem beyond what you are capable of doing. These are the conditions under which people often find God. Their lives have fallen apart. They are wounded and in pain. They are vulnerable and open to God's love in ways that are not possible when all seems well.

> *When you are physically stimulated—be it sports, exercise, martial arts, dance, or other forms of fitness—pathways to your inner emotional self, as well as to the deep centers of creativity and thought, become opened. In this state of mind and body, you are more receptive to personal growth and change; you are more willing to accept what you now see as truth, where beforehand, you may have become somewhat defensive and guarded.*
>
> JERRY LYNCH AND CHUNGLIANG AL HUANG

The runner consciously places himself in this situation. He starts his run knowing that it will certainly be strenuous, and that he will be called on to rise above the hardship. We respond to these physical challenges in much the same way that we react to the emotional, financial, and psychological upheavals that disrupt the stability in our lives. Such disruptions leave us feeling spent, in search of answers, and vulnerable. While the Divine lies in wait at all times, it is in these situations that we permit ourselves to listen to His voice. The run can be seen as symbolic, as a microcosm of the larger universe in which we exist. We live, and suffer, and if we are fortunate, open our hearts to the divine spark that lies in within us.

I am not suggesting that a physically active form of contemplation supplant a traditional quieter form of prayer or meditation. I continue to sit each morning for twenty to thirty minutes. This time is essential for maintaining a balance in my life. Traditional practitioners of meditation often recommend an additional twenty to thirty minutes

minutes in the late afternoon or evening. However, at this stage of my life, for several days a week, I run instead of sitting in the afternoon. If I spent my day engaged in physical work, I feel certain that a sitting meditation would be in order. However, probably like most of you, my day is spent largely sitting at a desk. A run after work allows the pent-up emotions and worries of the day to quickly dissipate and make room for prayer.

It takes a measure of discipline to integrate running meditation into a busy daily routine. However, I would suggest that running meditation be introduced gently into your schedule. Rather than forcing yet another activity into a busy existence, allow the practice to slowly become a part of the rhythm of your life. The noted Episcopal monk Martin L. Smith has suggested in his guide to praying with scripture that the word *discipline* "has overtones of unyielding regulation and stern subjection of spontaneity." Smith says that instead we should seek those "rhythms and patterns" that allow us to find the time and energy to find and develop our spiritual selves. As you experiment with the practice of running meditation, you are likely to find that the practice makes a place for itself within the rhythm of your days. Initially, if you can find only ten minutes to run, then that will suffice. If you have difficulty catching your breath after running fifty yards, then run that distance and walk until you can breathe more easily. Alternate running and walking, and gently increase the amount of time spent running. There is really no hurry.

I find that if some other demand on my time interferes and I miss my regularly scheduled run, I feel a marked sense of uneasiness, of restlessness. Most dedicated runners feel this disquietude, whether or not they regard their practice as a spiritual one. There seems to be an element of addiction, albeit a positive one, to the habit of running and to the benefits that surround the practice. If I miss a planned late-afternoon run, I feel its absence all evening. The effect is more pronounced the following morning and I will search my schedule for an opportunity to run that day. I sometimes wonder how much of my desire to run is based on a physical need to stretch my limbs in the outdoors and how much is a spiritual need to connect with God. I am led to the conclusion that this is a false dichotomy. I now find that my physical, emotional, and psychological demands cannot be separated from the spiritual. I once thought that the pleasure I received from running was due to the production of endorphins in my bloodstream. Now I see that those endorphins are of God as well. The warmth of the sun shining on my back as I emerge from the shadows is from God. God is in the physical.

Using the body to attain a deeper spirit of prayer is a well-recognized practice within the church. The body is no less useful in retaining that spirit of prayer outside the church doors. If we are willing to grant spiritual significance to various physical gestures customary within the church, why deny the spiritual significance of other prayerfully conscious physical actions practiced on tracks, running trails, and city streets?

As an Episcopalian, I have learned a form of worship that involves much movement throughout the traditional worship service. New Episcopalians are instructed to "sit to listen, stand to sing, and kneel to pray." We make the Sign of the Cross at significant moments during worship, genuflect when passing in front of the cross, bow when the cross-led procession of acolytes, clergy, and choir decorously march to the altar, and kneel while opening our hands to receive communion. All of these activities are performed in an orderly, prescribed manner. It is recognized that this physical activity not only keeps the parishioners awake on Sunday morning but also serves as a way of involving the entire being in the liturgy. Are we worshiping God any less with our bodies than we are with our hearts and minds? I have found that worship services requiring the attendee only to sit not only make one stiff and sleepy but are far less engaging. So it is with running. When I have grown tired and notice that I have begun to run flatfooted, the conscious act of regaining a lighter touch on the ground is an act of worship. I recognize that the energy that enables me to step more lightly on the earth comes from God. The act of raising my knees slightly higher, springing from the path instead of plodding, is an expression of thanksgiving that speaks with more sincerity than any verbal pronouncement I could ever offer.

In an article titled "Welcoming God with Our Bodies: The Role of Posture in Prayer," Gabriel O'Donnell, a Dominican priest, states that, "The body and the spirit pray together, one animating and supporting the other. When the mind is exhausted or the heart is too bruised to pray, the body, through kneeling or prostration, may provide the necessary stimulus for prayer." Likewise, the body and the spirit may pray together while running. It is not necessary to assume a traditional prayer pose. If one runs with an awareness of being, not necessarily with a specific physical form, but with the knowledge that your body is a part of the prayer process, then a natural attentive posture develops. If your arms are flailing about, if your body is bent over, if each foot lands with a loud plop, then a prayerful attitude is difficult to maintain. Cultivate awareness and the form will follow. Interestingly enough, if you focus on the physical form, a prayerful spirit will likely develop. There will be days when the mind is so troubled that attention to the physical aspects is all the concentration that can be mustered. Thankfully, that is usually sufficient to bring you into God's presence and mend your troubled soul.

Out of Body?

Running meditation, even when the runner is deeply engaged in the meditation, is not an "out of body" experience. In fact, the runner's body and its interaction with the physical environment become focal points of attention. There is a heightened awareness of all that surrounds the runner, and the "I" that experiences the environment firsthand notices even that awareness. Because running is such an intensely physical activity, the body is brought directly into play and cannot be ignored. Rather, the body—and its direct connection with the earth, the wind, heat and cold, scents and noises—becomes the stimulus that brings us closer to God, that reminds us of His presence. The seemingly incessant chatter in our brain can be stilled by attentiveness to the immediate relationship between body and milieu. Rather than being an out-of-body experience, running meditation takes you much more deeply into the body and then pushes the limits of its sensory experience.

> *You're water. We're the millstone.*
> *You're wind. We're dust blown up into shapes.*
> *You're spirit. We're the opening and closing of our hands.*
> *You're the clarity. We're this language that tries to say it.*
> *You're joy. We're all the different kinds of laughing.*
> *Any movement or sound is a profession of faith.*
>
> RUMI

For those who run the spiritual path, God is the source of strength, God is the footpath, and God is the finish line. When we run consciously, with intention to move closer to the presence of God, our movement, the sound of our breath becomes a profession of our faith. Each stride, the opening and closing of our hands, are ways of connecting with the spirit. John Broomfield, in his book *Other Ways of Knowing*, says that wisdom is stored in the body and in the body of the earth. Running meditation has a way of unlocking the wisdom that is stored in the body. It can open lines of communication between God and man. While running, we can use the body as another language in which to express our longing for God. Running artfully, our bodies become a beautiful liturgy of the physical.

Equating the Trinity with Body, Mind, Spirit

The question of the Trinity arises in my mind with some frequency, occasionally while running. On an early-morning hill run, while I focused on aspects of my body in motion, a way of considering the body-mind-spirit connection came into my thoughts. I equated this body-mind-spirit connection with the Trinity, with the Father being the mind and the Son the body, the Holy Spirit is felt as the breath. It is natural to think of the Father—the giver of laws, the seat of justice, the source of wisdom—as residing in the head. The Son—the embodiment of the Transcendent, God made flesh—is clearly at home in the body. The Holy Spirit, the source of life for both body and mind, is physically manifested in the breath. It is this interplay of mind, body, and spirit that allows us to be who we are. It is not merely that the body serves the mind or that the mind directs the body. Just as God became flesh, in his son Christ Jesus, the body is the physical manifestation of our Self. The body does not just assist us in prayer, but can become a part of a unified prayer of the trinity of being.

God-ing

Mountain Climb Drive starts off as a steady incline, continues climbing steeply for about a quarter of a mile, and then approaches verticality for about fifty yards. This hill has always been an excellent opportunity for me to practice running form. Saturday morning, as I made my way up the hill, I was brought to an acute sense of consciousness, an awareness of my place on the side of that hill. As I approached the steep finale, I held my gaze on the distant void that was formed by V-ing oak branches. I ran erect, conscious of my posture. My arms churned in perfect counterbalance with the knee-high strides of my legs. I lightly landed on the balls of my feet and finished each step rolling almost to my toes. My breath propelled, even orchestrated, each motion of my body. My attention was on form because it was form that moved me toward the summit. To the casual observer, it might appear that reaching the top was my goal, but in fact, my goal was to create the form that would enable me to make it to the peak. My breath, my arms and legs, my impact on the side of that hill were the place of my being. With my breath demanding my attention, the usual problem of extraneous thoughts creeping into my consciousness was not an issue. The words of my most common chant, "Toward the One," were realized as surely as the fact that each step brought me closer to the apex of the hill. Yet just as my focus was not on the end of the climb, neither was my focus on the objective of some sort of ultimate divine union. My aim was to find God with each step and each breath, by focusing on form.

Mechanically speaking, the physical form that I sought to achieve as I ran up the hill was perfectly functional. It was the form that would most efficiently take my body to the pinnacle. So was it a matter of form following function, or function following form? In this case, the form was the function. The loftier goal of "God knowledge" can only be achieved by focus on the form. My gaze may be firmly held on the summit, but it is only by maintaining a firm sense of presence in the moment that progress toward the summit is made. Blindly flailing about, making a mad dash toward the zenith, leaves the runner, and the pilgrim, at the end of a journey whose real destination remains elusive.

I have been reading Rabbi David Cooper's *God Is a Verb,* a description of the Jewish mystical path of Kaballah. Rabbi Cooper stresses that God should not be thought of as a "he," a "she," or even as an "it." He uses the term *God-ing* to describe the interactive nature of God. Using this idea as a springboard, I've come to realize that I think of running meditation not as a movement toward God, but as an interaction with God along the way. In effect, the running is God. Or in Rabbi Cooper's terms, running meditation is a way of practicing God-ing. He states that we can come closer to thinking of God as a process rather than a being.

When we run, we are brought into this process, this state of being that we call God. The run is a direct, physical way of practicing becoming who we are, our authentic selves, of bringing our lives into harmony with another ongoing action—this God-ing. We become cocreators.

Aristotle referred to God as "the unmoved mover." Inherent in this idea was Aristotle's conception of God and motion. Thinking of God in motion, not as static, but as an evolving, changing, moving God, it is easier to understand how we might more easily link with such a God when we are in motion ourselves. God is not static and neither are we. Recognizing that motion and flowing with it, letting go of a rigid conception of God, opens up vast, unlimited opportunities to connect with God in new, evolving ways.

Grace, Speed, and Play

Run in the present moment, not from something and not to something. Strive for a grace-filled as well as a graceful run. I urge you not to run for time, but to run for form . . . and for grace. That is not to say that you shouldn't run fast. Run as fast as you'd like. However, run with speed not in order to measure elapsed time, but to experience the fast run, to know fully the sensation of rapid, self-propelled motion.

Socrates practiced his dialogue in the gymnasium (a place to exercise naked), an open court with places for running and jumping. Here was a place of athletics for the body and mind. The way of dialogue was a method of exercising the mind through play. Running meditation is, in a similar manner, a way of exercising the spirit through play. Socrates taught that man should be careful of taking himself too seriously. He felt that lessons could be remembered better if they took the form of play. The same applies to lessons of the spirit. A sense of playfulness, not allowing the spiritual exercise to be taken too seriously, contributes to the joy of participation in the exercise and to the remembrance of the connection established.

running as a pilgrimage

It is said that when we human beings journey we are preceded by angels crying, "Make way! Make way! Here comes the image of God!"
ANCIENT RABBINIC SAYING

We shall not cease from exploration
And the end of all our exploring
Will be to arrive where we started
And know the place for the first time.
T. S. ELIOT

Ambrose Bierce defines a pilgrim as a traveler who is taken seriously. The runner who runs as a pilgrim is likewise on a serious journey. The run becomes more than an attempt to get in shape, reduce stress, enjoy the outdoors, feel better about yourself, or even win an Olympic medal. The runner, who approaches each run as a pilgrimage, is on a quest for the Divine. Like the pilgrim who often finds that the journey has more meaning than the destination, the runner finds fulfillment along the way, not just at the finish line.

Approaching each run as a pilgrimage, and knowing that the realization of the goals of the running pilgrim happen with each step taken, the runner is led down a sacred path. The running trail itself becomes holy. The runner who runs with the sense of the sacred in his heart transforms the earth beneath his feet into holy ground. Moving with the intention to find God, the runner becomes a pilgrim, and with the pilgrim's sacred intention, changes the most humble of paths into *El Camino Real*.

Running as a pilgrim, we don't just log miles, witnessing the journey as it progresses. The run becomes an act of devotion, a spiritual renewing. The pilgrim's view of what transpires as he runs is not mere sightseeing, but a development of the capacity to see what is sacred. A smile from a stranger, an expressive exchange between lovers, a young boy's sense of freedom while cycling alone, all become sacred when viewed with eyes expecting to find that which is authentic.

I have always run with a sense of release. I begin a run with the same sense of freedom I experienced as a fourth grader, part of a roaring tide of classmates flowing from the mouth of the ancient redbrick schoolhouse—filling the playground with ripples of laughter. Now my runs are more than an escape from the strictures of modern life. Each run is motivated by a sense of what Phil Cousineau, in his book *The Art of Pilgrimage,* calls "an unbearable longing." My days are no longer so confining; I have been blessed with the opportunity to pursue my calling, and I find the work joyful. Still, at the close of my workday, I long to connect with God and find that I can best do so by running toward the sacred.

When running, search for the Divine in the ordinary. Each run is not a pilgrimage to Chartes, to Mecca, to Jerusalem, but it is a pilgrimage nonetheless. The run may be nothing more than a quick trip around the neighborhood, or a jog on your favorite local trail. If the intention is to converse with God, you are a pilgrim. It is the very ordinariness of the run that enables it to become a central part of your life. If running were an extraordinary experience, its contribution to your daily life with God would be limited. The encounters of cosmic magnitude are few and they tend to be remembered with such awe that the memory is placed on a shelf where it can be occasionally recalled and admired. When God appears in the midst of the mundane, we are making progress toward him. When we reach out to God and it is not a time of crisis, when we do not feel forsaken by all we know and love, or, conversely, when we suddenly find ourselves the recipient of undeserved grace—then we are beginning to establish paths to the Divine. These are paths that can become familiar enough for us to find every day and do not require the illuminating power of great pain or great joy. With each run, you are embarking on a pilgrimage of the ordinary.

January 31, 1999—Pilgrimage, A Coming Home
I ran my usual Saturday-morning hill run on Sunday. I needed to run very badly. The day before had been very intense. I attended the funeral of Patsy Pike, the much-loved mother of my good friend Jack. All the members of "the Brotherhood," a collection of old college friends—Jack, Cass, Gary, and Chuck—came from across the country. The day before the funeral was filled with people, emotions, a late night, and too much whisky. I hadn't run since early in the week and I felt the deficit. About halfway through the morning run, I began to feel more like myself again. Without running and meditation, I quickly lose touch with who I am. Call it a connection with God, with the Self, with peace. I simply know that I feel a coming home to a place where I belong, when most of the world is a foreign land.

I am aware that I existed in this foreign land most of my life, and now that I recognize how to get to the place that feels like home, I want that feeling always. Through prayer, meditation, and particularly through my running meditations, I journey to that place. Moreover, I take some of that place back with me from each journey.

I feel that I am inching forward, though fitfully, to a condition where the sense of alienation I have felt in much of my life is evaporating. I long to experience all of my life as a meditation, where I can know the same peace, the same level of awareness I have known when running, in all of my being.

bibliography

Artress, Lauren. *Walking a Sacred Path: Rediscovering the Labyrinth As a Spiritual Tool.* New York: Berkley, 1996.

Baumann, Lynn C. *A Handbook to Practical Wisdom.* Telephone, Tex.: Praxis, 1997.

————. *The Praxis of Prayer,* An unpublished manuscript, 1992.

Boff, Leonard. *Sacraments of Life, Life of the Sacraments.* Translated by John Drury, Portland, Ore.: Pastoral Press, 1987.

Boorstein, Daniel. *The Seekers.* New York: Random House, 1997.

Boorstein, Sylvia. *It's Easier than You Think: The Buddhist Way to Happiness.* San Francisco: Harper, 1997.

Broomfield, John. *Other Ways of Knowing.* Rochester, Vt.: Inner Traditions, 1997.

Chittister, Joan, OSB. *Wisdom Distilled from the Daily.* San Francisco: Harper, 1991.

Cooper, David A. *God Is a Verb.* New York: Riverhead, 1997.

Cousineau, Phil. *The Art of Pilgrimage.* Berkeley: Conari, 1998.

Dante Alighieri. *Inferno: The Italian Text with Translation and Notes.* Translated by Allan H. Gilbert. Durhan, N.C.: Duke University Press, 1969.

Davis, Ellen F. "The Bailey Lectures," Austin, Tex.: All Saints Episcopal Church, 1999.

De Mello, Anthony. *Sadhana: A Way to God.* New York: Doubleday, 1984.

Doctorow, E. L. *City of God.* New York: Random House, 2000.

Eckhart, Meister. *The Essential Sermons, Commentaries, Treatises, and*

Defense. Translated by Edmund Colledge and Bernard Mc-Ginn. New York: Paulist Press, 1981.

Edwards, Betty. *Drawing on the Right Side of the Brain.* New York: Putnam, 1999.

Fadiman, James, and Robert Frager, eds. *Essential Sufism.* New York: HarperCollins, 1997.

Foster, Richard, and James Bryan Smith eds. *Devotional Classics.* New York: HarperCollins, 1990.

Godwin, Gail. *Evensong.* New York: Ballantine, 2000.

Goldberg, Natalie. *Writing Down the Bones.* Boston: Shambhala, 1986.

Goldman, Daniel. *The Meditative Mind.* Los Angeles: Tarcher, 1988.

Green, Barbara. *Jogging the Mind.* Dingmans Ferry, Penn.: Silverlake, 1995.

Hanh, Thich Nhat. *Living Buddha, Living Christ.* New York: Riverhead, 1995.

———. *The Miracle of Mindfulness.* Boston: Beacon, 1987.

Hemingway, Ernest. *The Old Man and the Sea.* Philadelphia: Chelsea, 1999.

Kapleau, Roshi Philip. *The Three Pillars of Zen.* New York: Doubleday, 1980.

Keating, Thomas. *Open Heart, Open Mind.* Amity, N.Y.: Amity House, 1987.

Kortge, Carolyn Scott. *The Spirited Walker.* San Francisco: Harper, 1998.

Lawrence, Brother. *The Practice of the Presence of God.* Springdale, Penn: Whitaker, 1982.

Leech, Kenneth. *Soul Friend: The Practice of Christian Spirituality.* San Francisco: Harper, 1980.

Lynch, Jerry, and Chungliang Al Huang. *Working Out, Working Within.* New York: Penguin, 1998.

Mass, Robin, and Gabriel O'Donnell, OP, eds. *Spiritual Traditions for the Contemporary Church.* Nashville, Tenn.: Abringdon, 1990.

McDonnell, Thomas P., ed. *A Thomas Merton Reader*. New York: Doubleday, 1974.

McGinn, Bernard. *The Foundations of Mysticism*. New York: Crossroad, 1991.

Merton, Thomas. *Contemplative Prayer*. New York: Doubleday, 1971.

Mitchell, Stephen, ed. *The Enlightened Mind*. New York: HarperCollins, 1991.

Mundy, Linus. *The Complete Guide to Prayer Walking*. New York: Crossroad, 1997.

Nabokov, Peter. *Indian Running*. Santa Fe, N.M.: Ancient City, 1981.

Reynolds, David K. *Water Bears No Scars: Japanese Lifeways for Personal Growth*. New York: William Morrow, 1987.

Rumi, Maulana Jalal al-Din. *The Essential Rumi*. Translated by Coleman Barks with John Moyne, A. A. Arberry, and Reynold Nicholson. San Francisco: Harper, 1995.

Salinger, J.D. *Franny and Zooey*. Boston: Little, Brown, 1955.

Segal, William, John Pepper and Jan Pepper, eds. *Opening: Collected Writings of William Segal, 1985–1997*. New York: Continuum, 1998.

Shehan, George. *Running and Being*. New York: Simon and Schuster, 1978.

Smith, Huston. *The Religions of Man*. New York: Perennial, 1989.

Smith, Martin L. *The Word Is Very Near You: A Guide to Praying with Scripture*. Cambridge, MA: Cowley, 1989.

Steindl-Rast, David. *Gratefulness, the Heart of Prayer*. Ramsey, N.J.: Paulist Press, 1984.

The Way of a Pilgrim. Translated by Olga Savin. Boston: Shambhala, 1996.